The Appearance of Impropriety

How the Ethics Wars Have Undermined American
Government, Business, and Society

PETER W. MORGAN

GLENN H. REYNOLDS

THE FREE PRESS

New York   London   Toronto   Sydney   Singapore

THE FREE PRESS
A Division of Simon & Schuster
1230 Avenue of the Americas
New York, NY 10020

THE FREE PRESS and colophon are trademarks
of Simon & Schuster Inc.

Manufactured in the United States of America

Designed by Carla Bolte

10 9 8 7 6 5 4 3 2 1

Library of Congress Cataloging-In-Publication Data

Morgan, Peter W.
        The appearance of impropriety : how ethics wars have
undermined American government, business, and society
/ Peter Morgan, Glenn H. Reynolds.
            p. cm.
        Includes bibliographical references and index.
        ISBN: 0-7432-4266-1
        1. United States—moral conditions.   2. Political ethics—United States.
        3. Business ethics—
United States.   I. Reynolds, Glen H.   II. Title
HN90.M6M69   1997
308'.0973—dc21   97-19261
                                                                 CI

For information regarding special discounts for bulk purchases, please contact Simon
& Schuster Special Sales at 1-800-456-6798 or business@simonandschuster.com

To Vicki, Sara, Elizabeth, and Christopher

—PWM

and Helen and Julia

—GHR

All that is gold does not glitter.

—*Tolkien*

Contents

Preface and Acknowledgments

In the summer of 1849, the *New York Herald* reported on a man who had been traveling around the city duping people out of their watches. Being "a man of genteel appearance," he was able to strike up conversations with complete strangers, during which he would ask his intended victims whether they had confidence in him to trust him with their watch until the following day. Many did, and never saw their timepieces again.

The man became known as the Confidence Man. His exploits generated considerable public discussion (and inspired early "con men" characters in American literature). Some commentators expressed understandable outrage at his preying on the trust of the citizens of New York. Others instructed on the dangers of placing too much weight on appearances: The "con" succeeded largely because its perpetrator *looked* genteel and trustworthy. Finally, a few observers cautioned the public against overreacting, noting that there are worse things than a country that gives birth to swindlers—for example, a land in which no one *can* be swindled because no one trusts anyone else.

These observations nicely frame one of the dilemmas presented by the ample supply of scandals of the last decades. There is a natural urge to try to identify every possible mountebank and to devise increasingly elaborate ways to prevent such scams in the future. Yet at some point the costs of vigilance outweigh the benefits. When we are always on guard, always alert to potential improprieties, for instance, we are by definition always distrustful, and thereby engender distrust—not confidence—in others.

There is one striking difference between the discussion about the Confidence Man and today's ethics debates, however. No one in 1849, to our knowledge, suggested that New Yorkers could restore community trust by paying more attention to how their conduct might appear to others. Manipulating appearances was the Confidence Man's game. In recent years, by contrast, there has been a rush to bolster public confidence by scrutinizing how ethical or unethical things *appear*. This book explores that phenomenon.

The book started as an article in the *Stanford Law Review*. For a number of reasons, including the luck of timing, the ideas expressed there seemed to resonate more loudly than the ideas in most law review articles. Eventually the writing of this book seemed a good idea. In particular, having ourselves become sensitized to the uses and abuses of appearances in contemporary society, we found it impossible to look at the world in the same way as before. And the more we identified similar appearance problems in different places, the more we thought it would be a good thing if more people saw the same things that we did.

This book explores appearance ethics, and related appearance issues, in several contexts: government ethics laws, business ethics, scientific and academic misconduct, criminal law, and the worlds of journalism and nonprofits. We could have easily covered more topics; the challenge was deciding what to leave out. We expect, however, that readers will experience the same thing we did: Once sensitized to the problem, they will see it all over. If that is the result, we will have succeeded. The rest, as the old math textbooks used to say, is left as an exercise for the reader.

A few of the examples used in this book concern matters with which one or the other of us had some personal involvement. One advantage of two authors is that any such examples had to be passed by the other, and they were only used if both of us believed they were accurate and appropriate.

No book is solely the product of its authors, and we have been fortunate enough to have received a great deal of help in writing this one.

First and foremost, our wives and families have suffered much, and contributed much, in this process. The Free Press's Bruce Nichols both suggested the project and provided invaluable editorial insights and discipline. In addition, our respective places of work, Dickstein Shapiro Morin & Oshinsky LLP and the University of Tennessee Law College, provided excellent support, with the latter's help being augmented by a faculty research fund established by the law firm of Kramer, Rayson, Leake, Rodgers & Morgan. Excellent research assistance was provided by Amy Aiken, Fran Durako, Elizabeth LeDoux, Shannon Lovins, Joe Meringolo, Mark Vane, Mary Ann Wacker, Lisa Walsh, and Kimberly Watson. Kathie Walvick provided her usual outstanding check on errors small and large throughout the drafting process. And a number of other individuals read all or part of the manuscript, or provided helpful answers to questions that came up. They include: Martin Battestin, Neil Cohen, Judy Cornett, Brannon Denning, Heidi Henning, Bruce Holcomb, Deborah Kelly, Dave Kopel, Roslyn Mazer, Scott Pace, Carol Parker, Charlie Parks, John Ragosta, Helen Smith, Paul Stevens, and Doug Weinstein. Superb secretarial support was provided by Jackie Bonvin and Julia Manns.

We live in an Age of Appearances, a time, oddly enough, in which it seems necessary to argue formally that substance should govern over image. Although this book undoubtedly contains errors, for which we ask the reader's indulgence in advance, we do not believe we are mistaken in the overall contention that the modern appearance fad is misguided—and indeed symptomatic of more serious, if less plainly visible, problems in American life.

The Appearance of
Impropriety

1

Introduction: The Failed Experiment

Insanity consists of doing the same damned thing over and over again, while expecting a different result.

—Anonymous

O ver the last twenty-odd years, this nation has engaged in a far-reaching effort to increase public confidence in institutions through the use of ethics rules that stress appearances and procedures. Governmental ethics rules have expanded exponentially, to the point where an entire bureaucracy exists just to interpret and explain them. In the corporate world, ethics codes have proliferated wildly, and business ethics consulting is itself a major industry, worth over one billion dollars a year by some estimates. Yet judged on its own terms, that experiment has been a failure. Although the post-Watergate explosion of ethics rules has produced enormous benefits for some parts of society—chiefly journalists, interest groups, ethics consultants, and political operatives—it has not produced confidence. In fact, faith in government and corporate America has probably never been lower.

Indeed, the problem has gone beyond simple withdrawal and disaffection, with a surprisingly large number of Americans—some number it in the hundreds of thousands—openly arming themselves against the possibility of outright revolution, and entertaining all sorts of far-fetched conspiracy theories about the plans of government officials to deprive them of their constitutional rights.[1] Nor can these Americans be dismissed as some sort of lunatic fringe: A recent *Los Angeles Times* poll showed 16 percent of all Americans described themselves as "sympathetic" to such views, with 3 percent describing themselves as "very sympathetic."[2] While there has always been what Richard Hofstadter called a "paranoid style" in American politics,[3] there is no question but that it has reached a new high.

How can this be? After all, many argue that American government and business have never been cleaner, and in a sense this is true. Campaign finance, formerly the domain (literally) of briefcases full of cash, is now heavily regulated, with Federal Election Commission filings for presidential candidates running in the tens of thousands of pages. Many unethical practices have been criminalized. And a vast array of laws bar not only the substance, but even the appearance, of impropriety. If asked, the political reformers of twenty or thirty years ago, and the business ethics gurus of the last ten years, would undoubtedly have predicted (in fact, they *did* predict) that such a situation would produce widespread confidence in government and industry, not its reverse.

With every political scandal, from Watergate, to Abscam, to Koreagate, to Iran-contra, to Whitewater, we have enacted more rules and regulations designed to create both the reality and the appearance of ethical behavior—but chiefly the latter. We live, in short, in an Age of Appearances. To an unprecedented degree, ethics legislation and rules have focused on appearances—both on the appearance of proper conduct by public officials and executives, and on the appearance of enforcement by authorities. The emphasis on appearances has been dramatic: A search of the NEXIS database yielded 1,016 mentions of the appearance of impropriety in 1995, as compared to 261 in 1985, and only 43 in 1980. Consider the public side of this phenomenon:

- There has been an explosion since Watergate in the use of "appearance" ethics in judicial opinions, political debates, scholarly journals, and news stories on the private and public behavior of government officials, candidates for public office, and judicial and cabinet nominees.

- The Office of Government Ethics has issued numerous advisory letters and formal opinions on appearance problems since its creation. And when one OGE director sensibly said that the "appearance" rule is merely aspirational, and that consequently "appearance" transgressions, standing alone, do not themselves constitute ethical violations, a Senate oversight committee quickly convened public hearings to interrogate the director, his predecessors who adopted a contrary view, and various "ethics experts." The OGE subsequently reversed itself.

- Every administration since Watergate has paid homage to the "appearance" principle. At the beginning of his presidency, for instance, President Bush repeatedly emphasized to members of his administration the importance of maintaining the appearance of propriety. After his commission on federal ethics examined the "appearance" standard in depth, Bush included the principle in a new executive order outlining the ethical responsibilities of government officers and employees. Even more rigorous pronouncements famously accompanied the inauguration of President Clinton.

- Most significantly, only in the post-Watergate era has the accusation of improper appearances by a senator or representative carried enough weight, by itself, to create the threat of sanction. We have even had nationally televised congressional hearings in the "Keating Five" case specifically to determine whether the senators should be punished for creating the appearance of impropriety.

Now consider how the appearance curse has spread beyond the federal government, to afflict American business and society:

- At Baylor University, a professor was denied tenure because rumors about romantic links to another faculty member created "the appearance of impropriety."[4]

- In Jefferson Parish, Louisiana, plans to connect school board members to the school system's computer network were held up for fears that doing so might create ethical problems. "To avoid even the appearance of impropriety," one board member said, "the school system should not provide hardware to board members."[5] It was, however, considered okay for the school system to provide phone lines.

- When another school board member, this time in Baltimore, made a $20,000 donation to the schools to support French language studies, the donation was criticized as creating an "appearance of impropriety." Although the board's ethics panel ultimately cleared the board member of any wrongdoing, it called for a ban on such gifts in the future to avoid improper appearances.[6]

- In California, gay rights advocates criticized a state judge's volunteer work with his sons' Boy Scout troop. The Scouts' disapproval of homosexuality on religious grounds, they argued, created an "appearance of impropriety" regarding his involvement. If he wanted to continue car pooling and supervising hikes, the judge was told, "for the sake of appearances, it might be best if he quit the bench."[7]

- Meanwhile, the Boy Scouts themselves, apparently afraid that their scoutmasters would not take the Scouts' disapproval of homosexuality seriously enough, issued rules against scoutmasters ever being alone with scouts so as to avoid improper appearances.[8]

- Albany's B'nai Sholom Reform Congregation goes even farther, barring unchaperoned youths from its building so as to avoid even an "appearance of impropriety."[9]

- But that's not the end of appearances in the religious world. In fact, there is an ethical "watchdog" group that oversees churches on financial grounds. That group, the Evangelical Council for Financial Accountability, deals mostly with fiscal, not physical, wrongdoing. Its goal is to "confront that which could bring dishonor to the cause of Christ," which it says means that churches should "avoid the appearance of impropriety."[10]

- And, speaking of watchdogs, the Animaland shelter for abandoned cats and dogs in Franklin, Tennessee, stopped allowing volunteers inside to care for animals when it lost its charitable status due to a technical violation of state corporation law (a failure to file records of directors' meetings with the Secretary of State). The reason was to "avoid the appearance of impropriety or any illegal acceptances of donations."[11]

Nor are these isolated examples. Businesses routinely counsel their employees to avoid even the appearance of impropriety in their work.[12] The "appearance of impropriety" was raised in discussions of whether Tonya Harding should have been allowed to skate in the Olympics.[13] It has been put forward (by the American Corn Growers' Association) as a reason why crop forecasters should not be allowed to trade in futures markets.[14] And it even played a major role in persuading the National Cheese Exchange in Green Bay, Wisconsin, to adopt an electronic trading system.[15]

All of this focus on appearances was intended, or at least professed, to promote honest government and to foster greater trust in business and charitable institutions, yet we have achieved neither. Nor is that lack of trust a result of paranoia or misapprehension. The public's suspicion that the rules and regulations are mostly for show, and that the reality of influence peddling, vote buying, and ruthless corporate behavior continues underneath a patina of ethical stringency, is, in fact, largely correct. The rules promote (at best) an appearance of propriety, not its reality.

Worse yet, the process of "reform" has had as its chief result the creation of an "ethics establishment" that itself possesses an active interest in keeping the flames of scandal burning even while soliciting funds to fight the fire. The growth of this establishment has caused appearance ethics, and its accompanying vices, to metastasize well beyond the political field, infiltrating many other aspects of society, from science, to academia, to the business world.

Although unprecedented in our lifetimes, obsession with appearances has marked at least one other society. In Augustan Age England, a nation that had just become the world's only superpower, a newly burgeoning professional class and a newly expanding bureaucracy focused on appearances as a means of getting ahead. This focus on appearances was sharply criticized by London magistrate and judicial reformer Henry Fielding, whose classic novel *Tom Jones* dealt with the good and bad sides of appearance ethics. Despite (or perhaps because of) their origins, Fielding's observations ring startlingly true today, and throughout this book we will examine contemporary institutions and controversies in light of Fielding's observations on the relative roles of appearances, virtues, and prudence. Fielding's analysis sheds a great deal of light on contemporary affairs, but it is not, as we will see, a very flattering light.

The following chapters will explore how our current unhappy situation came about, what its consequences have been, and what can be done about it. It is not a happy story, although it is occasionally a humorous one. It is, ultimately, a story of institutional breakdown and failure to take moral responsibility—a story of the substitution of appearances for substance, of technicalities for judgment, of opportunism for self-discipline. The phenomenon we describe is both a cause and a symptom of the dysfunctional politics of recent decades. Its cure will require more than the appointment of commissions or the enactment of new laws. It will require a willingness on the part of politicians, executives, community leaders, journalists, and even voters to make critical judgments and to take responsibility for them. It will, in short, require a move beyond appearances.

2

The Appearance of Propriety

The most formal Appearance of Virtue, when it is only an Appearance,
may perhaps, in very abstracted Considerations, seem to be rather less
commendable than Virtue itself without this Formality; but it will however be always more commended. . . .

—Henry Fielding, *Tom Jones*[1]

It is a safe wager that when someone invokes the odd-sounding "appearance of impropriety" principle today, few listeners think of the
Black Sox scandal of 1919 or the writings of Henry Fielding. This isn't
for lack of opportunity: When a high school band considers whether to
appear in a campaign rally featuring the President of the United States,
the debate is framed in terms of the potential for an "appearance of impropriety." When NYNEX adopts a companywide policy on accepting
holiday gifts, management invokes the "appearance of impropriety"
principle. By what common standard have we evaluated the conduct of
prosecutors, defense counsel, judges, jurors, congressional investigators,
and subjects of the various Whitewater inquiries? The "appearance of
impropriety."

The White House travel office controversy; the alleged racial insular-
ity of the Jazz at Lincoln Center series; the late Senator John G. Tower's

drinking; the seemliness of restrictions placed on an endowed chair in geology at a state college; former Secretary of State James Baker's withdrawal from a politically uncomfortable debate on global climate change; a gift of Denver Bronco tickets to Denver city council members; the conduct of the "Keating Five" senators; and a local zoning officer's complaint about a man's junk-car collection have all been scrutinized, debated, judged, or justified in terms of the "appearance of impropriety." Hardly anyone seems able to evaluate the rightness or wrongness of conduct these days without gravely considering how it *appears.*

A casual observer might think we have cleverly engineered a sturdy new strain of morality. Unfortunately, we haven't. As we discuss below, a somewhat similar (albeit smaller) "appearance ethics" experiment was undertaken in eighteenth-century England, and the roots of "appearance ethics" in America extend back to the Black Sox scandal. Moreover, experience teaches that there are inherent defects in trying to improve the moral climate by asking image-conscious Americans to pay more attention to how they and others appear: Appearance standards are very susceptible to abuse—both by individuals and by entire regimes.

Both types of abuses were well understood and examined by Henry Fielding, a prominent eighteenth-century lawyer, London judge, social reformer, and novelist, whose writings help frame this chapter's discussion of the small and great paradoxes of today's appearance ethics. Fielding's varying roles placed him in regular contact with thieves and prostitutes, the poor and the wealthy, calculating politicians and benevolent country squires, the great enlightened writers of his age and the literary *poseurs.* Fielding's comic masterpiece *Tom Jones* dissects the paradoxes of the rising appearance ethics with unsurpassed precision.

We call the paradoxes the Blifil Paradoxes (pronounced Bliff-full), after the comic villain of Fielding's novel. The first paradox, which we call Petty Blifil, lies in the utility of the "appearance of impropriety" principle as a political weapon, with the critic often being more unethical than the victim. By way of illustration, a landfill owner whose questionable dumping practices are beginning to catch the attention of a local city council member may dig up enough ethical "dirt" on the city council member to neutralize the official as an investigative threat. We call this Petty Blifil because Fielding's Master Blifil repeatedly tries to advance his own selfish interests by wrongly accusing Tom Jones of unethical behavior.

The second paradox, Grand Blifil, is much worse. It involves the manipulation of appearances at the *institutional* level. Grand Blifil is the paradox inherent in an ethos that, ostensibly to promote confidence, pushes people to create the appearance that our institutions are running properly and "ethically" even when they are not. This was the case in professional baseball in America as the 1910s drew to a close.

The Black Sox Scandal and the Arrival of Organized Appearance Ethics

On October 2, 1919, the heavily favored Chicago White Sox lost their second consecutive World Series game to the Cincinnati Reds. The next morning's *Chicago Tribune* pinned the 4–2 loss on "[a]lmost criminal wild pitching by Lefty Williams" and two squandered opportunities at the plate.[2] Twice Chicago first baseman Chick Gandil had come to bat with only one out, a runner at third base (once with a runner also at second), and the infield drawn in; twice Gandil had rapped the ball directly to a Reds infielder without advancing his teammates. During the season Gandil had been the Sox's best hitter in this situation, driving a base runner home more than two-thirds of the time.

The spectators in Cincinnati who watched Gandil kick the dirt in seeming disgust as he returned to the dugout did not know that just a few weeks earlier he had organized seven of his fellow Sox (including pitcher Lefty Williams) to throw the World Series in exchange for cash payments from big-time gamblers.[3] Nor did Gandil's performance on the field obviously give him away: Like a number of other ballplayers of the day, Gandil was skilled in the art of intentionally losing a game while appearing to play to win.

A shortstop might twist his body to make a simple stop seem like a brilliant one, then make his throw a bare split second too late to get the runner. An outfielder might "short-leg" a chase for a fly ball, then desperately dive for it, only to see it skid by him for extra bases.[4]

Although Gandil had not contributed to a single Chicago run by the end of the second game, he could flex a muscular batting average of .375, second highest on the club, and boast having successfully stolen a base in his only attempt. Cincinnati nonetheless stunned the baseball world by winning the fixed Series five games to three.

By the time of the 1919 Series, professional gambling's corrupting influence on baseball had become widespread. Baseball had begun booming in the early 1900s, as more and more Americans moved into cities and built grass ballparks to celebrate the game's mix of individual and team virtues. By 1919, baseball had become big business and a monopoly. The lack of competition allowed owners like Chicago's Charles Comiskey to exploit the players by severely underpaying them. This mistreatment in turn embittered the players and made them easy prey for gamblers. Gamblers openly bragged that they could control ball games as easily as they managed horse races or manipulated Tammany politicians.[5]

Baseball's owners, fearing the negative effect that publicity about the bribery would have at the turnstiles, routinely quashed investigations into gambling incidents in an effort to preserve appearances. But when the Philadelphia *North American* broke the story of the "Black Sox" scandal on September 27, 1920, under a headline proclaiming "The Most Gigantic Sporting Swindle in the History of America,"[6] the owners were forced to act.

On November 11, 1920, less than two weeks before an Illinois federal grand jury handed down indictments against eight White Sox players (the "Black Sox")[7] and five professional gamblers, the owners induced fiery U.S. District Judge Kenesaw Mountain Landis to become the first commissioner of baseball. The owners granted him expansive and unreviewable power to take whatever steps "he may deem necessary and proper in the interests of the morale of the players and the honor of the game."[8] Landis promptly initiated a long string of reform actions by proclaiming that, notwithstanding their acquittal of criminal charges by a Chicago jury, the eight Black Sox would be barred forever from the game.

Judge Landis's reforms as commissioner were designed to transform organized baseball from a state of thinly concealed corruption into a national sport that would be free from corruption in fact, not just in appearance. Ironically, the country's first codification of appearance ethics was not applied *by* Landis. It was applied *to* Landis, by his fellow lawyers. Judge Landis remained commissioner from 1920 until his death in November 1944. In 1921, however, the American Bar Association formally censured him at an annual meeting, and congressional critics moved for his impeachment. The cause of their displeasure was Landis's insistence that he continue to sit on the federal bench while drawing a large salary as baseball commissioner.[9]

Given the atmosphere of widespread corruption signified by the Black Sox scandal itself, the Landis matter induced the ABA to take action to bolster public confidence in the judiciary. In 1924, the ABA issued its Canons of Judicial Ethics[10]; Canon 4 commanded judges to avoid even "the appearance of impropriety" in their official conduct.[11] Soon America was in the Depression, however, and then World War II. Appearance ethics were the last thing on America's mind, and the federal courts never officially adopted the 1924 Canons. For fifty years the "appearance" rule lay dormant.

Watergate and the "Appearance" Reawakening

Ethics historians may debate exactly when and why the appearance standard reappeared in the late 1960s and early 1970s. We suggest in Chapter 4 that the galvanizing events were Vietnam and Watergate. It is true that for many years before Watergate, criminal and civil ethical codes had contained particularized rules designed to prevent the appearance of wrongdoing.[12] And there were stirrings in the 1960s over broader appearance rules. But it was the Watergate reform legislation that institutionalized appearance ethics and brought it to the forefront of public debate.

Attorneys tended to be in the front ranks of encouraging attention to appearances. Yet attorneys were sufficiently sensitive to the potential for abuse in an official "appearance standard" that they repeatedly rejected application of an "appearance of impropriety" disciplinary rule to their own conduct. When the ABA adopted its Model Code of Professional Responsibility in 1969, the ABA classified the "appearance of impropriety" principle as simply one of the ethical considerations to which a lawyer should *aspire*.[13] The ABA declined to embody the principle in a disciplinary rule, finding it too vague.[14]

In 1983, when the ABA replaced the Model Code with new Model Rules of Professional Conduct, the ABA jettisoned even the aspirational appearance principle. The reporter's notes criticized an appearance test as having no discernible limits and presenting "severe problems for both the public officeholder and the private practitioner."[15] The ABA was right. But this insight arrived too late for government ethics, which by the mid-1980s—in response to the increasing power, size, and failures of bureaucratic government—had taken on a life of its own.

The regulation of executive branch ethics illustrates the point. Largely in response to financial scandals of previous administrations, the Kennedy administration promulgated regulations directing federal employees to avoid the appearance of financial conflicts of interest.[16] In 1964, President Lyndon Johnson issued a landmark executive order urging federal employees to avoid any action that might result in or create the appearance of various improprieties, such as "impeding government efficiency or economy" or "affecting adversely the confidence of the public in the integrity of the government."[17] So there were already stirrings.

Yet these appearance provisions had little effect until the seminal post-Watergate reform legislation, the Ethics in Government Act of 1978, established the Office of Government Ethics, thereby institutionalizing a federal ethics program.[18] The Ethics Act breathed new life into the rule requiring public officials to pay particular attention to appearances. The OGE started issuing numerous advisory letters and formal opinions on appearance problems,[19] and in a few cases ethics regulators disciplined federal employees for creating improper appearances.[20]

The history of "appearance of impropriety" in the courts is similar to its history in the executive branch. In the late 1960s and early 1970s, the alleged misconduct of Supreme Court Justices Douglas, Fortas, and Rehnquist, and Supreme Court nominee Clement Haynesworth, raised questions about judicial ethics and renewed concern about judicial conflicts of interest. The ABA responded in 1972 by adopting the Code of Judicial Conduct. The keystone of the Code was Canon 2's directive that "A Judge Should Avoid Impropriety and the Appearance of Impropriety in All His Activities."[21] But it was not until 1975, soon after Watergate, that there was an explosion of articles on judicial ethics,[22] accompanied by an equally dramatic increase in judicial decisions using the language of "appearance of impropriety."[23]

Although the Senate has never enacted an "appearance of impropriety" rule governing its members' conduct,[24] it certainly recognizes the principle. Senators referred to the appearance standard periodically before Watergate,[25] but, again, without major repercussions. After Watergate, however, the members of the newly named Senate Select Committee on Ethics[26] invoked the principle to support the committee's findings and recommendations in two preliminary cases: the Korea Influence Inquiry[27] and the Senator David Durenberger Investigation.[28] "Koreagate," in the mid-1970s, centered on gifts and campaign contributions that a South Korean businessman had made to several members of Congress at a time when he was trying to influence congressional decision making on foreign policy. Senator Durenberger was denounced by the Senate in 1990 for financial improprieties, including reimbursing himself out of federal funds for fictitious "rent" he had paid himself while staying in his Minnesota condominium.

The committee formally embraced the "appearance of impropriety" rule shortly thereafter, in 1991, in the "Keating Five" case, when it cited Senators Dennis DeConcini and Donald Riegle for appearance violations.[29]

From the "Keating Five" to Whitewater

The televised "Keating Five" Senate ethics hearings focused on the substantial contributions S&L high-roller Charles H. Keating, Jr. had arranged for five senators' reelection campaigns, and the pressures the senators had exerted on federal regulators on behalf of Keating's Lincoln Savings & Loan. Special Counsel Robert S. Bennett argued in his opening statement that the committee should judge the senators' conduct under the "appearance standard."[30]

Bennett was sensitive to the criticism that improper appearances are uniquely in the eye of the beholder. So he articulated the following "appearance" principle: "A senator should not engage in conduct which would appear to be improper to a reasonable nonpartisan, fully informed person."[31] This was an artful formulation. Yet, by design, the majority and minority members of the Senate Ethics Committee *are* partisans—a truth they confirmed by including Senators John Glenn and John McCain in their public hearings despite Special Counsel Bennett's contrary recommendation. The two senators had played relatively minor roles in the Keating affair. Senator McCain was a Republican, however, and without him the televised hearing would have given the appearance that Democrats were responsible for the S&L crisis. Senator Glenn's presence, in turn, was necessary to provide the appearance of evenhandedness in reaching out for Senator McCain.

The hearings did instruct viewers on the underside of special interest influence in Washington. But as they were directed at punishing a few individuals, not reforming institutional corruption, they left few watchers satisfied that any real lessons had been learned.[32] Moreover, even Senators Dennis DeConcini, Donald Riegle, and Alan Cranston were able to cloud the ethical waters with charges of institutional hypocrisy and the evils of vague disciplinary standards. Senator Cranston confused matters further by trying to "plea bargain" to an appearance "violation" in lieu of a formal reprimand. Thus the appearance standard made it more difficult to identify wrongdoers, impeded efforts to get at the underlying problem of influence peddling, and encouraged elected officials to redouble their efforts to control how they *appear* in the press.

The hearings made one other point rather clear. In the jargon of news reporters, this "appearance" principle "has legs." It is now firmly embedded in the rules governing government officials. And raising appearance questions has become a fashionable way for journalists to show they care not only about actual wrongdoing, but even the appearance of misconduct.

Just a tiny slice of news articles over the past several years concerning one person—Hillary Rodham Clinton—confirms how entrenched appearance analysis has become. The First Lady has been asked to justify the *appearances* created by her failure to produce subpoenaed attorney billing records, her past association with Whitewater's McDougals, her role in the White House travel office firings, her past profiting in commodity market trades, and her representation of private interests before state regulators when her husband was governor of Arkansas.

More broadly, as we show in the Appendix, judges, prosecutors, defense counsel, jurors, and congressional investigators have all exchanged appearance charges and countercharges during the various Whitewater investigations. These mini-appearance "scandals" have dominated Whitewater news accounts, frustrating almost every attempt to draw some moral lessons from the tale (such as: why *did* Hillary Clinton consider it necessary to devote her legal talents in Little Rock to representing private interests before state regulators who worked for her husband?).

We live, in short, in an appearance ethics heyday. Because we are now so bent on measuring others' morality by how their conduct *appears,* it makes sense to return to England's appearance ethics experiment in the eighteenth century and Henry Fielding's demonstration that a preoccupation with mere appearances inevitably leads to the concealment of substantive abuses.

Appearance Ethics and the Augustan Age

During the cultural period in British history known as the Augustan Age (1660–1750), the practice of law became a licensed profession and attorneys began regulating themselves.[33] This trend toward greater professionalism yielded a number of public benefits, enhanced the reputation of practitioners as a group, and helped generate considerable private wealth. The regulation of professional conduct thus advanced both public and private interests, though not necessarily public and private ethics—a situation that reinforced, and was reinforced by, the Augustan aristocratic preoccupation with maintaining the appearance of propriety.

Many Augustan essayists and novelists, such as Samuel Richardson, portrayed personal virtue as "a commodity readily convertible into hard cash and social rank."[34] The more attention one paid to "ethics," these writers instructed, the more likely one was to prosper. Not surprisingly, the English public eagerly purchased ethical "how to" books. The texts' pervasive theme was this: One must possess a good reputation in order to rise in society; therefore, one must maintain a proper appearance. This, in turn, demands acting with "prudence"—meaning, to the authors, a self-interested discretion that requires concealing one's defects.

The most successful handbook, William de Britaine's *Humane Prudence: or, The Art by Which a Man May Raise Himself and His Fortune to Grandeur*,[35] advises the reader "to try in the first Place to subdue your Passions, or at least so artificially to disguise them, that no Spy may be able to unmask your Thoughts; here to dissemble, is a great Point of Prudence; for by this means you so cunningly hide all your Imperfections, that no Eye shall be able to discover them."[36]

This manipulative approach to ethics met one of its strongest critics in Henry Fielding. Fielding became an active reformer.[37] One of his more interesting efforts in the war against crime (about which he wrote in such pamphlets as *An Enquiry Into the Causes of the Late Increase of Robbers, &c.*) was to organize a London detective force, the "Bow Street Runners," which became Scotland Yard. He also advocated stringent laws to control a rising crime wave, made a number of practical proposals to strengthen the hand of law enforcement officials,[38] and urged a complete reexamination of the nation's administration of its poverty laws.[39]

When Fielding became the so-called Court Magistrate in London in 1749, the year *Tom Jones* was published, he promptly began attacking the root causes of corruption in the judicial system: underpaid magistrates who had made themselves financially dependent upon the people who appeared before them. Fielding knew that by allowing the magistrates to receive compensation for outside work, the existing system encouraged widespread bribery and extortion.[40] He therefore fought for legislation granting magistrates a salary[41] and worked to remove dishonest "trading justices" from the bench.[42] Fielding also saw his own judicial income decline almost by half as he resolved disputes instead of inflaming them for the judicial fees he could earn.[43]

In *An Essay on the Knowledge of the Characters of Men,*[44] Fielding criticized appearance ethics for nourishing both the corruption he saw in government and the crime he saw in the streets.[45] He said it was "no Wonder that [Deceit] should grow to that monstrous Height to which we sometimes see it arrive," since the ethics of the day "taught rather to conceal Vices, than to cultivate Virtues."[46] This lesson, he continued, is "the very Reverse of that Doctrine of the Stoics; by which Men were taught to consider themselves as Fellow-Citizens of the World, and to labour jointly for the common Good, without any private Distinction of their own."[47]

Fielding—with Jonathan Swift and Alexander Pope[48]—especially decried what he saw as the debasement of the classical virtue of *prudentia,* without which, Aristotle believed, "it is not possible to be good in the strict sense."[49] *Prudentia,* poorly translated today as *prudence,* is the virtue of practical intelligence, of knowing how to apply general ethical principles in specific situations.[50] In *The Nicomachean Ethics,* Aristotle praised "Pericles and men like him" for having this practical wisdom: "they can see what is good for men in general; we consider that those can do this who are good at managing households or states."[51]

One important aspect of *prudentia* is knowing how to make one's ac-

philosopher. They fume after Allworthy leaves the room. Thwackum, "whose Meditations were full of Birch," provides all sorts of scriptural support for the proposition that Squire Allworthy's pardon was "wicked Lenity," which encouraged "the Vice of Lying." Square can't reconcile Tom's behavior with the "Idea of perfect Virtue" and therefore concurs in the need for additional corporal punishment. Both men applaud Blifil for bringing the truth to light. The servants, however, understand Tom's motivation and honor him "with the Appellations of a brave Lad, a jolly Dog, and an honest Fellow."

"Born to Be Hanged"

Despite his generosity and bravery, Tom is introduced to the reader as a person "certainly born to be hanged," for he lacks the classic virtue of *prudentia*. After Tom and Sophia fall in love, Sophia learns that Tom earlier had allowed himself to be seduced by the gamekeeper's promiscuous daughter, Molly Seagrim. Just as Sophia is beginning to reconcile herself to Tom's earlier lapse, Tom carelessly places himself in a worse predicament: Unable to contain his joy at hearing that Squire Allworthy will recover from what seemed to be a fatal illness—an illness that prompted others to squabble over their respective inheritances while Tom was consumed with concern about Allworthy—Tom celebrates with an exuberant bout of drinking. Then, still intoxicated, Tom goes for a walk outdoors and encounters Molly by chance; he ends up with her in a nearby thicket.

Blifil and Thwackum spy Tom with Molly and, like a pair of investigative reporters, track the couple to expose them. The episode ends in a nose-bloodying brawl. Allworthy receives a distorted account of Tom's behavior, painting him as a heartless drunkard, whoring and fighting while Allworthy lay dying. Allworthy, thus deceived by Blifil, banishes Tom from Paradise Hall.

After a further string of adventures and misadventures, leading to his imprisonment for a murder he did not commit, Tom is ultimately exonerated and restored to Sophia and Allworthy. But this redemption does not occur until after Tom recognizes that his own lack of prudence, not fortune, is to blame for his predicament. Fielding explains, so that others will not neglect the lesson:

> Prudence and Circumspection are necessary even to the best of Men. They are indeed as it were a Guard to Virtue, without which she can never be safe. It is not enough that your Designs, nay that your Actions are intrinsically good, you must take Care they shall appear so. If your Inside be never so beautiful, you must preserve a fair Outside also. This must be constantly looked to, or Malice and Envy will take Care to blacken it. . . . Let this, my young Readers, be your constant Maxim, That no man can be good enough to enable him to neglect the Rules of Prudence; nor will Virtue herself look beautiful, unless she be bedecked with the outward Ornaments of Decency and Decorum.[57]

Fielding's instruction on the importance of *prudentia* and attention to appearances is in many ways consistent with the teachings of the ethical handbook writers of his day. Unlike his contemporaries, however, Fielding understood the paradoxes and incongruities of appearance ethics. For instance, no one pays more attention to appearances in *Tom Jones* than the villainous Master Blifil, "sober, discreet, and pious beyond his Age." In front of his instructors—Thwackum and Square—Blifil carefully and purposefully builds a reputation for religious and philosophical correctness.

Blifil's disguise as a paragon of propriety allows him to make Tom, who is more virtuous but not so self-regarding, seem to others to be a selfish reprobate. Tom's lack of sensitivity to appearances, on the other hand—and, yes, his youthful passion—make him an easy mark.

Petty Blifil

Petty Blifil is the term we use to describe the ease with which unscrupulous individuals use our ethical standards to attack relatively innocent individuals with accusations of "impropriety." This paradox is named after Master Blifil, because in him we see a truly unethical person manipulating society's preoccupation with appearances in order to achieve unethical ends: Blifil not only fabricates his own ethical reputation by *appearing* to be quite proper, he almost completely eliminates Tom as a rival by constructing—out of appearances—such a grave case of immorality against Tom that the thoroughly decent Allworthy feels compelled to expel him from Paradise Hall.

Petty Blifil has many contemporary manifestations. One dramatic contemporary example involved the manipulation of appearance ethics by Charles Keating and other high-rolling S&L operators. In 1986, Federal Home Loan Bank Board Chairman Edwin J. Gray began trying to slow the deregulation of federally insured savings and loans. Gray's decision may or may not have been perfect, but it was plainly contrary to the wishes of the more freewheeling S&L operators, and unquestionably free of any corrupt motive. The *Wall Street Journal* and the *Washington Post* nonetheless ran several front-page stories in the summer of 1986 criticizing Gray for apparent improprieties in his and the Board's expense practices.[58]

Though Gray had been following past Bank Board practices[59] (as well as the advice of Bank Board counsel), the press accused him of being too close to the savings and loans he was supposed to be regulating. As it turned out, the detailed expense information and other materials upon which the stories were based were supplied to the newspapers by Keating's underlings in an effort to drive Gray out of office. Keating believed, correctly, that Gray was an obstacle in the path of unrestrained deregulation. By discrediting Gray, Keating hoped to force the appointment of someone more willing to push for deregulation, allowing his bank to invest its federally insured funds any way it chose.[60]

Keating, who later went to prison, appeared suitably pious and ethical before the clergy and moral elite. His charitable gifts led even Mother Teresa to panegyrize him to Senator Dennis DeConcini.[61] Others admired Keating's work as an antipornography crusader.[62] Senator DeConcini has said that he was impressed with Keating's good deeds.[63]

At the end of his term in June 1987, Gray left office with his reputation muddied by sensational press accounts and ensuing government ethics investigations (none of which recommended any remedial action against him). Today, the most comprehensive books on the S&L disaster portray Gray as a well-intentioned public servant who warned about the impending disaster while jousting with S&L speculators; their lawyers, accountants, and hired experts; the thrift lobby; White House Chief of Staff (and Keating friend) Donald Regan; and such prominent members of Congress as House Speaker Jim Wright and the Keating Five.[64] In the end, questions about the appearance of Gray's expenses have been supplanted by questions about exactly how many hundreds of billions of dollars the American taxpayer lost in what has been called the "worst public scandal in American history."[65] Our preoccupation with appearances allowed those guilty of real misconduct to neutralize Gray when it mattered most.

There are other, less apocalyptic examples: a judge disqualified on the basis of appearances at the behest of a party seeking a purely tactical advantage, a political candidate laid low by opponents who make accusations of impropriety in lieu of engaging in serious policy debate, an Independent Counsel eliminated on appearance grounds so that a more favorable one might be appointed (see the Appendix), and so on. Examples of Petty Blifil have proliferated. In substantial part, this is due to the richness of the soil: increasingly complex ethical rules teeming with ambiguous provisions and exceptions, fertilized by appearance ethics capable of growing ethical controversies even when the seeds of suspicion are carelessly scattered about. And the ersatz scandals sprouting up everywhere tend to obscure our vision of old-fashioned corruption. When everything's a scandal, nothing's a scandal.

As the ethical rules become more and more technical, furthermore, more and more people scheme to avoid them, and the rules are delegitimized. One of the reasons Tom Jones has difficulty learning the importance of prudence in his own affairs is that the models of propriety his elders place before him are persons whose "grotesque prudence" hardly recommends the virtue.[66] Appearance ethics is often just as hypocritical and therefore similarly unappealing.

Indeed, sometimes those with the best character become rule violators. Consider what might have happened to someone like Dwight Eisenhower, a rock of integrity, under today's rules of ethical engagement. He might not have survived West Point (and become the future Supreme Commander of Allied Forces) if West Point had not had the good sense to calibrate its rules of conduct so that even scores of minor transgressions did not disqualify a cadet from military service:

> Cigarette smoking was strictly forbidden. "So," Eisenhower recorded laconically, "I started smoking cigarettes." He smoked roll-your-own Bull Durhams. His roommate did not approve; other plebes were worried; Eisenhower smoked anyway. When caught by an officer, he walked punishment tours or served room confinement for a number of hours. He continued to smoke.
>
> This was only one of his small acts of rebellion. He could not or would not keep his room neat as the regulations required, was frequently late for formation or guard mounting, often failed in his attempts to dress according to the regulations. For all these, and other, sins, he paid a price in demerits, which counted against him in his final class standing. Of the 164 men in his class who graduated, he stood 125th in discipline. It hardly bothered him; he later admitted that he "looked with distaste on classmates whose days and nights were haunted by fears of demerits and low grades." During World War II, he expressed astonishment at the news that one of his classmates had made general office rank: "Christ," he said, "he's always been afraid to break a regulation."[67]

Convoluted ethical systems not only chase out good individuals, however; they also actively sort for individuals who are *so* determined to acquire power, or adoration, or whatever, that they will endure just about anything to get it. This is not a recipe for producing Washingtons, or even Eisenhowers, in the White House. It is instead an advertisement for image-conscious and ethically thick-skinned professional politicians.

Moreover, our incessant ethics controversies—like the negative campaign advertising they often generate—have profoundly ill effects on public confidence. When Congress and an army of independent or special prosecutors are incessantly investigating violations by just about everyone, it is unlikely the public will maintain confidence in *either* the investigated or the investigators.

Such distrust fuels, and is fueled by, what has become almost a national obsession of finding an appearance of bias or conflicts of interest in the conduct of public actors. Daniel Boorstin observed at the beginning of the 1960s that Americans' distrust of each other's motives had been heightened by overattention to the teaching of Marx and Freud that the actions people take are often smoke screens for hidden (economic and psychological) interests.[68] The sixties—and Vietnam and Watergate in particular—reinforced this distrust. Today, almost as a matter of course, we try to uncover evidence of bias as soon as someone takes a visible stand on an issue.

The "appearance" standard tends to legitimize this approach by focusing on the apparent bias in one person's "links" to another, or to some group. A simple but instructive example occurred in the sexual assault case against William Kennedy Smith:

> [N]o sooner did one of Mr. Smith's lawyers, Mark P. Schnapp of Miami, offer a routine motion to admit one of his two Washington-based colleagues, Herbert J. Miller Jr. and Randall J. Turk, to the case than Ms. [Moira] Lasch raised a sharp objection.
>
> Complaining that the two lawyers had failed to respond to a letter in which she had sought information about their backgrounds, Ms. Lasch said she was concerned that their admission to the case might raise an "appearance of impropriety." She did not specify what might be improper, but questioned whether Mr. Miller, who has taught at Georgetown University Law School, might have known the judge in the case, Mary E. Lupo, who once studied there.[69]

This would be merely so much silliness if such distrust weren't pervasive and if the same logic weren't employed repeatedly with great effectiveness in matters small and large every day.

What is that logic? In the same breath with which Ms. Lasch invoked the principle that public actors should be above suspicion—the Caesar's wife standard—Ms. Lasch herself manufactured such suspicion by trying to draw completely unremarkable personal interconnections—interconnections that anyone familiar with "small world" studies would know were bound to exist. The most famous of these "small world" studies was conducted in the late 1960s by Yale University psychologist Stanley Milgrim.[70] To gauge just how interconnected Americans are, he asked several hundred people in Kansas and Nebraska to transmit a letter to an identified stranger in Massachusetts by sending it through people who knew each other. The average number of intermediaries was fewer than six (hence the title of the John Guare play *Six Degrees of Separation*). The *Washington Post* recently showed that in the Washington, D.C. area, each citizen is probably only "three people away" from President Clinton.[71] When the pool of people is further drained to leave only attorneys and judges, it would be shocking if we didn't see them swimming near each other.

In looking for these sorts of "links," we are applying to lawyers, executive officials, school board members, and city council members an "appearance of impropriety" standard originally crafted in the 1920s for judges. Judging, however, is a special activity. It cannot sustain public support unless seen as essentially nonpartisan and unbiased. Political decisions are different. The "appearance" standard's extraordinary rise in prominence since Watergate has created mischief in substantial part because political decisions are not the same as judicial decisions, yet in an effort to elevate moral standards, we have pretended that they can and should be.

Indeed, even Julius Caesar's oft-repeated insistence that an emperor's wife must be above any suspicion of wrongdoing was politically motivated and unrelated to ethical concerns. ("I wish my wife to be not so much as suspected," he reportedly said.[72]) The mythology that developed around Caesar's "mere suspicion" standard for high officials illustrates, in microcosm, how we have deceived ourselves into believing that a rule forbidding the "appearance of impropriety" somehow separates ethics from politics.

Caesar's remark was made in response to a scandal created by Publius

Clodius Pulcher's slipping into Caesar's palace during the women's festival of Bona Dea; Clodius's ostensible intention was, in today's euphemism, to "lunch" with Caesar's wife, Pompeia.[73] When Caesar heard of the incident, he immediately sent a messenger to Pompeia declaring their divorce. The incident allowed Caesar to rid himself of a wife "whose aristocratic connections were rather embarrassing than useful now that he was in open war with the aristocratic party."[74] Caesar invoked the "appearance of impropriety" principle in response to an inquiry as to how he could simultaneously divorce Pompeia and proclaim that he had no evidence with which criminally to charge Clodius.[75] Caesar's response—that he was forced to divorce his wife because she had to remain above the appearance of wrongdoing—allowed Caesar to abandon Pompeia while retaining the unscrupulous, but popular, Clodius as a valuable political ally.[76]

These examples of Petty Blifil justify the advice that Squire Allworthy offers Tom Jones near the end of Fielding's epic:

> Prudence is indeed the Duty which we owe to ourselves; and if we will be so much our own Enemies as to neglect it, we are not to wonder if the World is deficient in discharging their Duty to us; for when a Man lays the Foundation of his own Ruin, others will, I am afraid, be too apt to build upon it.[77]

Grand Blifil

If the effects of appearance ethics were confined to individual cases, less cause for concern would exist. But the misuses of appearance ethics are not restricted to individuals. Appearance ethics has also been used to shield bureaucracies and regulatory programs from often accurate charges of corruption or ineffectiveness. We call this paradox Grand Blifil, for it involves the manipulation of appearances on a grand scale, to create an image of *institutional* propriety.

Grand Blifil is the paradox of an ethical *system* that promotes the appearance of propriety at the expense of substance—one which rewards people for concealing vices rather than for cultivating virtues. Grand Blifil has two intertwined consequences. The first, and most obvious, is that when we require professional and public officials to maintain proper appearances, proper appearances are primarily what we get. James Q. Wilson captures this problem in his book on bureaucracy:

> "You learn very quickly that you do not go down in history as a good or bad Secretary in terms of how well you ran the place. . . ." In these words, Michael Blumenthal summarized the difference between his experience as secretary of the treasury, where good administration was not rewarded, and as chief executive officer of the Bendix Corporation, where it was.
>
> . . . The head of a public agency is judged and rewarded on the basis of the *appearance* of success, when success can mean reputation, influence, charm, the absence of criticism, personal ideology, or victory in policy debates. . . . Michael Blumenthal put it bluntly: In Washington, "you can be successful if you appear to be successful . . . appearance is as important as reality."[78]

Those who try hard to *appear* to be addressing a particular problem, furthermore, often spend their limited resources on the details of political stagecraft rather than on the behind-the-scenes work necessary to actually understanding the problem and trying to solve it. The student who strives to *appear* to be attentive, Sartre once observed, often exhausts himself and hears very little.[79]

How, for example, did Bob Dole deal during last fall's presidential campaign with criticism that he had denounced Hollywood's "sorry values" without actually having seen any of the movies he attacked? By studying up on the subject? By consulting a spectrum of First Amendment experts? By viewing a half dozen or so problem films? Nope. As the *New Republic* reported, the producers of Dole's campaign instead arranged a staged visit to a Los Angeles movie theater to see a patriotic film, *Independence Day*. The campaign aides scripted Dole's "reaction" to the film in advance. Only the Doles (no one else) bought tickets to the flick—"to create the illusion that this is a regular trip to the movies."

The Doles also bought popcorn and a box of Goobers. A Fox employee commented, "The nice thing about this place is that you can create anything in it."[80]

The second consequence of Grand Blifil is that even the best-intentioned professionals and public servants become involved in efforts to conceal the truth from the public. When these people attempt to create the proper appearances upon which we so fervently insist, they almost inevitably conceal unsightly facts that, if left in plain view, would destroy the overall image of propriety. The problem with this approach is that we cannot fix what we cannot see. Government programs (and S&L industries) don't fail because they look bad; they collapse when they are poorly constructed or recklessly maintained.

Many seasoned veterans now protect appearances in advance by not writing down controversial thoughts or by eliding less-than-rosy assessments of how things are going. Suzanne Garment's *Scandal* makes the point succinctly:

> "Nothing goes on paper." The political appointee was explaining how top managers in her federal agency make their official decisions. "Any comments we want to make to one another are made on yellow stick-on paper that later gets thrown away. And we have oral government: I've had to learn to absorb things by ear and rely on people who are good at giving oral briefings."[81]

As a result, we lose the discipline inherent in requiring written communications within channels; important decisions are made for reasons that never appear in the record. "Off the books" operations, formerly the province of intelligence agencies, become a standard way of proceeding at the most humdrum agency or department. Negative assessments of the situation produce bad press and therefore are edited out to bolster public confidence.

The Grand Blifil response to a cry for reform in legal or government ethics is to project the image of reform without undertaking the hard task of actual structural change, which can be quite messy, laborious, and expensive. This image-building "reform" often involves grave pronouncements about the evils of the activity in question, followed by layers of detailed regulation involving subtle "ethical" distinctions, but never actually addresses the fundamental problems. This phenomenon is illustrated by an 1892 letter from the Attorney General of the United States to a railroad president reassuring the executive that the Interstate Commerce Commission could be "of great use to the railroads" because "[i]t satisfies the popular clamor for a government supervision of railroads, at the same time that the supervision is almost entirely nominal."[82] Since the conduct we regulate in this fashion typically includes behavior that is plainly improper, we end up dressing both proper and improper conduct in the ornaments of decency and decorum. The result is a cover-up of problems and, frequently, serious improprieties.

The Ethics in Government Act is a prime example of Grand Blifil. Regardless of any legitimate interests the Act may advance, it has properly been criticized for giving "the public the false impression that procedural reforms would end ethical problems in government service."[83] Recall President Carter's zealous proclamation the day he signed the Act: "[F]rom now on, your public officials will have to account to you, and it will not only make them honest, but it will keep them honest."[84] Hardly. Or consider how the Act entices us to believe that the label "Independent Counsel" actually insulates a prosecutor from conflicts of interest and divided allegiances that persist nonetheless.

Nowhere in government ethics, however, is Grand Blifil more pronounced than in the area of campaign financing. In 1993 in Illinois, in a sort of foreshadowing of the Clinton administration's problems with fund raising at the White House, there was an outcry over the behavior of a riverboat-gambling lobbyist, who had pulled state legislators off the House floor to hand them campaign contributions. Critics charged that this gift giving near the House chamber gave the appearance of influence buying. The legislative response? A proposed "appearance" bill declaring *state premises* to be off limits to such activities in the future. In other words, it's okay for the holders of the ten extraordinarily valuable state-issued riverboat-gambling licenses to give money to the state legislators—just keep it out of the State House because that looks bad.

A recent example of Grand Blifil at the federal level is the House of Representatives' celebrated adoption of new gift rules. The rules generally bar members, officers, or employees of the House from accepting gifts from lobbyists. Like most post-Watergate ethics rules in Washington, the rules are both overbroad and underbroad, as well as subject to various hair-splitting exceptions.[85] More fundamentally, they provide cover to a highly questionable system of enormous special interest influence.

Examine the case of Bud Shuster—head of the powerful House Transportation and Infrastructure Committee—and transportation lobbyist Ann Eppard. In February 1996, the Capitol Hill newspaper *Roll Call* reported that Shuster had confessed to staying overnight many times at Eppard's recently purchased $823,000 waterfront home. Eppard, a former Shuster aide, in one year had enjoyed a meteoric rise from being Shuster's chief of staff at an annual salary of around $100,000 to heading her own lobbying firm, which earned more than $500,000 during the year's start-up and boasted such big-time transportation clients as Federal Express, United Airlines, and the American Road and Transportation Builders Association.

After becoming a transportation committee lobbyist, Eppard had continued to work on Shuster's campaign payroll as his top political aide, overseeing a fund-raising operation that netted over $655,000 during 1995 (including amounts contributed from Eppard clients and their PACs). She also chaired the Bud Shuster Portrait Committee (estimated value of portrait: $40,000). She was charged with raising funds for his son's congressional campaign. And she had decorated her personal car with the official-looking license plate, "US House PA 9." Bud Shuster's congressional district was Pennsylvania's ninth.

This might raise questions about improper closeness to someone unschooled in congressional ethics. The best defense to such charges in today's Washington, however, lies in the ethics committees and rules themselves. Both Shuster and Eppard said they were fastidious about clearing their activities with the House ethics committee. Thus, when Eppard's associates walked officials from the Pennsylvania Highway Commission into Shuster's office, Eppard stayed home.[86] Similarly, although Eppard had regular contact with the Chairman and was seen entering or leaving his office almost daily when Congress was in session, she and Shuster "set up walls" so as not to discuss issues of concern to Eppard's clients.[87] Eppard likened the arrangement to family members' agreeing not to discuss a contentious issue at the dinner table.[88] "If somebody mentions Amtrak," Shuster assured, "she gets up and leaves the room."[89] Eppard agreed, "If we're guilty of anything, it's being meticulous."[90]

The *Roll Call* reporter consulted what he called "a bipartisan assortment of Congressional ethics experts," who advised him that there might be a possible violation of the new House gift rules. If Shuster had not paid rent for the overnight stays, the experts unanimously agreed, the arrangement might be suspect. "The $64 question for you is, 'is there rent being paid?'—and at fair market value," former House ethics counsel Stan Brand advised *Roll Call.*

The House gift rules contain an exception for gifts provided on the basis of personal friendship. Such gifts are exempt from the ban—unless the member, officer, or employee has reason to believe that a particular gift was made because of his or her official position. The recipient is supposed to make this determination for gifts of up to $250; gifts exceeding $250 require the committee's approval.

Shuster and Eppard wisely attempted to fit his overnights under the protective umbrella of the friendship exemption. The pair repeatedly pointed out to members of the fourth estate that they had been friends for twenty-six years. Shuster and Eppard were quick to add, however, that the friendship did not extend to all of the rooms of Eppard's townhouse. Shuster, in fact, lambasted *Roll Call* for supposedly trying to circulate a "maliciously untrue innuendo" to the contrary, and his office released a "statement by the Shuster family," which said that other members of the Shuster family also have stayed at Eppard's home many times.[91]

A congressional ethics expert would have known, however, that if Shuster and Eppard *had* been sleeping together, they could have proved they weren't in bed together—at least not within the meaning of the

House ethics rules. Shuster and Eppard would have had an irrefutable case that the gifts of lodging were intimately bound up with their personal friendship. The House Committee on Standards of Official Conduct in such event would have had to dismiss any allegation of improper favors based upon the overnights.

Thus do we attack problems of government ethics in the United States. On the one hand, we use heavy weaponry against the relatively trivial sin of free overnights. On the other hand, we operate under rules of engagement that prohibit our examining—much less attacking—the source of the ethical problem: the overwhelming degree of congressional dependence on the financial contributions from lobbyists' clients. Ann Eppard, after all, is merely a conduit. If she were run out of town, other lobbyists would take her place. Fundamentally, nothing would change. As Dave Kopel observed in the context of campaign spending rules, these rules of financial etiquette, although often well-intentioned, are "like the amusement arcade game of Whack-a-Mole. The faster you hammer one mole into the ground, the faster another one pops up from a different hole."[92]

At the height of the publicity over the Keating Five controversy, former Senator William Proxmire proposed that members of Congress should refuse to accept campaign contributions from the special interests over which their committees have jurisdiction.[93] Senator Proxmire stressed that under this modest reform proposal, congressmen could still accept contributions from persons who did not work in industries over which the members' committee assignment had given them "special power"—the "unique power to push legislation through Congress that will bring, for example, millions of dollars of benefits to banks, savings and loans, real estate firms, and housing developers."[94] Proxmire described the congressional reaction to this proposal:

> You would think I had just insulted their mothers. It was "What do you take us for?" and "Do you think I would sell out my office . . . ?"
>
> The legislators said I was playing to the wild public prejudice that all Members of Congress are on the take. Was I serious?

You better believe I was serious. Here is the heart of the problem: After serving 31 years in the Senate, every day of that time on the Senate Banking Committee, eight years as chairman, I am convinced good moral people serve on that committee.

I am also convinced they are sincerely, honestly hypnotized by a system of thinly concealed bribery that not only buys their attention but frequently buys their vote.

The special interests that make these contributions know exactly what they are doing. They know just what changes they want to make. . . .

. . . Any Senators or House Members who believe they are getting this big money because the lobbyist admires their character or personality are kidding themselves.

These contributions to members of committees with jurisdiction over the contributor's industry are bribes, pure and simple.[95]

Charles Keating, when asked whether his financial support had influenced some politicians to take up his cause during the days of S&L deregulation, remarked, "I want to say, in the most forceful way I can, I certainly hope so."[96]

Frustrated with elected officials' apparent inability to comprehend his point, Senator Proxmire resorted to an analogy he hoped they would understand:

Imagine that you're watching a World Series baseball game. The pitcher walks over to the umpire before the game begins. The pitcher pulls a wad of $100 bills out of his pocket and counts out 100 of them, $10,000, and hands the whole fat wad to the plate umpire.

The umpire jams the bills into his pocket, warmly thanks the pitcher and settles down to call that same pitcher's balls and strikes.

. . . How does this differ from what the lobbyists for banks, realtors, S&Ls, and security dealers do when they contribute mega dollars to the Members of Congress who have prime power to call the balls and strikes in their industry?

Yes, the game is fixed.[97]

Real ethics reform addresses these problems instead of camouflaging them with detailed, appearance-oriented rules. It attacks root causes— whether, in eighteenth-century England, underpaid magistrates' financial dependence on the persons who appeared before them; or, in the Black Sox era, the problem of embittered and underpaid ballplayers beckoned by the big bucks of organized gambling; or, today, legislators' enormous dependence on the financial support of special interests.

Grand Blifil pulls in the opposite direction, treating symptoms instead of causes. A preoccupation with appearances encourages the U.S. Senate to referee "ethical" questions concerning the rights of possession and retention of office furniture purchased with excess campaign funds[98]—what columnist Stuart Taylor calls the "more aesthetically felicitous ways of doing things"[99]—rather than to address the undeniable conflicts of interest created by the donation and receipt of those funds in the first instance. In the process, the Senate squanders the opportunity to engage in a meaningful debate as to which sorts of private influences are acceptable and which are not.

We discuss in later chapters in this book—in describing the effects of the new appearance ethics in science, business, journalism, criminal law, and other areas—additional examples of the resulting paradoxes. One final point about Fielding's analysis of appearance ethics in *Tom Jones* bears mention here, however. It has to do with how Fielding brings order out of the novel's apparent chaos. The vehicle for this resolution is Sophia, whom Tom is allowed to marry once he appreciates the relative values of *all* of the virtues.

Sophia

Sophia possesses the qualities that Fielding associates with "real Greatness."[100] In her, we see "the Union of a good Heart and a good Head."[101] Sophia is both "thoroughly good and innocent,"[102] and also supremely perceptive. She alone sees through Blifil from the beginning. Most importantly, Fielding takes care to show us that she accomplishes this by correctly perceiving Blifil's *motives:* malice and envy.[103] In the process,

Fielding underscores how crucial an ingredient motive is in moral analysis, and demonstrates what may be the ultimate paradox in the novel—that "Simplicity, when set on its Guard, is often a Match for Cunning."[104]

These points lead to several conclusions about appearance ethics. First, appearance ethics is problematic because it distracts our attention from the primary ethical referent, *motive.* Motive, after all, is how we distinguish a murder from an accident. And it is a strange ethical system indeed that diverts our eyes from the actor's intent. It is, in truth, a strict liability ethics, under which we inevitably judge some conduct too harshly and some too leniently.

Second, as the public begins to perceive that admitting to an appearance "violation" is a way of seeming to confess wrongdoing without actually admitting anything substantive, it becomes a convenient ethical plea bargain, which is precisely what Senator Cranston attempted in the Keating Five case. Thus, White House aide George Stephanopolous counseled White House Counsel Bernard Nussbaum during the early days of the Whitewater investigation, "Just say it was an appearance of impropriety."[105]

The final point relates to Fielding's hypothesis that unethical people who try to create the false appearance of virtue typically fail. Cornell economics professor Robert H. Frank argues that these insincere people do not succeed for two reasons: first, because too many practical difficulties inhere in an opportunist's *pretending* to be altruistic,[106] and second, because, as Fielding contended,[107] sensitive observers are adept at spotting fakes. If these propositions are true, then it is "imprudent" even in the corrupted sense of the word to try merely to *appear* to be honest and generous; the path to preferment, ironically, may be smoother for those who *are,* in fact, honest and generous.

We should recall in this connection that despite the attention to appearances, the truth about both the Black Sox and the Keating crowd was ultimately exposed in one way or another. As early as the end of the second game of the 1919 World Series, journalist Ring Lardner concluded that rumors about the Series being fixed were true. Lardner walked into the losing White Sox dressing room derisively singing, "I'm forever blowing ball games."[108] Similarly, while members of Congress debated the fine points of appearance ethics during the Keating Five controversy, the public and news media condemned the conduct of the three most culpable senators, Cranston, DeConcini, and Riegle; and Charles Keating headed for jail. In the long run, it does indeed prove quite difficult to conceal improper behavior beneath the appearance of propriety.

Fielding once said that all treatises on ethics are merely comments on the Golden Rule.[109] From this he deduced two rules of propriety. "First, That every Person who indulges his [own] Ill-nature or Vanity, at the Expence of others . . . is thoroughly ill-bred," however exalted he may appear.[110] Second, that whoever sincerely endeavors to contribute to the comfort and happiness of others, "hath, in the truest Sense of the Word, a Claim to Good-Breeding," however lowly he may appear.[111]

These are as simple and obvious as the Biblical mandates that we should avoid all appearance of evil,[112] but not judge according to appearances.[113] Yet it is a measure of how far afield we have strayed with appearance ethics that maxims like these, or the idea that we should look at motive in judging conduct, seem novel or even radical.

3

The Convenience of It All

Judge not according to the appearance, but judge righteous judgment.
—John 1:24

The ability to think rationally is pretty rare, even in prestigious universities. We're in the TV age now and people think by linking images in their brains.

—Neal Stephenson[1]

The post-Watergate Ethics Explosion was the product of a desire to increase trust in government and other institutions. Has it worked? Hardly.

Judged on its own terms, that experiment has been a failure. Although the post-Watergate explosion of ethics rules has produced enormous benefits for some parts of society—chiefly journalists, interest groups, and political operatives—it has not produced greater faith in government, in science, in industry, or in the other institutions that have adopted this approach. In fact, faith in these institutions has probably never been lower.

As columnist Maureen Dowd writes in the *New York Times,* public hostility to the government has reached levels that would have shocked

39

most Americans even at the height of Vietnam and Watergate. One spontaneous display of feeling came at previews of the movie *Independence Day*, in which

> the White House is shown quietly at night when suddenly it explodes into a big orange fireball. It is detonated by space aliens, not Republicans.
>
> In movie houses everywhere, audiences wildly cheer the preview when they see the White House vaporized.[2]

Dowd is not unsympathetic. She goes on to say:

> It figures. This city has not only alienated aliens, but earthlings, too.
>
> It is said that people get the governments they deserve, but can we possibly be bad enough to deserve this one? . . . It's exhausting listening to all their convoluted excuses and backtracking and lawyerly rationales and demands for executive privilege.[3]

Nor are such sentiments limited to spontaneous demonstrations. Poll after poll demonstrates that they are widespread, and deeply felt. In 1964, Americans trusted the government to do the right thing 76 percent—more than three-quarters—of the time. By 1995, they trusted the government to do the right thing 25 percent of the time.[4] When asked, "Do you think elected leaders in Washington are really interested in solving the nation's biggest problems, or do you think that they are just interested in *appearing* to solve them," 65 percent answered, "Only want to appear to solve them."[5] In the same poll, 54 percent said that they thought the "overall level of ethics and honesty in politics" had fallen over the previous ten years; only 12 percent thought it had risen.[6]

An optimist might hope that decreased trust in government has been offset by increased trust in other institutions, but the story is the same across the board: Churches, corporations, universities, even (perhaps especially) the news media are all trusted much less today than they were before the Big Bang. Having followed the government's lead in adopting appearance-based approaches to ethics, these institutions have suffered more or less the same fate. (The sole exception to this loss in public trust is the armed forces, which are more esteemed today than in the past. Interestingly enough, since the Vietnam debacle the armed forces have invested significant effort in avoiding appearance-based approaches.)

How did we create such a mess? Why did we spend so much time and energy focusing on appearances? After all, warnings against judging by appearances are ancient and numerous. From catch phrases like "Don't judge a book by its cover," to folk tales like Cinderella, the Frog Prince, or Beauty and the Beast, to Biblical admonitions like the one at the beginning of this chapter, the dangers of judging according to appearances are literally legendary. Such warnings no doubt say something about the frailties of human nature: Folk wisdom often distills human folly into warnings. But folly and frailty are one thing; deliberate action is another. How could we possibly have *deliberately* created and maintained a system based on appearances in the face of such an extensive store of wisdom to the contrary?

As it turns out, there are a number of explanations. Some are historical, as set out in Chapter 4. The Ethics Explosion grew out of a set of political and partisan pressures generated by Watergate and Vietnam, and probably never would have taken place without them. But even so, what can account for the particular path things took? With so much history warning against an appearance-based approach, what can account for its appeal at the time, and for its continuing appeal in many sectors even today when it has manifestly been a failure? The answer must be found in the incentives, and institutions, involved. Appearance ethics, and all the superstructure that goes with it, has a number of traits that appeal to participants in the system in spite of their larger disadvantages for society. These traits account for the way in which appearance ethics has flourished, and for the damage it has done.

It's Easy

Everyone has heard the cautionary tale about the drunk looking for a lost coin under the street lamp, instead of where he dropped it, because "the light's better." Like most cautionary tales, it illustrates an enduring trait of human foolishness. Also like most cautionary tales, it is often ignored.

One reason for focusing on appearances is that it's just easier. Ethical problems are by nature hard. Did someone commit scientific fraud? To answer that question properly, it is necessary to know a great deal about science and a great deal about ethics, and to do a great deal of investigating and thinking—and even then it's hard. It is so much easier to look at whether a form has been filled out properly or a notebook kept neat. Similarly, questions of plagiarism require considerable knowledge not only of the work being plagiarized and the alleged copy, but also of the field of literature involved, since what might superficially look like a case of copying might instead be a case of two works that both draw upon the same archetype.

All that takes effort, and it is too much to expect our free-roving ethics police to master such arcana—particularly within the same news cycle as the accusation. Part of the appeal of appearance ethics is that it makes such mastery unnecessary. The entire problem can be short-circuited: Instead of having to learn about the matter in question, critics and commentators can opine sagely that it creates a bad appearance, that a bad appearance undermines confidence just as much as a bad reality, and that thus the Ed Grays and David Baltimores of the world have obviously done something wrong even if it is never entirely clear just what. Indeed, once appearance questions have been refined sufficiently, negative comment is enough to produce a bad appearance, meaning that journalists and pundits need only read one another's columns to address appearance issues.

The problem, of course, is that whether or not bad appearances undermine confidence as much as bad realities, good appearances do not build confidence as much as good realities—so a system that rewards or punishes based on the cultivation of appearances turns out not to build confidence, or even preserve it, over the long term. But on a day-to-day basis, an approach based on appearances is ideally suited to our frenetic culture, and to a journalistic profession increasingly dominated by journalism graduates who never studied anything substantive before entering their profession.

It's Safer

Appearance ethics also provides a degree of security to its practitioners, in the (surprisingly uncommon) event that their miscues generate criticism after the fact. Substantive analysis requires judgment, and judgment implies responsibility. Someone who analyzes the facts and draws a substantive conclusion—this was wrong, this was right—is taking responsibility for that conclusion. If the conclusion is in error, that reflects badly on its formulator, suggesting that he or she is deficient in either knowledge or judgment. This is doubly true when questions of motive enter into the analysis, as we suggest they often should.

One who analyzes another's motives, after all, faces several risks. One is the risk of error: We are often unsure of our own motives, so how much more difficult might it be to judge the motives of others? An even greater risk is the pot-and-kettle problem: One who condemns another's motives must face the risk that his or her own motives will be called into question. Far better to stand above the fray, to declare that appearances are the problem, and that it is thus unnecessary to inquire into motives. With any luck, this will divert attention from one's own motives in favor of one's own appearance, which will invariably be that of upright defense of truth and goodness.

It's Zeitgeist-Friendly

One of the big demographic changes of the post–World War II era has been the expansion of the professional and managerial classes. In previous generations most Americans were involved in work—like farming or manufacturing—that emphasized the concrete. Now an unprecedented number are involved in work that emphasizes the abstract: law, accounting, public relations, education, or whatever. Such workers are likely to feel more comfortable with questions that revolve around appearances, since much of their daily work involves the manipulation and creation of intangibles.

Even among those who are not part of the professional class, today's entertainment-oriented culture encourages this emphasis on appearances. Whether it is silicone implants to create the appearance of large breasts, Armani suits to create the appearance of broad, muscular shoulders, gold credit cards to create the appearance of wealth, or computer graphics that create the appearance of long-dead movie stars consuming the latest soft drink, today's culture is, to say the least, friendly to superficiality.

Appearance ethics faces a particularly easy reception among professionals, a group that wields disproportionate political and journalistic influence. Since the "ethical" rules adopted by virtually every profession tend to involve artificial distinctions and, usually, outright hypocrisy, those who have become acculturated to the professional world typically find it hard to become shocked at similar sins elsewhere. Indeed, most professional schools, despite efforts to the contrary, tend to produce in their students an attitude of knowing cynicism toward all such rules. Those graduates then go on to occupy positions of influence in society, carrying such attitudes with them.

It is hardly surprising that appearance ethics thrives amid such a culture, which very much resembles that of the Augustan Age, when Henry Fielding criticized the sorts of problems that we have spelled out here. Just as in Fielding's time, the past several decades have seen the United States rise to the level of the world's only superpower (as England did after 1763), the rapid growth of a professional class with aspirations to higher status, and the tremendous growth of a bureaucracy no longer checked by traditional legal and political restraints.

It's Victim-Friendly

In spite of its appeal, appearance ethics would not have flourished as much as it has if those with the greatest incentive to object—those accused of violating appearance rules—didn't get something from it as well. And they do. While appearance ethics allows accusers to make mountains out of molehills by turning almost anything into an appearance problem, it often allows the accused to make molehills out of mountains by deflating even serious offenses into "mere appearances." The result is a strange cooperation between accusers and accused.

Not everyone goes along, of course, but enough buy into the system to help preserve its credibility. Yet we should be concerned about an ethical system that is endorsed mostly by those guilty of crimes worse than those that they are charged with. Such an endorsement may help the political viability of an appearance-oriented system, but it can hardly help to promote faith in the honesty of government or other institutions.

It's Comforting

Employing appearance ethics is not only easy, safe, culturally correct, and victim-friendly, it is also comforting. Why? Because it gives the illusion of control and precision. Substantive ethical analysis is hard. Done properly, it acknowledges the complexity of the real world. See, for example, the Talmud.

Appearance ethics, on the other hand, promises certainty and simplicity. Well, once the various regulations and interpretations intended to clarify what is an appearance violation and what is not start coming out, simplicity is lost. But certainty isn't. Look at all the rules! And just as importantly, look how hard we're *working* at being ethical! Surely all this effort at writing regulations, filling out forms, and attending conferences must make us better people. Like so many sacrifices to the gods of propriety, the complexities of ethical compliance themselves become sources of comfort and lead to belief in our own righteousness.

There are, of course, disadvantages; indeed, those disadvantages are what this book is all about. But every ethical system has disadvantages. Those based on tradition tend to be too rigid. Those based on religious authority often make no sense to those not fully conversant with the religion. Those based on philosophical argument are often unconvincing.

But what makes the disadvantages of the post–Big Bang system most striking, and most pernicious, is that they are disadvantages for society, but advantages for all of the players in the system.

If a successful ethical system is one that provides incentives for individuals and institutions to act in ways that are beneficial to society, then what is there to say for a system that provides incentives for individuals and institutions to act in ways that are inimical to society? Not very much. Yet that is the system that we have developed over the past twenty-five or thirty years. In later chapters we will discuss what to do about that problem. In short, we must try for a system in which we focus more on substance, and character, than on appearances.

4

The Big Bang

Vietnamese realities did not matter, but the *appearances* of Vietnamese realities mattered because they could affect American realities.
—David Halberstam

Now damn it, we just can't have an appearance of cover-up.
—Richard Nixon

This chapter explores the *how* of the late 1970s' explosion in ethics reform—a sort of cultural Big Bang, which began on August 5, 1974, in Washington, D.C. Although several dates might be chosen to represent the exploding public mistrust following Vietnam and Watergate, we date the Big Bang by the last great Watergate disclosure: the White House's August 5, 1974 release of the "smoking gun" tape. Nixon resigned four days later, ending what President Ford called "our long national nightmare," and within a matter of months we collectively threw ourselves into the most sustained and comprehensive public effort at "ethics reform" in American history.

We generated new ethical restrictions and requirements at every level of government and among the leading professions. We created ethics

47

agencies, boards, and commissions to interpret, implement, and police the often complex ethical regulations. We established private ethics centers and new public-interest watchdog groups. We began requiring graduate students to study professional ethics, which then became a practice specialization. We started consulting ethics counselors and retaining ethics testimonial experts. And we encouraged a proliferation of investigative reporters, who—spurred on by the Pulitzers and lucrative book contracts and speaking engagements that rained down on the journalists who uncovered scandals during Vietnam and Watergate—pursued tales of public misfeasance and private immorality with virtually unprecedented vigor. In short, the Big Bang gave birth to a modern Ethics Establishment.

How did all of this come about? After all, during the Eisenhower era, America's public confidence in its institutions was at a high point. By the mid-'70s, however, it was at a low—from which we still have not emerged. The story of our descent, traced briefly here, is the story of duels at the Gaps: the Missile Gap, the Credibility Gap, and the 18½ Minute Gap.

It might seem strange to begin this story with a false statement from President Eisenhower. Dwight Eisenhower was excruciatingly honest, and so was his administration. "In eight years under Eisenhower's direction," historian Stephen Ambrose has noted, "the government was so free of scandal that the best the Democrats ever came up with was that Sherman Adams had accepted a coat from Bernard Goldfine, and President Eisenhower was so far from abusing the power of his office that the chief Democratic complaint was that he did not do enough."[1] Yet this is where the trail curiously begins: at a lie President Eisenhower uttered for reasons of national security in response to a Soviet charge of American espionage.

There was a tacit understanding at the time between the President, on the one hand, and the Congress, the press, and the public, on the other, that the Commander in Chief would take necessary steps to protect the country from nuclear attack or other defeat at the hands of the Communists, spare everyone the often unpleasant details, and even lie if required for the greater good. Unfortunately, this Cold War rationalization led to the use of more and more deceptions—from the relatively innocent "spinning" of stories to protect executive policy (or bureaucratic backsides), to larger and more complex deceptions designed to advance narrow political interests, and, ultimately, to conceal criminal misconduct within the White House itself.

May Day, 1960

On May 1, 1960, while top Communist Party and military officials of the Soviet Union were reviewing the May Day military parade from the stands above Lenin's tomb, the head of Soviet defense forces approached Premier Nikita Khrushchev and whispered in his ear.[2] Hours before, about 1,300 miles inside Soviet territory, a Russian surface-to-air missile had blasted an American reconnaissance plane out of the sky.

President Eisenhower was aware of the dangers of sending a "spy plane" deep into Soviet airspace at the height of the Cold War. The high-altitude U-2, however, had been supplying U.S. officials with invaluable photographs of Soviet nuclear-missile production and deployment sites, which the President had used to gauge the sufficiency of America's nuclear deterrence. Moreover, Eisenhower had controlled against the risk of a shoot-down by personally scrutinizing the details of each flight plan, and the CIA had assured the President that no pilot could survive a downing in the fragile U-2. The President was therefore confident that the Soviets could not prove that the plane had been involved in intelligence gathering.

Concerned that a frank admission of "spying" would jeopardize the prospect for concluding a nuclear test ban treaty with the Soviets at an upcoming Four Power summit, President Eisenhower authorized his spokesmen to deny the accusation when the Soviets made it. The U-2 was merely a weather plane, U.S. officials assured, which "may have drifted across the Russian border" as a result of the pilot's losing consciousness.[3] Eisenhower did not know that the CIA had given the pilot, Francis Gary Powers, a parachute. Nor that Powers had managed to eject and float to earth. After the White House issued its denial, the Soviets convened a press conference before a worldwide television audience and unveiled Powers and scraps of incriminating evidence gathered from the plane's wreckage. Eisenhower admitted he had lied, and assumed responsibility for the flight.

The U-2 crisis involved uniquely difficult national defense issues, and Eisenhower was certainly not the first President to lie. Still, it was humiliating and startling for Americans to see Eisenhower snared in a lie by a table-pounding totalitarian, especially since Eisenhower justifiably believed his reputation for honesty was his greatest single asset as President.[4] And it was a formidable reputation. Before the U-2 incident, Americans believed Eisenhower without hesitation. When Indonesian President Sukarno accused the United States and Taiwan in 1958 of providing weapons and planes to antigovernment rebels, for example, the *New York Times* leaped reflexively to Ike's defense. It was enough, the *Times* lectured Sukarno, that "the President himself" had been emphatic about U.S. neutrality.[5]

Eisenhower would later say his greatest regret as President was "the lie we told about the U-2."[6] It was not a comment for moral show. It was a general's reflection on a mistake made under battlefield-type pressure, like sending troops forward into an ambush despite signs counseling retreat to high ground.

The Missile Gap

Unfortunately, one lie made for national-security reasons led to an unintentional but important falsehood made for political gain, when Senator John Kennedy seized upon the U-2 affair during his fall presidential campaign against Vice President Nixon. Citing the incident as further evidence that the Eisenhower administration was mishandling the Soviet threat, Kennedy charged that the administration had allowed a "missile gap" to develop between the United States and the Soviet Union. The claim was untrue. It was based on incomplete information reportedly leaked to Kennedy and others by allies in the intelligence community. President Eisenhower could have refuted the charge with intelligence from the U-2 flights. But Eisenhower consistently refused to share the fruits of the U-2's surveillance for fear of compromising the intelligence effort, and he would not reverse this policy for the campaign season. As a result, candidate Nixon unexpectedly found himself on the defensive on foreign policy issues. Nixon later blamed his election loss in part on the U-2 affair and the "missile gap."[7]

Robert S. McNamara made the "missile gap" his top priority when he became Secretary of Defense under President Kennedy in January 1961. McNamara spent many days during that first month on his office floor personally evaluating hundreds of aerial photographs of Soviet ICBMs.[8] When he was done, he knew the truth. "There was a gap—but it was in our favor!"[9]

Yet JFK had ridden to victory in substantial part on the contrary charge. During McNamara's first background briefing with members of the press, he was asked whether the Soviets had more operational missiles than the United States. So far as he had been able to tell, McNamara responded, the U.S. seemed to be ahead of the Soviets, not the other way around. The remark generated an AP "Bulletin" and caused a sensation in Washington.[10] The White House tried to limit the political damage by saying the press stories were "wrong" because the Pentagon didn't have a "study" showing no missile gap existed.[11] The response sidestepped the question whether the Defense Secretary had concluded there was no missile gap.

In an effort to contain the problem, McNamara began denying he had ever said the United States was ahead of the Soviets. He went so far as to inform Congress that the United States did lag behind the Soviets in operational missiles and that the "gap" might not be closed until 1963.[12] These declarations shocked Defense Department reporters who had attended the press briefing and heightened suspicion of subsequent Pentagon statements on budget issues, arms programs, and the smoldering conflict in South Vietnam.

The Credibility Gap

The term "credibility gap" first appeared as a play on "missile gap" in the title to an editorial criticizing Johnson administration misstatements during the Vietnam War. The June 1964 editorial in *Aviation Week & Space Technology* complained that the Johnson administration had developed a "credibility gap" at the very time the President needed to build public support for the campaign to repel Communism in Southeast Asia.[13] Newspapers and news magazines later repeated the term. So did American GIs in Vietnam, who began wearing buttons reading, "Ambushed at Credibility Gap."[14]

Typical of the news articles was a December 1965 story in the *Washington Post*.[15] The *Post* article described an "accumulated feeling" that official utterances were routinely couched in disingenuous circumlocutions and far too often shown by subsequent events to have been altogether false. The article cited a variety of official statements on a number of subjects. But the core accusation concerned misstatements on Vietnam—such as the administration's string of false denials that U.N. Secretary General U Thant had attempted to bring the United States and North Vietnam together for peace talks. After months of silence, U Thant contradicted the administration's pronouncements and upbraided the United States with Aeschylus's observation that truth is the first casualty of war.

The Johnson administration may have been singularly successful at liberating pronouncements on Vietnam from the facts. But Vietnam had become a credibility issue as soon as President Kennedy explicitly chose the country as the place to make U.S. power "credible."[16] To begin with, the Kennedy administration misstated the nature and scope of U.S. military assistance in Vietnam from the outset. William Truehart, the U.S. deputy ambassador to South Vietnam, later explained that American officials were trying to avoid convicting themselves out of their own mouth of violating the governing Geneva Accords. But signs of the escalating U.S. military presence in Vietnam were visible everywhere to even the casual observer—in such things as the sight of a gigantic American aircraft carrier steaming up a South Vietnamese river or the arrival of new U.S. military "advisers" and equipment. As a result, the military's relations with the press were strained from the start. As Truehart later conceded, the administration's approach was not very realistic. "It was at the root of the really bad problems we had with the press, this no-comment kind of position on things that were self-evident to anyone on the ground."[17]

Furthermore, even discussing a war in terms of "credibility" revealed that Americans didn't really feel threatened by the enemy—certainly not as they had by the Germans or Japanese in World War II—and this casualness created its own long-term "credibility" problems. In World War II, when America had been fighting for democracy's survival, its leaders had insisted on unvarnished assessments of the military situation—not to maintain "credibility," but to avoid cataclysmic defeat. Eisenhower, for example, had relieved generals who brought him overly upbeat reports[18] and had inspired confidence by his "searching and positive" self-criticism.[19]

In Vietnam, it was the Vietnamese Communists who followed such an approach. As one North Vietnamese major general later recalled, the Communists were well aware they were fighting against the world's most powerful military and knew it would not be enough just to make propaganda saying that they were winning.[20] So they established a system that encouraged military officials to report all of the bad news about their operations.[21]

Not so the Americans. It became standard practice to downplay problems with the American and South Vietnamese war effort. An early celebrated example was the exhaustive report written by Lt. Col. John Paul Vann in 1963, after the South Vietnamese defeat at the Battle of Ap Bac. Vann's superior, Colonel Daniel Boone Porter, forwarded the report to the senior U.S. military advisor, General Paul Harkins, under an endorsement memo that described the report as "possibly the best documented, most comprehensive, most valuable, and most revealing" of any of the reports of the previous year.[22] Colonel Porter said the operation revealed glaring weaknesses in the South Vietnamese military and recommended a series of open and frank conferences with South Vietnamese officials to review what needed to be done. General Harkins treated the report with disdain, however, and threatened to dismiss Vann for generating such a document.[23]

General Harkins had resolved to measure American and South Vietnamese success in other ways—specifically, in progress reports containing statistical graphs and charts of such things as the now-famous "body count" and "kill ratio," as well as the number of operations undertaken, the number of aircraft sorties flown, and the amount of bomb tonnage dropped.[24] It was an impressive-appearing approach, tailored to satisfy Defense Secretary McNamara's penchant for statistical analyses. It worked. "Every quantitative measurement we have," McNamara reaffirmed, "shows that we're winning the war."[25]

The Army also gave the *appearance* of stressing counterinsurgency: Studies were conducted, boards were convened, troops were briefed, and course descriptions at the Command and General Staff College were edited to add a few lines about the possibility of encountering "irregular forces," thus enabling administrators to report offering 437 hours in courses covering counterinsurgency.[26]

In a similar vein, the counterinsurgency plan for Vietnam that Army planners developed—the Geographically Phased National Level Operation Plan for Counterinsurgency—was so thick and forbidding ("about the size of the Washington telephone directory") that the South Vietnamese promptly ignored it.[27] They opted instead for the "strategic hamlet" program. The "strategic hamlet" program was designed to isolate and protect farmers from Communist influence by uprooting them from land they had worked for generations and transferring them into thousands of small, barbed-wire-enclosed refugee camps built around the countryside with U.S. funds (less amounts skimmed by corrupt South Vietnamese officials).[28] At best, the hamlets offered only "cosmetic resistance" to Vietcong recruitment and political organization[29]; at worst, they drove the peasants into the arms of the Vietcong.[30] South Vietnamese officials nonetheless eagerly passed along to their American advisors impressive statistics on the creation of thousands of pacified hamlets.

American policy, as David Halberstam later observed, increasingly became "a policy based on appearances; Vietnamese realities did not matter, but the *appearances* of Vietnamese realities mattered because they could affect American realities."[31] Colin Powell would later write of his Vietnam days during the early 1960s that there was a "conspiracy of illusion" in which the Army pretended to be fixing things in the apparent hope that then they would fix themselves.[32]

"Highly Conflicting" Press and Government Interests

This official emphasis on presenting a positive face to the public on Vietnam aggravated tensions between reporters and government officials. President Kennedy's relations with the Washington press corps may have been as convivial as the wine and cellos at a White House banquet, but not so with the handful of print reporters assigned to Vietnam. President Kennedy complained that his relations with these Vietnam journalists were the worst press relations in the world,[33] although Presidents Johnson and Nixon subsequently would have longed for the minimal press coverage Vietnam received during most of the Kennedy era. Then, only the *New York Times* among America's newspapers had a full-time correspondent in Vietnam. And televised news reports were limited to the network anchor's reading from excerpts from wire reports during the fifteen-minute evening news shows.

President Kennedy personally pushed for the removal of certain critical correspondents. He particularly targeted the *Times*'s David Halberstam. The President ordered the CIA to analyze Halberstam's stories line by line in the hope of showing that he could not be trusted. Kennedy accused Halberstam of running a political campaign and being unpatriotic and a coward. And Kennedy pressed the *Times*'s management to bring him home.[34]

In March 1963, John Mecklin, the U.S. press attache in Vietnam, met with President Kennedy to urge a new approach. Mecklin had himself attacked reporters for displaying "a self-righteous witlessness." Yet he nonetheless argued to the President that the policy of not confiding in reporters was proving counterproductive, and that Kennedy should personally instruct U.S. officials in Vietnam "to cease excessively optimistic public statements, to stop complaining about unfavorable stories . . . and most of all to take the newsmen into their confidence." The President doubted any press policy would succeed, however, because press and government interests had become "highly conflicting." Kennedy nonetheless instructed press secretary Pierre Salinger to work something up.[35]

The Pentagon Papers

By the fall of 1966, three years and 400,000 American troops later, the public was beginning to turn against what was then "Johnson's War," and reporters were openly incredulous of government briefings. Antiwar demonstrations also were rising. When McNamara visited Harvard University to speak with students in a seminar taught by Dr. Henry Kissinger, McNamara was shaken by the ferocity of student demonstrators who surrounded his car. The Defense Secretary admitted at a faculty dinner that the war was not going as planned. He suggested the need for a study of the history of U.S. involvement for use by future scholars. In the summer of 1967, McNamara made his idea concrete, commissioning the 7,000-page top-secret "History of U.S. Decision-Making Process on Viet Nam Policy," subsequently known as the Pentagon Papers.[36]

McNamara recalls instructing the researchers "not to hold back"—to "let the chips fall where they may."[37] And that's how the researchers interpreted their assignment: to provide an accurate history of decision making in Vietnam, not an upbeat "progress" report. McNamara drafted a handwritten list of 100 questions to be addressed. They included items that were being discussed in daily press briefings, policy papers, and news magazines: "How confident can we be about body counts of the enemy? Were programs to pacify the Vietnamese country-side working? What was the basis of President Lyndon Johnson's credibility gap?"[38] Thirty-six researchers and analysts were pressed into service. The authors, promised anonymity to protect their careers, were selected from the military services and various "think tanks" for their technical skills, intelligence, and discretion.

One Rand Corporation analyst years before had helped the Eisenhower administration evaluate the "missile gap." In Vietnam, he had become best friends with John Paul Vann. Vann remained dedicated to the American war effort, however, while the Rand analyst, Daniel Ellsberg, chose a different path. In the fall of 1969, he began photocopying pages of the Pentagon Papers. A year and a half later, he forwarded the duplicates—in violation of an assortment of U.S. laws—to Neil Sheehan, one of Vann's journalistic proteges in Vietnam, who had moved to the *New York Times.*

On Sunday, June 13, 1971, the *New York Times* published a front-page article on the Pentagon Papers under the bland lead "Vietnam Archive: Pentagon Study Traces 3 Decades of Growing U.S. Involvement." The story was accompanied by excerpts from Defense Department cables and memoranda. Managing editor A.M. Rosenthal later said the *Times*'s Pentagon Papers articles revealed no great secrets. Their principal benefit, Rosenthal allowed, was in showing how successive administrations had pressed forward in Vietnam without coming to grips with the failures and problems encountered at each step of escalation.[39] This was undoubtedly true.

Yet it is also correct to say the Pentagon Papers distorted history. As Vietnam historian Stanley Karnow has written, they conveyed the false impression that every bureaucratic plan reflects official policy.[40] This misimpression may have flowed naturally from the general view that official government statements on the Vietnam War were unreliable and therefore that the truth lay elsewhere—in secret memos, undisclosed cables, and the like. Washington is flooded with draft plans and proposals, however, which often are not even seen by higher authority, much less approved.[41] Nonetheless, in the years following the Big Bang, early drafts of government reports, memos written by relatively low-level officials, handwritten notations, glib comments offered in electronic mail from one White House aide to another, and similar material would be endowed with an aura of credibility precisely because they were not seen or edited by higher-ups.

President Nixon initially shrugged off the June 13 *Times* story. To begin with, the article had been met largely with silence from other news organizations.[42] Second, Nixon believed disclosure of the Pentagon history—ending as it did in 1968—would simply damage Presidents Kennedy and Johnson.[43] Henry Kissinger, however, expressed an opposite view. Kissinger was involved in sensitive secret talks with the Chinese and North Vietnamese at the time. He argued that the theft and publication of top-secret internal memoranda about a war in which the United States was still actively engaged were outrageous acts—which, if unchecked, would make the Nixon administration appear weak and untrustworthy of diplomatic confidences. Kissinger also bridled at Ellsberg's portrayal as some sort of hero.

Nixon ultimately agreed on the need for action. He ordered a high-priority legal offensive against further publication, criminal prosecution of the leaker, countermeasures to prevent further leaks, and a full-scale attack on the reputation and credibility of Ellsberg and other antiwar critics.[44] The first directive led to the filing of historic lawsuits against the *Times* and the *Washington Post*. (The *Post* had followed the *Times* in publishing the Pentagon Papers after a federal court temporarily enjoined the *Times* from further publication.) The Sturm und Drang surrounding these legal battles soon drowned out discussion of the Pentagon Papers' actual content.

Nixon lost the legal war, 6–3, in a landmark Supreme Court case, *New York Times Co. v. United States*. Justices Potter Stewart and Byron White cast the deciding votes. Both believed revelation of at least some of the documents would substantially damage the national interest, and both more or less invited the government to pursue criminal prosecutions. Neither could say, however, that disclosure would surely result in "direct, immediate, and irreparable damage to our Nation or its people"—the heavy burden the government shouldered under the First Amendment to justify a prior restraint on publication.[45] In language President Nixon could have penned, Justice Stewart wrote about the "enormous power" and "awesome responsibility" the Constitution grants the Executive in the realm of national security. Justice Stewart then added a plea, however, based upon "moral, political, and practical considerations," that this responsibility not be exercised in cynical or careless ways for reasons of self-protection, for "when everything is classified, nothing is classified." A "truly effective internal security system," he volunteered, would press toward "the maximum possible disclosure, recognizing that secrecy can best be preserved only when credibility is truly maintained."[46]

Justice Stewart's words sounded a fitting tribute to days gone by—to a period when the *New York Times* safeguarded the confidentiality of top-secret information about U-2 overflights out of respect for the President. The *Times* and *Post* victories in the Pentagon Papers case, as one prominent law professor noted, "signaled the passing of a period when newspapers could be expected to play by tacit rules in treating matters that government leaders deem confidential."[47] The *Post*'s success also led to the creation of a new *Washington Post,* managing editor Ben Bradlee later observed,[48] a *Post* confident enough to spearhead a direct assault one year later on Nixon's presidency.

Nixon's order to prosecute leakers led to Ellsberg's indictment under the Treason Act. Nixon's directive to plug leaks gave birth to the White House Special Investigations Unit, known to posterity as the Plumbers. The Plumbers were a group of White House aides organized under John Ehrlichman's supervision with Special Counsel Chuck Colson's frequent guidance. The Plumbers actually didn't much bother themselves with trying to plug leaks. Instead, like a band of modern Blifils, they set out to implement another Nixon directive—to discredit Ellsberg and other Nixon administration "enemies." Thus began the precipitous decline toward Watergate.

Forged Cables, Planted Literature, Scattered Drugs

"Enemies" was broadly construed to encompass political opponents, both dead and alive. Accordingly, Plumber E. Howard Hunt forged top-secret diplomatic cables to make it appear that John Kennedy had ordered South Vietnamese President Diem's assassination[49] and tried to exhume filth on Teddy Kennedy.[50] Chuck Colson, now an evangelical prison reformer, went so far in his effort to smear George McGovern's supporters as to try to plant "left-wing literature" in Arthur Bremer's apartment after Bremer had attempted to assassinate presidential candidate (former Alabama Governor) George Wallace. Colson informed Nixon of his plan at the time by telephone ("he'll be a left-winger when I get through"), in one of the more chilling White House tape excerpts now publicly available at the National Archives.[51]

In the summer of 1971, however, the Plumbers' sights were trained on Ellsberg. After receiving a disappointingly bland "psychological profile" on Ellsberg from a reluctant CIA, the White House dispatched the Plumbers to burglarize the office of Ellsberg's former psychiatrist, Dr. Lewis Fielding (no known relationship to Henry Fielding), to search for concrete evidence of mental instability or sexual misconduct. The break-in was supervised by G. Gordon Liddy, now a radio talk-show host, who had previously overseen one of the first military-type actions in the War on Drugs: Operation Intercept, a chaotic twenty-day blockade of the Mexican border.[52] The Plumbers left empty-handed, after ransacking Dr. Fielding's patient files and leaving drugs strewn about to make the invasion appear to have been the work of a narcotics thief.

John Ehrlichman later called the Fielding break-in the "seminal Watergate episode."[53] Indeed. It was an illegal burglary that exposed the perpetrators to enormous legal and political risk, yielded no actual intelligence, and yet proceeded from the conviction that it was a street-smart way to play hardball politics. It also was but a short step to the Plumbers' infamous break-in at Democratic Party headquarters at the Watergate in 1972.

"Stay Close to the P.R."

When the first Watergate stories appeared in June 1972, Nixon instructed chief of staff H.R. Haldeman, a former advertising executive, "to stay close to the p.r."[54] The comment reflected Nixon's sensitivity to appearances. He wrote in *Six Crises* that he had made a "basic mistake" in his first television debate with John Kennedy: "I had concentrated too much on substance and not enough on appearance."[55] It was an error he did not intend to repeat as President. And he didn't. He personally reviewed the most minute details of the arrangements for social functions, examined the comments visitors made about the paintings in the west lobby, decided where the military should stand when he drove up the driveway, inspected the White House Police uniforms, and double-checked inventories of White House cuff links and ashtrays.[56] He would handle Watergate with similar attention to its publicly visible details.

Not so federal prosecutors or *Washington Post* investigative reporters Bob Woodward and Carl Bernstein. Criminal investigators and the two unlikely journalists (Woodward, who was twenty-nine, had been with the paper only nine months and was working the police night beat; Bernstein, twenty-eight, was largely out of favor with *Post* editors) promptly began uncovering clues that would link the five arrested burglars to the Committee to Re-Elect the President ("CREEP") and indeed to the White House itself.

The first tape-recorded Watergate-related conversation involving Richard Nixon occurred around noon on June 20, 1972. The conversation, with H.R. Haldeman, lasted eighteen minutes and twenty-eight seconds.[57] Erased after the existence of the White House taping system became public in July 1974, the conversation is now memorialized as "the 18½ minute gap."

The next day, June 21, President Nixon told Haldeman and Colson that Watergate was a "credibility issue." They were used to thinking of "credibility" in terms of Vietnam, Nixon said, "but Vietnam's gone away."[58] The problem was how to respond to this new "credibility" problem. Staying "close to the p.r.," Haldeman suggested that if

E. Howard Hunt were to disappear and if G. Gordon Liddy were to assume full responsibility for the break-in, the damage could be contained. That, Haldeman offered, was "the beauty of the Liddy scenario."[59]

On June 23, President Nixon and his chief of staff discussed the problem of the FBI's not being "under control."[60] The exchange would later be labeled the "smoking gun" conversation. The FBI's investigation was "leading into some productive areas," Haldeman advised Nixon, "because they've been able to trace the money." Haldeman calculated that the best way to handle the problem would be "for us to have [CIA deputy director Vernon] Walters call [acting FBI director L. Patrick] Gray and just say, 'Stay the hell out of this . . . this is ah, business here we don't want you to go any further on it.'" Nixon agreed. He then himself scripted a call in which the President would be portrayed as being very concerned that further investigation would "open the whole Bay of Pigs thing up again." Nixon regretted former Attorney General John Mitchell's involvement, but again "[t]hank[ed] God it wasn't Colson" (who, Nixon later remarked, had worked on "the Pentagon Papers thing"[61]).

Nixon categorically assured the public throughout the summer of 1972 that the White House had not been involved in any way with the Watergate break-in. He also expressed sensitivity to the need for full disclosure, editorializing at one point during an August press conference in an oft-quoted remark, "What really hurts is if you try to cover it up."[62]

"The Outward Appearance of Total Cooperation"

February 1973 opened with a unanimous Senate vote to establish a bipartisan, seven-member select committee (the "Ervin Committee") to explore the Watergate matter and other charges of wrongdoing by both political parties. The White House adopted "the strategy that we should keep the outward appearance of total cooperation but our objective internally should be maximum obstruction and containment, as not to let the thing run away with us."[63] Thus, on the one hand, Nixon directed White House Counsel John Dean and others to "stonewall" the investigators, ordered the invocation of executive privilege "in order to get on with the cover-up plan," advised Dean as to how they could get a million dollars in cash to help silence Hunt, counseled Dean to feign lapses in recollection if called before the grand jury, and singled out John Mitchell's convenient memory for special praise.[64] At the same time, Nixon repeatedly cautioned his aides, "Now damn it, we just can't have an appearance of cover-up."[65]

Haldeman's diary entries for March make the point succinctly. March 15: Nixon begins working with White House Counsel Dean "every day on trying to develop ways of finding some statement that we can put out that shows we're not just covering up."[66] March 20: The President "feels strongly that we've got to say something to get ourselves away from looking like we're completely on the defensive and on a cover-up basis."[67] March 26: Nixon "thinks the key now is that we've got to change our appearance of cover-up."[68]

A New P.R. Counteroffensive to Restore the Credibility of the Presidency

As the Senate Watergate hearings approached, Nixon told Haldeman they had to do something to restore the credibility of the presidency. "Yeah, of course," Haldeman agreed, "you know the credibility gap in the old days."[69] Nixon laid out his main public relations counteroffensive in an April 30 television address, announcing resignations by Haldeman, Ehrlichman, Dean, and Attorney General Richard G. Kleindienst—their resignations accepted on the pretense of addressing a "Caesar's wife" problem.[70] In one breath, Nixon promised "no whitewash at the White House" and full control of the Watergate investigation by his new nominee for Attorney General, Elliot L. Richardson. In another, Nixon lied that he had gained no knowledge of any involvement by any members of his administration in the Watergate break-in, despite his persistent questioning, until March 21, 1973. This latter statement formed the core of the factual defense around which Nixon intended to stake his presidency.

The day before the Ervin hearings began, Nixon intensified his public relations initiative by proposing creation of a federal election reform commission and urging "sweeping" campaign reform. In similar fashion, just days before Judge John Sirica imposed maximum sentences on the Watergate burglars—an act Nixon privately called "outrageous"—Nixon had announced a new anticrime program involving restricted bail and—in keeping with today's fashion—greater use of the death penalty and mandatory minimum sentences.[71]

On May 17, 1973, the Ervin Committee convened the first round of nationally televised hearings into the planning and execution of the Watergate wiretapping and break-in and the alleged cover-up. Nixon had told Haldeman and Dean two months before the hearings to expect "rather considerable . . . attrition." By the time North Carolina's folksy, large-eyebrowed Senator Sam Ervin gaveled the hearings to order before the klieg lights and flashing camera bulbs, there had been attrition indeed. L. Patrick Gray had resigned from the FBI, following reports that he had destroyed documents Ehrlichman had given him from Hunt's White House safe. Haldeman, Ehrlichman, and Dean were gone from the White House. Attorney General Kleindienst had resigned from the Justice Department. And SEC Chairman G. Bradford Cook had resigned amid charges that he had altered an SEC complaint against financier Robert L. Vesco under pressure from former Commerce Secretary and chief Nixon fund raiser Maurice H. Stans, both of whom, together with former Attorney General John Mitchell, were under indictment (and later acquitted by the grand jury) for conspiracy to violate federal campaign contribution laws. To say the least, it was a complicated series of downfalls.

John Dean went before the Ervin Committee on June 25. The televised hearings had already held the nation spellbound, but Dean's appearance heightened the drama. In front of a nationwide television audience, Dean delivered a 245-page opening statement that repeatedly contradicted Nixon.

It was still largely Dean's word against that of the President of the United States, however. This equation changed on Friday, July 13, when former White House aide Alexander P. Butterfield revealed in a witness interview that Nixon had installed and used a taping system to record presidential conversations.

The Tapes

Senate investigators hurried to John Dean's home to gauge his reaction to the news of a taping system. When they informed Dean on Saturday, July 14, he broke into a huge smile: Butterfield had handed him a para-chute.[72] The debate in the Nixon White House swirled around whether the tapes should be destroyed. On Monday, July 16, Butterfield appeared as a surprise "mystery" witness before the Ervin Committee and made his stunning revelation on television.

On July 18, the Ervin Committee asked to hear relevant tapes. A court subpoena for nine White House tapes was issued the next day. It had been requested by Archibald Cox, the Harvard Law School professor appointed Watergate special prosecutor by Attorney General Elliot Richardson. The President refused both tape requests on grounds of executive privilege. An eight-month legal fight followed. After losing in the district court and in the court of appeals, Nixon proposed a compromise under which Senator John C. Stennis (D-Miss.) would prepare a summary of the tapes' contents. The proposal prompted jokes about the ailing, seventy-two-year-old Stennis's being hard of hearing.

Cox rejected the offer. A summary would have been subject to question and unusable in a court of law. Nixon ordered Cox to accept the compromise, but Cox still refused. Nixon directed Attorney General Richardson to fire Cox for disobeying a presidential order. Both Richardson (whom the President had promised full control over the investigation) and Deputy Attorney General William D. Ruckelshaus resigned rather than carry out Nixon's order.

On October 20, Solicitor General Robert H. Bork became acting attorney general and fired Cox, igniting a firestorm of hostile reaction across the country to what became known as the "Saturday Night Massacre." An order to secure the Watergate investigative offices during the transition to a new team of prosecutors appeared horribly on television as "coup-like" and "Gestapo-like." Twenty-one resolutions to impeach Nixon were introduced when Congress reconvened on Tuesday, October 23. White House attorney Charles Alan Wright quickly announced that Nixon would comply with the tapes subpoena after all.

The 18½ Minute Gap

On October 26, Nixon pledged "total cooperation" with whomever acting Attorney General Bork would appoint new special prosecutor. Yet White House attorney J. Fred Buzhardt was soon telling Judge Sirica that tapes of two of the nine subpoenaed conversations did not exist, and then, on a second occasion, that one of the subpoenaed tapes was missing 18½ minutes of recorded conversation.

News reports related a convoluted story from Nixon's personal secretary, Rose Mary Woods, concerning how she could have accidentally caused the erasures. Woods later amended her testimony to say that her mistakes could have caused only up to five minutes' worth of damage. In one measure of the decline since Eisenhower's days, Americans believed three to one that Nixon had made the erasures; indeed, three out of five Americans had predicted before the fact that the tapes would be doctored to protect Nixon.[73]

On January 30, 1974, in his State of the Union address, Nixon called for an end to the Watergate probes. But both the House of Representatives and new special prosecutor Leon Jaworski (through Judge Sirica) subpoenaed scores of tapes of specific presidential conversations involving Dean, Haldeman, Ehrlichman, and Colson. On April 29, Nixon responded in a nationally televised speech. Sitting before stacks of blue-bound volumes of edited transcripts, the President announced the release of 1,308 pages of material.

The transcripts showed the President discussing such things as how to raise cash for the Watergate burglars. They generated a huge negative public reaction, in substantial part because they were laced with "expletives deleted." This masking device would have been just as appropriate if Lyndon Johnson or a number of other Nixon predecessors had found themselves in Nixon's predicament. Indeed, it is hard to see how, say, disclosure of transcripts of President Kennedy's White House conversations with Judith Campbell concerning their sexual liaisons or Mafioso Sam Giancana could have caused less public shock.[74] But Nixon was President, not Kennedy or Johnson, and there was no denying the transcripts' tawdriness. Republican stalwart Senator Hugh Scott, upon reading the record of what he called Nixon's "immoral activities," retracted his long-standing support for the President.[75] The House Judiciary Committee accused Nixon of violating its subpoena and on May 9 formally opened impeachment hearings.

United States v. Nixon

On July 24, 1974, the Supreme Court announced its decision in *United States v. Nixon*—the President's final attempt to prevent production of unedited White House tapes to special prosecutor Jaworski. Chief Justice Warren Burger spoke for a unanimous Court. The Supreme Court agreed with the President concerning the need for confidentiality in communications among high government officials. Indeed, the Court found the point "too plain to require further discussion," for "[h]uman experience teaches that those who expect public dissemination of their remarks may well temper candor with a concern for appearances and for their own interests to the detriment of the decision making process."[76] The Court nonetheless held that such an undifferentiated claim of public interest must give way to a specific, narrowly defined need for information necessary to pursue criminal wrongdoing. Chief Justice Burger's observation about the power of the "concern for appearances" among government decision makers marked a fitting, if unknowing, eulogy for the Nixon White House's tragically failed Watergate strategy and presaged some of the adverse consequences that would flow in the years to come from the wave of institutional reforms adopted in the wake of Watergate.

"One Too Many Lies"

On July 27, the House Judiciary Committee voted 27 to 11 to recommend impeachment to the full House under Article I of the proposed Articles of Impeachment, charging the President with obstruction of justice. Two days later, the Committee added Articles II and III, alleging abuse of power and defiance of committee subpoenas. On August 5, after delivering the subpoenaed tapes to Judge Sirica, the White House publicly released the transcripts. Included was the "smoking gun" conversation of June 23, 1972, in which the President had directed Haldeman to have the CIA pressure the FBI to limit its Watergate investigation.

The "smoking gun" transcript contained strong evidence of Nixon's direct involvement in an effort to obstruct justice. On the other hand, so did previously released transcripts in which the President told Dean how to obtain cash to buy the silence of the Watergate burglars and recommended the virtues of convenient memories. For more than a year, however, the heart and soul of Nixon's public defense had been his repeated assurances that he had possessed no knowledge of efforts to impede federal investigators until March 1973, when, he said, he and his White House Counsel had begun meeting to try to uncover the truth. The "smoking gun" tape showed this story was completely false. All eleven Republicans on the Judiciary Committee who had voted against impeachment on Article I reversed themselves after reading the new transcripts. Senator Barry Goldwater, a barometer of the public's outrage, stormed during a meeting of Senate Republicans, "There are only so many lies you can take, and now there has been one too many."[77]

The Big Bang

The public's collapsing confidence had indeed reached critical density. And it did so at a moment (owing largely to Nixon's own foreign policy successes) when there was no sufficient Cold War counterforce (such as fear of Soviet nuclear attack) to restrain the public's anger against the Commander in Chief. The result was a powerful domestic explosion—a

Big Bang, which threw Nixon and then his successor (after pardoning Nixon) out of the White House, as well as about 100 Republicans from Congress, clearing the way for a new President from outside Washington arriving on the campaign theme that he would never lie to the American public.

The Big Bang's aftershocks generated waves of investigations and reinvestigations, and then waves of reforms. There were hearings into CIA and FBI spying on American citizens, the adequacy of Justice Department investigation and prosecution of criminal misconduct by executive-branch officials, intelligence failures in Vietnam, internal agency checks on corruption, alleged assassination plots involving foreign leaders, the reliability and integrity of the original investigation into the assassination of John Kennedy, covert action in Chile, the necessity for public access to internal executive-branch documents, the need for disclosure of the personal finances of government officials, and the lack of privacy protections for government-held information on individual citizens. These inquiries stimulated reforms at the federal, state, and local levels, as well as among America's professions.

There were separate lines of investigation into the "lessons" of Vietnam and Watergate. At times the inquiries proceeded in parallel; at other times, in oddly opposite directions. House intelligence committee hearings into intelligence failures in Vietnam, for example, approached the issue under investigation with post-Watergate appreciation for dark conspiracies. One publicized session featured CIA analyst Samuel Adams's highly charged allegation that top-level U.S. military officials had conspired to lie about enemy troop strengths through deliberately inflated enemy "body counts." (The accusation would eventually lead to a "CBS Reports" exposé and then a prominent libel trial between CBS and General Westmoreland.) This charge and various high-official denials were duly covered in the next morning's papers.

The news articles did not mention the testimony of a less sensational witness, Colonel Henry A. Shockley, who had been chief of intelligence collection in Vietnam. Colonel Shockley described how well-intentioned and highly dedicated public servants within the U.S. mission in

Vietnam, feeling themselves to be in "a beleaguered camp," independently had begun editing the bad news out from official reports in an effort to counterbalance what they saw as overly negative press stories. Their objective, he said, had been to help restore the public's sinking confidence in the American war effort. One congressman summed up Shockley's testimony as attributing intelligence failures largely to a widespread effort in Vietnam "to make things look good."[78]

The Appearance Explosion

Government officials in the Watergate-reform hearings described post-Watergate Washington in analogous terms to those Shockley used to characterize the mistrust U.S. officials had sensed from their outpost in South Vietnam. "All of us, to a greater or lesser degree, are under suspicion of misconduct," Senator Lawton Chiles intoned in opening hearings on a proposed Public Integrity Act. "Read the papers, talk to people: More and more they speak less and less of a few rotten apples. Now, they look with skepticism at the entire barrel."[79] Although the reform hearings would yield real substantive changes—some good, some less good, some bad—time and time again government witnesses and outside reformers stressed the need to "make things look good" in Washington in the face of a seemingly ravenous press and a skeptical citizenry.

A proposed new special prosecutor's office—designed to be entirely free of influence from the two officials historically entrusted to enforce the nation's laws, the President and the Attorney General—was recommended in large part, for example, because in "the shadow of Watergate . . . the appearance of justice is almost as important as justice itself."[80] The issue of financial conflicts of interest was approached in similar terms. Not merely actual conflicts of interest, but every "appearance of a conflict," was to be avoided.[81]

The centerpiece of the federal war against public distrust was the Ethics in Government Act of 1978. The law established the Office of Government Ethics, created a special prosecutor's office (today's Office of Independent Counsel), imposed financial disclosure obligations on high-level executive-branch officials, and instituted a variety of related reforms. The Ethics Act was accompanied by legislation broadening the public's right to information under the Freedom of Information Act; federal privacy legislation; a law providing public financing for presidential elections; a statute requiring Presidents to notify Congress of U.S. covert actions; the Federal Corrupt Practices Act; the Civil Service Reform Act of 1978, granting official protection for whistle-blowers; and the Inspector General Act, which created a dozen new Inspectors General with the obligation to make independent reports to Congress.

A score of states adopted ethics reform measures similar to the Ethics in Government Act. State ethics agencies, boards, and commissions sprang up. Stung by the highly publicized fact that many of the Watergate principals were lawyers (including President Nixon, Attorneys General Mitchell and Kleindienst, White House Special Counsel Chuck Colson, White House Counsel John Dean, White House counselor John Ehrlichman, CREEP counsel Gordon Liddy, acting FBI director L. Patrick Gray, Plumber Egil "Bud" Krogh, CREEP deputy director Robert Mardian, and Nixon's personal lawyer, Herbert W. Kalmbach), the American Bar Association for the first time required accredited law schools to teach at least one ethics course. The ABA also recognized "legal ethics" as a practice specialty, transmitted the names of attorneys involved in Watergate to state bar groups, and began drafting new model ethics rules. Commercial arbitrators, prosecutors, legal assistants, and even law libraries adopted ethics codes.

Other professions reacted similarly. Within months of Nixon's resignation, the Board of the American Society of Newspaper Editors replaced its half-century-old "Canons of Journalism" with "A Statement of Principles" intended "to preserve, protect and strengthen the bond of trust between American journalists and the American people." The American Medical Association's Judicial Council recommended that the AMA's ethics code likewise be revised. And centers for legal ethics, business ethics, government ethics, and medical ethics arose. The Big Bang, in short, led to the largest and most pervasive government and professional ethics reform effort undertaken in American history and to the creation of the modern Ethics Establishment.

America's approach to Vietnam was distinguished by both the massive use of firepower and the self-imposed constraints of "limited war." On the one hand, the United States dropped on North Vietnam triple the bomb tonnage released on Europe, Asia, and Africa during World War II.[82] On the other hand, we refrained for years from pursuing North Vietnamese soldiers when they retreated to their Cambodian sanctuaries.

America's response to the domestic "credibility" crisis has borne similar markings and unfortunately similar results. We have bombarded major breaches of trust as well as slight improprieties with some of the largest weapons in our arsenal: federal, state, and local government ethics bureaucracies; increasingly complex and pervasive professional society regulations; specially retained "independent" criminal investigators and prosecutors; ever-expanding federal criminal-ethics laws; elaborate, often sensational legislative oversight hearings; and relentless and intensive media scrutiny. At the same time, we curiously have refused to attack certain persistent problems at their source.

The result has been a further sharp and indisputable drop in public trust from the then disturbingly low points of Vietnam and Watergate. This failure may not be as dramatic as television footage of American helicopters pulling away from the rooftop of the U.S. embassy in Saigon while the North Vietnamese made final preparations to enter the city, or of President Nixon's helicopter banking away from the White House lawn one last time after Nixon had flashed his signature "V" for "victory." But the defeat is just as real. And given our talents and resources as a nation, it is in certain ways just as troubling.

5

The Ethics Establishment, Part I: Government

To do good is noble, but to teach others how to be good is nobler—and no trouble.

—Mark Twain[1]

One of the first consequences of Watergate was the enrichment and empowerment of virtually everyone who participated in the Watergate scandal. In rough order of enrichment, those included Bob Woodward and Carl Bernstein, the investigative reporters who broke much of the story and whose career success and first major book contracts resulted from that scandal; the *Washington Post,* itself, which under Ben Bradlee's leadership climbed aboard the public-interest rocket to become the nation's third most important paper; lawyers ranging from Sam Dash, to Fred Thompson, to Hillary Clinton; and members of Congress ranging from Sam Ervin, to Peter Rodino, to Howard Baker, to the many "Watergate babies" elected in the 1974 and 1976 waves of anti-GOP backlash. Those who went to jail, of course, were an exception—though some of them came out all right in the end, too, as the successful post-Watergate careers of G. Gordon Liddy and Charles Colson illustrate.

The political scene suddenly featured large numbers of individuals and organizations with agendas that had not existed before. Journalists knew that their careers could take off if they uncovered the right scandal. Members of Congress, especially (but not exclusively) Democrats, had wrested power from the presidency, and they used it to pass the Ethics in Government Act. Newly minted experts in the new ethical rules stood to benefit from the rules even (or especially) if those rules were confusing and ultimately ineffective. Political groups and politicians could use the rules as both a shield and a sword, discrediting opponents for improper appearances, while defending their own transgressions as mere technical violations of rules so arcane that no one really understood them anyway.

The creation of an Ethics Establishment—that complex of interest groups, journalists, consultants, government ethics officers, and legislators owing its existence to the Watergate scandal—may have been the most significant impact of the Big Bang. In short, the Ethics Establishment became an institutional infrastructure to support the Watergate syndrome. Rules and statutes matter, but are often ignored. Self-interest, on the other hand, is seldom ignored, whether by individuals or institutions. ("Follow the money," Deep Throat advised Woodward and Bernstein.) As the Framers of our Constitution knew, self-interest is a more reliable guide to action than patriotism or civic virtue. Successful systems are thus those where self-interested behavior by individuals and organizations produces behavior that is good for society. Unfortunately, the ethical system created by the Big Bang is not such a system.

This chapter will survey some of the institutions that were created or empowered by the Ethics Explosion and discuss some of the ways in which the interests of these players depart from what most people would regard as the public interest. We emphasize that we are embarking on a survey of conflicting *institutional* interests. Many of the individuals who work for these institutions, of course, are very dedicated and well-intentioned. But applying traditional standards of conflict of interest to these *institutions* (many of which devote enormous energy to pointing out conflicts of interest in others) reveals much about why the gears of the new ethics machinery seem to be making more and more clanking noises and yet producing fewer and fewer useable products.

Some parts of the Ethics Establishment have already been explored in one aspect or another: the press, for example, in James Fallows' *Breaking the News* or Larry Sabato's *Feeding Frenzy*, the "public interest" world in Hedrick Smith's *The Power Game,* or the overall Beltway culture in Suzanne Garment's *Scandal.* We will not revisit that ground. Instead, after a brief survey, we will point out some of the ways in which appearance standards serve these institutional players' interests more than those of the public. We will also look at the likely consequences of empowering such groups, consequences that will be further explored in subsequent chapters.

The Independent Counsel

There was no more dramatic event during the Watergate scandal than the so-called "Saturday Night Massacre," in which executive control of the Justice Department was used in an effort to hinder prosecution of White House officials, including the President. After the resignation of President Nixon, Congress set out, with broad support from the press and people, to ensure that such a thing could never happen again.

The result was the creation of an Independent Counsel. Although often dubbed a "special prosecutor," the Independent Counsel is something rather different. A special prosecutor is a prosecutor appointed by the Attorney General to handle a particular case—whether because of special expertise or, more often, because lawyers in the Justice Department possess a real or perceived conflict of interest in that case. But although a special prosecutor is brought in from outside and handles only the case for which he or she is appointed, as a Justice Department appointee the special prosecutor remains under the control of the Attorney General. He or she can—as the Saturday Night Massacre proved—be fired at will by an administration willing to bear the political costs.

The Independent Counsel is a different creature altogether. Under law, an Independent Counsel is not appointed by the Attorney General.

Instead, the procedure works like this: Upon receiving a complaint concerning the behavior of an executive-branch official, the Attorney General must investigate. If he or she finds the complaint to be without basis, then no further action is needed. But if there is any evidence that the complaint might be valid, then the Attorney General must petition the U.S. Court of Appeals for the District of Columbia Circuit for the appointment of an Independent Counsel. That court (through a "special division" whose sole function is the appointment of Independent Counsels) will then appoint a Counsel who is to serve until the investigation and prosecution of the matters under his or her jurisdiction are complete.[2]

The Independent Counsel differs from an ordinary prosecutor, or even a special prosecutor, in a number of important ways. The most obvious is that he or she is freed from political control. In light of the Watergate history that led to the creation of the office, that makes sense. But there are other differences as well. One major constraint on ordinary prosecutors is budgetary. Because they are judged in no small part on their win/loss record, and because resources are limited, they have a powerful incentive not to devote large amounts of time and energy to marginal cases. Since marginal cases are precisely those in which prosecutorial harassment or "targeting" is likely to be the biggest problem, that is a significant protection for potential defendants. Another constraint is political: If prosecutions appear to be politically motivated, it reflects badly on the prosecutors and their superiors, ultimately (where federal prosecutors are involved) including the Attorney General and the President.

By contrast, an Independent Counsel has an effectively unlimited budget. Nor must he or she balance work on a particular matter against work on other cases—Independent Counsels, after all, deal with only a single matter. Nor is track record a constraint: Independent Counsels are judged not on how they do an overall job on many cases, but on how flawlessly they handle a single case. That encourages a no-stone-unturned style of prosecution that is certainly thorough, but that is often far harder on defendants than run-of-the-mill prosecution. And since the Independent Counsel is independent, he or she is largely immune from complaints of political bias, though "independent" is not necessarily the same thing as "unbiased."[3]

None of this is necessarily bad, of course. When a President or close advisor is being investigated or prosecuted for serious misconduct, we probably should want the job to be more thorough, and freer from politics, than is the case in run-of-the-mill prosecutions. The rights of a top-rank government defendant, after all, are not superior to those of a bottom-rung drug dealer, but the public interest in preventing misconduct by the former may well exceed the public interest in convicting the latter. When drug dealers are put away, others rapidly appear to take their place. One hopes that the same is not true for corrupt officials.

But the Independent Counsel law is not limited to top officials accused of serious misbehavior. Instead, it has been expanded to cover all sorts of fundamentally trivial—or at least fundamentally noncriminal—behavior. The prototypical example is the Independent Counsel investigation into accusations (later discredited) of cocaine use by Carter official Hamilton Jordan. Jordan rang up $70,000 in legal expenses vindicating himself from charges that wouldn't have even prompted an investigation in the case of an ordinary citizen in Washington at the time.[4]

The Independent Counsel law has since been amended in various ways in an effort to treat high-profile targets more like ordinary citizens are treated by ordinary prosecutors. Predictably, this has proved to be an impossible undertaking—and not only for the institutional reasons mentioned above. Ordinary citizens simply aren't subject to the same dizzying array of complicated government ethics regulations that govern the conduct of government officials, the violation of any of which typically can be transformed into a criminal case.

For example, Reagan counselor Edwin Meese III was criminally investigated (and later cleared) for such things as receiving cuff links from a foreign government and inadvertently failing to report on his annual Standard 278 Financial Disclosure Report such items as a $299.00 payment from the San Diego Museum of Art to the Department of Defense to cover the cost of Mrs. Meese's return airfare from Los Alamitos Naval Air Station to Andrews Air Force Base in connection with a trip the Meeses made to a museum fund raiser. The intentional failure to disclose required information on such forms would have been a felony.

Similarly, the Ethics in Government Act's criminal "revolving door" provisions obviously apply only to (former) government officials, not to ordinary citizens. The statute criminalizes certain types of lobbying by officials after they leave government. The objective of preventing former officials from cashing in at the public's expense is commendable. But the "revolving door" statute is so complex and full of loopholes that the first subject of such an Independent Counsel prosecution, Reagan political director Lyn Nofziger, with ACLU support, had his 1988 conviction reversed by a federal appeals court[5] and was never retried.

The Independent Counsel who investigated former Reagan White House deputy chief of staff Michael Deaver for similar postemployment lobbying didn't even attempt to prove a violation of the "revolving door" statute in light of its complexity. Instead, he brought only perjury charges arising out of testimony Deaver had given in an effort to *explain* his lobbying to Congress and a grand jury. By the end of the Deaver prosecution, even the *Washington Post* was siding with Deaver, saying his influence peddling "is done every day in this town," and calling the "preachily titled Ethics in Government Act . . . feel-good legislation" that draws "arbitrary lines" leading to "cutesy evasions" that "spawn as much corruption as they cure."[6] (Independent Counsel Whitney North Seymour, Jr. criticized the *Post*'s editorial at Deaver's sentencing, by which time Seymour had already sent out numerous copies of a promotional letter advertising his postemployment availability as a "paid speaker" to discuss the Deaver case and ethics in Washington. NYU legal ethics professor Stephen Gillers told the *New York Times* that Seymour's letter "was not a violation of legal ethics, but raised concerns about the appearance of a conflict of interest."[7])

Like the appearance standard on which it depends, the Independent Counsel law has been used as a shield as well as a sword. More than once, allegations of misconduct have been defused by the appointment of an Independent Counsel. Doing so turns debates about right and wrong into discussions of criminality and turns a finding of "not actually criminal" into something that is politically advertised as a vindication. It is not clear that doing so helps to promote ethical behavior by our public servants.

Furthermore, the Independent Counsel also represents a further step in the targeting of law enforcement. Traditionally, one first identified a crime and then went looking for the criminal. Nowadays, however, law enforcement officials often first target an individual and then start looking for evidence that individual has broken some law somewhere or other.[8] One result: No American under the age of sixteen has lived under a President who has not been the subject of an Independent Counsel investigation.

So what? Aren't lawbreakers lawbreakers? Well, no. The problem with targeting is that virtually no individual can withstand such scrutiny— particularly where political ethics laws, which are notoriously technical, complex, and counterintuitive, are concerned. Criminal law professors traditionally open their classes by announcing to their students that every single one of them is a felon, whether he or she is aware of it or not. And they are right. While some of the felonies may be silly ones (oral sex in Georgia), or at least "youthful indiscretions" (pot smoking in college), most people have some such wrongdoing in their past. Normally, we rely on prosecutorial discretion to prevent such prosecutions. That has its problems (there have been cases in which seldom-enforced laws have been used against political rivals), but it generally works fairly well.

But an Independent Counsel has different incentives. He or she has been told to investigate someone and has no other responsibilities. There are no other cases to occupy resources, or to make up part of a track record. An Independent Counsel is likely to leave few stones unturned in investigating a target, and less likely to exercise discretion by not prosecuting for merely technical or minor offenses. This is particularly significant given that political ethics laws are known for producing large numbers of technical or minor offenses.

The appearance of impropriety standard is useful for both sides in this situation. The Independent Counsel can charge appearance violations, simultaneously showing that he or she is doing the job without accusing the target of actual wrongdoing. The target can claim that he or she did nothing wrong, but merely committed a technical violation involving only appearances, not substance: "Of course I am guilty of being careless of appearances," Michael Deaver confessed in typical fashion after his perjury conviction.[9] These benefits from pleading to an appearance "violation," as noted in Chapter 2, partly explain the popularity of appearance ethics on Capitol Hill.

The Hill

Of congressional hearings, at least, there was no shortage. Although Congress had traditionally avoided calling attention to executive-branch improprieties (much less its own), in the wake of Watergate and the Ethics in Government Act all that changed. For it could not escape notice that many members of Congress gained enormous stature and influence—with both the public and their peers—as a result of Watergate.

Senator Sam Ervin, previously a little-regarded opponent of desegregation, emerged from the Watergate hearings a hero, perhaps even an icon. Peter Rodino, chair of the House Judiciary Committee, became a household name. Senator (later Senate Minority Leader and White House Chief of Staff) Howard Baker got his start at national prominence with his question "What did the President know and when did he know it?" And many lesser lights, such as New York Congresswoman Elizabeth Holtzman, Texas Representative Barbara Jordan, and Maine's then-freshman Representative Bill Cohen, first entered the national stage as a result of Watergate hearings.

While Watergate was hardly the first time that members of Congress used televised hearings to gain national stature (the McCarthy subversion hearings and the Kefauver organized crime hearings of the fifties were precedents), it was a much more dramatic event. And, coming as it did just before the explosion in appearance ethics, it set in motion a powerful tendency for such hearings to become the norm, rather than the exception, in how government business was conducted. This tendency was exacerbated by two related phenomena. One was the weakening of the traditional party system. Without that system, politicians who wanted to advance had to do so largely through publicity seeking. Another was the rise of "public-affairs" journalism: political talking-head shows, newsletters, cable TV networks such as C-SPAN and NET, and so on. All of these outlets needed new material on a constant basis and rewarded those who fed them with fame, and often fortune. Add to this (as either a symptom or a cause) a massive expansion of congressional staffs, providing the necessary legwork for more hearings and press conferences, as well as revolving-door career paths between the Hill and the other institutions of the Ethics Establishment, and the stage was set for an explosion of ethics scandals, real or invented. There were plenty of both.

The Bureaucrats

Nothing is real in Washington unless there is a bureaucracy dedicated to it, and ethics is no exception. There had, of course, been House and Senate ethics committees for some time before Watergate, though they became considerably more active afterward. But the real action was in the executive branch, and in state and city governments across the country.

Under the Ethics in Government Act,[10] the key agency is the Office of Government Ethics.[11] It communicates with the various executive agencies and departments through Designated Agency Ethics Officials, known as "DAEOs." Memos to the DAEOs are known within the trade as "DAEOgrams." The following *excerpts* from a five-page, single-spaced DAEOgram provide a flavor of the overarching complexities:

May 1, 1984

MEMORANDUM

SUBJECT: Summary of Acceptance and Disclosure of Travel
           Expenses and Related Gifts

FROM: David H. Martin
           Director

TO: Designated Agency Ethics Officials, General
           Counsels, and Inspectors General

Because this Office has consistently received a number of questions regarding the acceptance and disclosure by executive branch employees of travel reimbursements and related gifts from private sources and because the annual filing deadline for public financial disclosure reports is again drawing near, we believe it is important to provide you with the following outline of the considerations involved in answering any questions regarding this subject.

———

If the traveling employee is on *official* business—

1. When an executive branch employee is offered payment for travel expenses from a private source for expenses incurred in carrying out his or her *official duties,* the travel reimbursement expense payments can only be accepted, if at all, by the agency employing the individual on the individual's behalf. The employee may *not personally* accept the travel expenses without potentially violating 18U.S.C. 209.

2. The agency may accept the travel expenses *only* if it has statutory gift acceptance authority to do so or if the gift qualifies under 5 U.S.C. 4111 discussed in paragraph 3 below. Otherwise the agency will be improperly augmenting its appropriations and running afoul of the Comptroller General's Decision B-128527 dated March 7, 1967 (46 Comp. Gen. 689). Authority to accept gifts, if it exists, will generally be found in your agency's organic statute.

The authority may limit the acceptance to gifts for specific purposes and your agency must have a process to determine which offers of gifts can be accepted under that authority. An agency's authority to accept gifts, including travel expenses, cannot be granted by regulation; the grant must be made by statute. (Note: Most agencies do *not* have this statutory authority.)

3. If the donor is a non-profit, tax exempt institution described by 26 U.S.C. 501(c)(3), the Employees Training Act, codified at 5 U.S.C. 4111, authorizes an employee to accept the payment of travel expenses from that donor if the agency follows the regulations set forth in 5 C.F.R. 410.701 *et seq.* These regulations require prior written authorization for acceptance of such travel expenses and that acceptance of the expenses does not create an actual or apparent conflict. The important considerations involved here are two: First, the organization *must* be categorized by the I.R.S. under section 501(c)(*3*). There are many tax-exempt non-profit organizations which do *not* fall under subsection (c)(3). The I.R.S. reading room can confirm the status of the organization if you provide the exact name of the organization and the state of incorporation. Second, simply because the organization is categorized under section 501(c)(3) does not mean that the offered travel expenses are always acceptable. If the organization seeks grants from your agency or does business with your agency, especially if its staff deals directly with the employee involved, such offered reimbursements should, in most cases, not be accepted. Again, refer to the implementing regulations.

Example: A grants official at an agency is asked to speak at a University in his official capacity and the University offers to pay his travel expenses. The University is a 501(c)(3) corporation but it has one grant and is seeking others from the agency. The employee should not be allowed to accept the travel expenses because of the appearance of a conflict of interest.

4. If your agency does *not* have gift acceptance authority and the donor is not a 501(c)(3) corporation, neither the agency nor the employee may accept payment for travel expenses of the employee on official business. Further, the agency may not put the employee in non-duty status to carry out what is essentially official business simply to allow the employee to accept the travel expenses.

———

If the traveling employee is *not* on official business—

6. The employee may not accept any travel expenses or any gift from any organization which
1) has, or is is seeking to obtain, contractual or other business or financial relations with his or her agency;
2) conducts operations or activities that are regulated by his or her agency; or,
3) has interests that may be substantially affected by the performance or non performance of his or her official duty.

These standards are set forth in 5 C.F.R. 735.202(a). Agencies may have regulations which are more strict and they may also have certain exceptions based on those in 5 C.F.R. 735.202(b).

———

Public Disclosure (SF 278)

An employee required to file a public financial disclosure report (SF 278) should disclose travel expenses meeting the $250 threshold in the manner set forth below. Note that the law treats in-kind services such as travel tickets, hotel rooms and meals as one disclosure requirement and cash reimbursements for any of those same items as a separate disclosure requirement.

If the employee is on official business—

1. When the agency has gift acceptance authority and has made the appropriate determination to accept travel expenses for an em-

ployee's travel prior to the expenses being incurred, then the employee need not disclose these expenses as the agency has accepted them, not the employee. If for any reason prior approval was not received, these expenses must be disclosed because at the time they were accepted, it was the employee not the agency making the acceptance. For the employee's sake the agency may note subsequent approval on the form if it occurred.

2. When the employee accepts the travel expenses from a 26 U.S.C. 501(c)(3) corporation pursuant to 5 U.S.C. 4111, these expenses must be disclosed. Section 4111 specifically allows the *employee* to accept, albeit with agency approval, and because it is a personal acceptance it is governed by the public financial disclosure requirements. Again, the agency may wish to note on the form the date the agency gave acceptance approval.

3. If an employee accepts travel expenses without the benefit of agency gift acceptance authority or coverage of 5 U.S.C. 4111, the expenses must of course be disclosed.

If the employee is not on official business—

4. All travel expenses meeting the threshold values must be disclosed unless they are paid by a relative or are required to be reported under 2 U.S.C. 432.

Gifts from a foreign government—

5. Because the reporting threshold for gifts from a foreign government covered by the Foreign Gifts Act is lower than the $250 threshold for reporting under the Ethics in Government Act, all such travel expenses should be disclosed under the procedures established pursuant to 5 U.S.C. 7342 and are therefore exempt from disclosure on the SF 278. (See Section 209(8)(B) of the Ethics in Government Act.) Note, however, that a gift *other* than reimbursement of travel expenses need only exceed the more than $100 threshold of the Ethics in Government Act disclosure requirements. Therefore, any

gift, other than travel expenses from a foreign government valued at more than $100 but within the "minimal value" that triggers the acceptance and disclosure requirements of the Foreign Gifts Act, would have to appear on the SF 278. (In March, 1984, the GSA adjusted the "minimal value" to $165 or less.)

> Example: An employee is asked by a foreign government to participate in a symposium hosted by the government. The employee's travel expenses outside the United States are paid for by the foreign government and as a participant she is also given a small piece of sculpture. The travel expenses have a value of $500 and the sculpture $125. The Foreign Gifts Act "minimal value" at the time was $140 or less. Because the travel expenses are more than the "minimal value" for Foreign Gifts Act purposes and are therefore subject to disclosure under 5 U.S.C. 7342, she need not disclose them on her SF 278. However, because the sculpture is within the "minimal value" for Foreign Gifts Act purposes but more than the over $100 reporting requirement of the Ethics in Government Act for gifts other than travel expenses, she must disclose the receipt of the sculpture on her SF 278.

> ————————

If you have any questions concerning the acceptance of travel expenses, please feel free to contact this Office.

If your eyes glazed over somewhere between mention of Comptroller General Decision B-128527 and discussion of the availability opf the IRS's reading room for cross-checking the bona-fides of a 501(c)(3) corporation, then you can appreciate the problem federal employees confront. And the mistakes *they* make can trigger all sorts of questions about their ethics—to say nothing about potential *crimes*.

The DAEOs are responsible for overseeing the application of ethics rules at their respective agencies. These include not only the travel expense rules and gift-acceptance rules mentioned in the above DAEOgram, but also the "revolving door" rules, other conflict-of-interest rules, other financial disclosure rules, and so forth. In addition, under the Inspector General Act of 1978 each department has an Inspector General whose duty is to oversee the propriety of actions within the department, report to Congress, and make criminal referrals to the Justice Department where appropriate.[12]

The day-to-day encounters of most federal employees with the ethics laws begin and end with the regulations promulgated by these ethics bureaucrats. For example, a federal employee who was given a free ticket after his flight was delayed five hours while he was on official travel was told that the ticket belonged to the federal government. The employee argued that he was being compensated for the airline's poor performance: The government concluded instead that the ticket was "promotional" because it was intended to "enhance a company's image or customer service" and hence was government property. The employee argued that since the government would have allowed him to keep the ticket if he had gotten it in exchange for giving up his seat voluntarily on an overcrowded flight, he should be allowed to keep a ticket given to him in exchange for suffering a lengthy delay. The government responded that "payment for voluntarily relinquishing a seat, however, is unique in that it advances the Government's regulatory policy requiring airlines to encourage volunteers to give up their seats on oversold flights." The government went on to note that "the Federal Travel Regulation explicitly prohibits employees from keeping compensation when an airline involuntarily bumps them from a flight," and that "an involuntary delay is more analogous to an involuntary bump than the excepted circumstances."[13]

Even the government's chief ethics officer couldn't make sense of a 1989 congressional ban on outside income. OGE director Steven Potts said the law—the "Honoraria Prohibition" of the 1989 Ethics Reform Act—was "not sensible" and undermined respect for legitimate restrictions on federal workers. Peter G. Crane, a Nuclear Regulatory Commission lawyer who writes about Romanov-era Russian history in his spare time, also complained about the law's absurdity. For the sake of appearances, Crane explained, the law forbade federal workers from accepting pay for writing articles or giving speeches even on topics unrelated to their work:

> No other form of moonlighting (selling real estate, repairing cars) [is] banned—just writing and speech.

> ———————

> It bans articles but not books, nonfiction but not fiction, and individual speeches but not a series of speeches.

> ———————

The regulations implementing the law read like "1984" updated by Monty Python. In a January 1991 Federal Register notice, the Office of Government Ethics declared that a federal worker can legally accept pay for a "comic monologue"—unless, that is, the government decides that the talk was actually an "amusing speech," in which case the federal worker could be fined $10,000 and drummed out of the government.[14]

The National Treasury Employees Union quickly challenged the provision in court. The federal workers began piling up predictable legal victories on First Amendment grounds, including in the Supreme Court.[15] Many people wondered why Congress ever went down this rocky path to virtually certain court disapproval. Crane had the answer:

> The answer lies in the now largely forgotten history of Congress' attempt to pass a long overdue pay raise in the late 1980s. A first pay increase, hurried through Congress, was scuttled after talk show hosts and Ralph Nader mobilized intense public opposition. At about the same time, questions were raised in the media about House speaker Jim Wright's book deal and about honoraria to senators for token appearances.

Congress's answer was to reenact the pay raise, but this time with an "ethics reform" attached: In return for higher pay, Congress would forswear "honoraria" for speeches and articles. In the name of "uniformity," the ban would apply to the whole federal government. Senior government executives also got a large pay raise.

Uniformity quickly went out the window, however, because senators (historically the recipients of many more honoraria than representatives) voted to reject the pay raise and keep their honoraria. The statute also included an exemption for writing books. Thus the two kinds of abuse that gave rise to the law—a book deal and payments to senators—remained unaffected by the new law. For Congress, it was a perfect solution. House members got a pay raise but could proudly tell their constituents they had renounced their outside earnings. Senators got to keep their outside earnings but could proclaim that they had refused the offer of a pay raise.

On the other hand, the several million federal workers who were not senior executives had their right to outside earnings curtailed but got no raise to make up for it. That meant the mailroom clerk in my agency who supplemented her modest salary by writing articles about horse shows had her outside income—and with it, a hobby that had given her joy—taken away. But a senior executive whose moonlighting did not include writing articles or giving speeches could continue to earn outside income, on top of the hefty new pay raise.[16]

It is fair to say that this world of regulatory ethics *is* rather complicated, and that the "ethics" label we place on these sorts of reforms is hardly proof of where the public interest actually may reside. Indeed, the "public interest" groups in the *National Treasury Employees Union* case were on opposite sides of the issue: Common Cause supported the honoraria ban as "part of a careful and deliberate choice by Congress to guard against conflicts of interest and the appearance of impropriety."[17] Public Citizen and People for the American Way, however, sided with First Amendment groups and the federal employees.[18]

The Interest Groups

The post-Watergate era saw the blossoming of all sorts of "public interest" groups aimed at policing (or at least exposing) official misconduct. These groups, with names like the Center for Public Integrity, Common Cause, Public Citizen, and so on, were organized in response to an appealing notion. The notion was that these groups would serve as lobbyists for ordinary citizens: While special interests, business, and so on were represented by big-time Washington lobbyists, these groups would advance the issues and agendas that special interests ignored, those aimed at the common good rather than the narrow concerns of selfish manipulators.

The interest groups certainly brought a different perspective and agenda to Washington and undoubtedly highlighted some serious problems and accomplished many good things. But as time passed—and the groups proliferated—it became clear that "public interest" groups could be just as self-interested as anyone else. Unlike business or labor groups, after all, "public interest" lobbyists could not simply turn to their parent organizations and ask for an allowance. Instead, they had to seek out paying clients of their own.

There are many ways of doing this, but far and away the most popular was that staple of late-twentieth-century politics and advocacy, direct mail. Direct-mail fund raising offers many advantages: It allows groups to combine advocacy with fund raising ("mail this postcard to your Senator, and mail us a check so we can send out more postcards"), it allows groups to claim legitimately that they are not "fronts" bankrolled by particular individuals or organizations, and it gives many citizens the feeling that they have some kind of influence in the political process.

Direct-mail fund raising also has some significant disadvantages. The most publicized disadvantage is fraud: Many groups that ask for money do little else, and some are outright scams. But there is a less publicized, but perhaps more fundamental, disadvantage to direct-mail fund raising. Over time, it begins to set the agenda of an organization, causing it to direct its actions in ways that promote fund raising, not necessarily its stated agenda.

Organizations that raise money by mail keep or rent mailing lists of members and likely targets. Such lists must be "maintained" by frequent mailings or they become less fruitful. The success or failure of a particular mailing can mean a lot to a group: often the difference between layoffs at headquarters or a bonus for the Executive Director. The pressure to undertake activities that will help boost direct mail yields is strong, and often becomes overwhelming.

Organizations that rely on direct mail thus tend to stage confrontations and p.r. events; things that get an organization's name in the news boost the returns on direct mail substantially. And those organizations often look for high-profile events or causes to tout in their mailings, or promise new projects in their mailings more because they hope to encourage recipients to open their wallets than for any other reason.[19] And the hyperbole and emotionalism that are essential elements of direct-mail solicitation serve as an incentive to exaggerate, shade the truth, or even lie outright.

As Katherine Dunn reports in the *New Republic,* many widely repeated "facts" have more to do with nonprofits' fund-raising activities than the truth. More suicides during the holidays? Nope, they actually go down—but charities raise most of their money near the end of the tax year, and by no coincidence, those dealing with suicides and the suicidal flood the news media with heart-wrenching stories at about that time. A sudden flood of child abduction by strangers in the mid-1980s? Nope— just a flood of nonprofits raising money by giving that impression. Super Bowl Sunday "the biggest day of the year for violence against women"? Nope—just a way to raise money, reports Dunn: "The entire campaign was a lie."[20]

One might dismiss this sort of thing as simply another example of late-twentieth-century hype, though perhaps with a certain measure of concern regarding the impact on parents (and children) of exaggerated stories of child abduction or the impact on marriages of advocacy mailings to women (like one from a p.r. firm in New Hampshire) saying, "Don't remain alone with him during the game."[21] But the impact of this phenomenon on public interest organizations specializing in promoting government ethics is significant, too. The reason is the relationship between direct-mail fund raising, the public relations efforts needed to sustain it, and the proliferation of appearance standards in the government ethics realm.

Appearance ethics is ideally suited for such advocacy groups. First, the promotion of appearance standards allows such groups to adopt a posture of strictness: "We're not just for clean government, we're for government that doesn't even *look* dirty." Second, appearances provide ready-made grist for public relations and direct-mail mills. Showing impropriety may require real work, but showing the *appearance* of impropriety is often much easier: a few vaguely worded statements about an official's "links" to unsavory characters, a raised eyebrow at some campaign contributions, and *voila!* a scandal (or at least a mini-scandal) likely to last long enough to get mailings out and money back. A few press releases, a few items on the evening news and in newspapers, a little footage of the Executive Director standing in front of the Capitol, and the organization has created an image as a real go-getter. If its charges lead to the appointment of an Independent Counsel, it can claim victory in its next fund-raising letter.

If the Independent Counsel decides not to prosecute, that's okay—it's on to a new fund-raising cycle. Or, the whole thing can be called a cover-up, and more money can be requested so that the truth can be exposed. If the Independent Counsel does prosecute, then victory can be declared again, and more money can be requested for more such triumphs. The constant factor in all of this should be obvious.

The Press

More than any other institution, of course, the press was the big victor in the aftermath of Watergate. The *Washington Post,* not previously known for its willingness to offend those in power, suddenly became the world's most famous and admired newspaper. Bob Woodward and Carl Bernstein, the reporters who broke the main Watergate story, were idolized as no journalists before or since. One can do worse than be portrayed on the silver screen by Robert Redford, as Woodward was—or even by Dustin Hoffman, as Bernstein was. Across the nation, ambitious and idealistic undergraduates decided to major in journalism. And, also across the nation, ambitious (and sometimes idealistic) journalists decided that the path to fame and fortune was the breaking of political scandal stories.[22]

In Tennessee, Democratic Governor Ray Blanton fell to a sort of mini-Watergate. The events leading to his downfall were dramatized in the movie *Marie,* which led to the real-life Marie Ragghianti's lawyer, former Watergate special prosecutor Fred Thompson, playing himself in the film and beginning an acting career that ultimately led him to a seat in the U.S. Senate. The journalists who broke the story were no doubt inspired by Woodward and Bernstein. Similar scenes played out across the country. From small towns to college campuses to Washington itself, once investigative journalism became the path to fame (and occasionally fortune), journalists began looking for scandals to uncover to a degree never dreamed of by the "muckrakers" of decades gone by.

The post-Watergate ethics reforms made their jobs much easier. Though Woodward and Bernstein were "outsiders" to the mainstream Washington journalistic establishment, Woodward and Bernstein's reporting had been hard-fought traditional journalism. The facts that they documented involved slush funds, illegal break-ins, abuse of intelligence agency resources, and more. Even in Ray Blanton's case, the crimes involved were traditional—involving bribes for liquor licenses and criminal pardons—and so were the methods of discovering and reporting them. Such journalism was hard work.

But thanks to the rise of post-Watergate appearance ethics, the work of journalists became much easier. Now the "appearance" of impropriety, or of a conflict of interest, was enough. Such appearances were far easier to uncover than the sort of things involved in Watergate, making the path to journalistic success easier.

Of course, such ease came at a price. When the Watergate story broke, it was something unparalleled in American history: rampant and serious abuse of power, meticulously documented by the press, and unconvincingly denied by the administration. Later scandals, based on appearances, had less resonance. In part, of course, that was because few could equal the importance of Watergate. But it was also because the scandal currency had been debased. With appearance ethics making scandals easy to create, more were created. But although the supply of scandal increased, demand, by all appearances, did not. Such matters were grist for hearings and investigations, but not, it seems, for moral outrage.

The Consultants

Such technicalities, however, called for expertise to match them, and in very short order there developed an entire industry built around compliance with ethics rules. Like most such things, it featured newsletters, conferences, and—most especially—high-priced consultants.

The consultants offered advice, much of which was useful in the narrow sense. Those entering government service were often encountering the complexities of post-Watergate ethics laws for the first time. Since those laws often involved disclosures and forms that most individuals found daunting and difficult to decipher, it is natural that they would turn to professional help, just as so many Americans turn to accountants and tax lawyers at tax time each year. (One Washington lawyer even claims a specialty in "ethics and congressional spouses."[23]) Of course, Americans expect taxes to be complicated. They might be forgiven for wondering why matters of right and wrong have to be equally difficult. The short answer, of course, is that failing to treat ethics laws with the same kind of respect as tax laws can produce equally unpleasant results.

As we discuss elsewhere, there has been a proliferation of ethics consultants since Watergate, not only in government ethics but also in the professions and in business. In medicine, for example:

In much the same way that a rheumatologist or a dermatologist might be called in by a GP to consult on a patient with especially puzzling joint or skin problems, an ethics consultant is called in to give advice on cases which present particularly difficult ethical problems. The consultant will typically interview and perhaps examine the patient, review the case with the health care team, and consult with the patient's family. Like any other consultant, he or she will usually leave a note in the patient's chart with recommendations for the patient's management.[24]

This practice enables the doctor to abdicate responsibility to a presumed specialist, who in turn can seek safety in published professional codes and opinions.

Hiring *government* ethics consultants offers another benefit, which accounts for much of their appeal. Many of those consulting on ethics matters have special expertise gained while serving on the staff (or occasionally as members) of House or Senate committees that draft ethics laws, or on the staff of special prosecutors or Independent Counsels enforcing them. Hiring such individuals serves not only as a source of advice, but also of insurance: Because of their experience, these individuals carry weight with their successors in such positions, who can't help but imagine themselves out there earning high consulting fees later on. What better source of insulation against ethics charges than to be able to say, "I hired a leading expert in the field, a former Watergate special prosecutor, who told me I had no problems"?

Such individuals, of course, are often called upon to advise legislators on the drafting of new ethics rules. With their encyclopedic knowledge of the minutiae of existing rules, and the likelihood of future consulting work at least in the back of their minds, the advice offered by these consultants is, not surprisingly, often to make rules that further complicate matters. With luck, the consultants can then testify at congressional hearings on the new rules, further underscoring their expertise.

The Iron Triangle

Indeed, the combination of revolving-door career paths and political favor trading among all of these institutions has created a true "establishment" in the political ethics world. Although the term "Iron Triangle" was coined to describe the relationship between the Pentagon, its contractors, and its allies in Congress,[25] it is just as applicable here. Sometimes also called "issue networks," these loose but powerful assemblages have several key characteristics. One is that they act in their own (shared) interests, not necessarily in the public interest. Another is that they resist reform. A third is that they are poorly understood by the public. And a fourth is that they are seldom reported on by journalists because journalists are often too involved in the horse trading that goes on to be objective.

All of these characteristics are true of the Ethics Establishment. The relationship between ethics bureaucrats—whether permanent or *ad hoc,* like Independent Counsels—and the Congress and interest groups is marked by constant interaction and trading of favors. Congressional staffers get "dirt" from interest groups who, for example, oppose the confirmation of a particular judge or the implementation of a particular policy. Then they leak the information to journalists, and hold hearings that generate more news and that allow interest groups an opportunity to testify and otherwise get their message out. Journalists investigating the scandals get still more leaks from government officials close to the scandal, often in exchange for not linking those officials to what went wrong—or even occasionally in exchange for defending those officials in columns or on political talk shows. All of this provides interest groups with opportunities for publicity and direct-mail fund raising. And when the scandal is over, often new legislation is introduced in response, adding yet another layer of legal requirements (often quite technical ones) that increase the opportunity for more such events in the future. As Milton wrote, "Chaos Umpire sits, And by decisions more embroils the fray, By which he Reigns."[26]

The Results

None of the above is to say, again, that the individuals involved have, or ever had, evil intent. As appearance rules themselves are supposed to recognize, however, even those with pure intent can have their judgment distorted by conflicts of interest. And the Ethics Establishment itself possesses a huge unacknowledged conflict of interest: The kinds of rules that benefit the Ethics Establishment are not the kinds of rules that promote ethical behavior. With this in mind it should come as no surprise that appearance rules, and the tangle of technical regulations that go with them, have done nothing to curtail scandal.

To the contrary, these rules and regulations—like the new House "gift" rules, which were praised by groups like Common Cause at the time—have simply added more fuel to the fire. Thus, lobbyist Ann Eppard's "gifts" of overnight lodging to Congressman Bud Shuster (discussed in Chapter 2) prompted the Government Accountability Project to demand a criminal investigation and Common Cause to seek a House ethics committee investigation, while a bevy of ethics experts publicly debated the fine points of a "hospitality" exception to the House rules. Similarly, a conservative "public interest" group responded to House Minority Whip David Bonior's lodging of about seventy-five ethical charges against Speaker Newt Gingrich by demanding a House ethics committee investigation of Bonior's alleged misuse of staff and funds to write his own book. As a result of these sorts of charges and countercharges, the number of ethics complaints filed in the House of Representatives in the past several years has been "skyrocketing," far outpacing staff resources.[27]

Perhaps the real surprise would have been the adoption of elaborate ethical rules and regulations that did curtail scandal. Such were not to be had. As a cynic might have predicted, the products of the Ethics Establishment did far more for the welfare of the Ethics Establishment than for the promotion of ethics. By the 1990s, even the Ethics Establishment itself was admitting the problem:

At no time in the history of our country has government ethics been more intensively scrutinized and extensively regulated.

Yet something is wrong. The more zealous the effort to identify and legislate against wrongful conduct, the more elusive the goal of achieving ethical behavior has become. Each reform initiative has added another layer of regulation. The result is a complex and formidable rule structure, whose rationale is increasingly obscure and whose operation is increasingly arcane. Ethics is in danger of becoming an elaborate legalistic ritual, in which the application of multipart tests substitutes for the internalization of values, and the establishment of multi-level clearance processes replaces the development of a supportive institutional culture. For government employees who must negotiate this ritual, the result is frustration and alienation. For citizens who hear all the ethics fanfare but nonetheless see government "as usual," the result is disillusionment and cynicism.[28]

The diagnosis is correct. The Ethics Establishment has produced rules, regulations, and fanfare galore. But the average citizen, while not familiar with the intricacies of the rules, can plainly see that the ethics emperor is naked: Government is not appreciably more ethical than it was. Nonetheless, the damage is spreading, as the Ethics Establishment now reaches far beyond the governmental context into a variety of other institutions. Unfortunately, the results have been no better.

6

The Ethics Establishment, Part II: Business

If I had a company and was tasked with changing the culture, I would make sure that I understood exactly the current culture. I would communicate thoroughly to the employees what part we were changing and what we were changing it to. Then I'd go overboard in reinforcing the culture that we wanted to move to.

—Mike Maples, Former Microsoft Executive Vice President[1]

After the whole Drexel Burnham thing exploded, there was a push to codify ethics. A big-ass policy book came out. No one read it.

—Anonymous Harvard MBA Alumnus[2]

By the time Drexel Burnham Lambert chief executive Michael Milken began furiously trying to convince investors, on October 20, 1987, that junk bonds remained a sound investment despite the stock market's previous-day record loss of 500 points, federal prosecutors were building an insider-trading case against him as part of their continuing assault on Wall Street traders; and Milken's alma mater, the University of Pennsylvania's prestigious Wharton School, had joined other leading business schools in a scramble to emphasize business ethics.

Wharton was particularly sensitive to criticism that America's business schools had fallen down on the job. For one thing, in 1986, another Wharton alumnus, Drexel director Dennis B. Levine, had earned the distinction of being the first Wall Street trader to be indicted. Then there was arbitrageur Ivan F. Boesky's celebrated visit to Wharton. Some months before Boesky agreed to pay a $100 million penalty to the SEC for insider trading (and help prosecutors pursue Milken), Boesky had jetted down to join Wharton's students in an enthusiastic cheer for "MONEY!"[3]

Wharton also had a perception problem involving its alumni Hall of Fame. The Hall of Fame celebrates a select group of about a dozen-and-a-half alumni for "outstanding achievement and contribution to society." In 1987, not far from the picture of Donald Trump '68, the Hall of Fame proudly displayed a photographic plaque honoring Michael Milken '79. The plaque was discreetly removed in 1990, when Milken agreed to plead guilty to six felonies and to pay $600 million in criminal fines.

The insider-trading scandals of the late 1980s ushered in a true bull market for business ethics. To be sure, the assorted crimes of Watergate—especially corporations' illegal use of political slush funds—had prompted Bentley College to establish one of the nation's first business ethics centers and had spawned a cottage industry of business ethics codes, courses, and conferences during the 1970s.[4] Government contracting scandals of the early 1980s drew further attention to business ethics.[5] But the insider-trading scandals of the late '80s sent business schools scurrying to emphasize business ethics.[6] And, in 1991, when Congress passed sentencing guidelines for corporations convicted of federal crimes, the boom was on.[7]

Today, the "market" for business ethics consultants is estimated to exceed one billion dollars per year.[8] "Since the sentencing guidelines there are more ethics consultants per square inch than you can shake a stick at," reports Barbara Ley Toffler, a former Harvard professor turned ethics consultant.[9] The guidelines offer substantial advantages to corporations that adopt internal "compliance" programs.[10] This is not merely a matter of academic interest: During the 1970s alone, about 11 percent of America's largest corporations were convicted of crimes.[11] One scholar has advised that it would be professional malpractice not to establish a compliance program in light of these guidelines.[12] Insiders call the guidelines "The Ethics Consultants Full Employment Act of 1991."[13]

The business ethics market received another boost in 1991: the sensational testimony of Anita Hill in the Clarence Thomas confirmation hearings. Those hearings caused a rush among businesses to put sexual harassment policies in place. Shortly after a San Francisco jury ordered the prominent law firm of Baker & McKenzie to pay $6.9 million in punitive damages in a "Court TV" sexual harassment case in 1994, sexual-harassment consulting firms became perhaps the fastest-growing segment of the business ethics market.[14]

Financial journalist Dan Cordtz was thus understating things several years ago when he identified business ethics consulting as "a growth industry":

LOOKING FOR A CAREER WITH BETTER than average prospects in the years ahead? You could do worse than to enter the business ethics industry.

Although there was a more-or-less general (if vague) notion of what constituted acceptable business conduct 20 years ago, it was rare when a company took the trouble to spell everything out. And the idea of establishing formal ethics departments was virtually unheard of.

But in the past decade there has been a whirlwind of activity among social activists, business school faculties, management consultants and corporate leaders aimed at improving the ethical standards and conduct of U.S. companies.

According to a survey conducted by the Center for Business Ethics at Bentley College: "Some 9096 of the nation's largest corporations have now adopted written codes of ethics that prescribe what is and isn't acceptable in their day-to-day operations. Almost one-third of the country's biggest firms have designated an ethics officer—an individual given formal responsibility for seeing to it that all employees know, accept and observe the code of ethics. One firm in five has actually established an ethics department devoted to monitoring performance and engaging in an ongoing program of training."

There is even an Ethics Officers Association, organized three years ago, that already has 50 sponsoring corporations and more than 100 practicing members.

That's not all. People in the business estimate that two dozen management consulting firms now derive a significant share of their fees from giving advice on ethics, helping their clients write codes and showing them how to establish systems designed to make sure they work. Moreover, something like a hundred business ethics "solo practitioners" devote themselves full-time to such activities.[15]

This might all be cause for celebration if the twenty-year trend line charting the rise of the business ethics market were accompanied by, say, even a modest increase in public confidence in the integrity of business leaders, or by a small upturn in workers' attitudes concerning what's right and wrong in the workplace. Unfortunately, these latter trend lines appear to run downhill. A small sample:

- In 1968, 70 percent of Americans believed that American businesses tried to strike a balance between profits and the public interest.[16] Twenty years later, a Gallup poll ranked big business last on a list of ten institutions in which Americans had confidence,[17] and a Harris poll said 82 percent of Americans believed business is primarily motivated by greed.[18]
- A 1990 *New York Times* poll said that only one-third of Americans thought that business does even a pretty good job of behaving ethically.[19]
- In 1991, 15 percent of the public expressed a "great deal" of confidence in large corporations[20]; by 1996, this number was down to 6 percent (by comparison, 32 percent had "a great deal" of confidence in the military).[21]

- A 1996 study published in the *Journal of Business Ethics,* sounding concerns about "a potential crisis in business ethics," reports that 47 percent of top executives and 76 percent of graduate-level business students said they would commit fraud in various scenarios by understating their firm's write-offs against profits, especially if the likelihood of job promotion were linked to higher profit numbers.[22]

Whatever conclusions one might draw from these and similar statistics, it seems fair to say, at a minimum, that the business ethics reforms of the past two decades have not succeeded notably in building public confidence or alleviating fears that we haven't quite fixed things.

Reformers might point out how difficult it has been to recapture the public's respect in the face of a tidal wave of negative media. And they could offer impressive data in support. One study has calculated, for example, that almost 90 percent of all business characters on television during the 1980s were portrayed as corrupt.[23] And there is little dispute that for decades the news media have pounded away at various business scandals: government contracting frauds, S&L scams, insider-trading crimes, toxic waste scandals, exploding gas tanks (both real and staged), and so on. But to argue that, say, the proliferation of new business ethics codes obviously couldn't be expected to cope either with this onslaught of bad publicity or with real wrongdoing is itself to confess to some of the fundamental errors in looking primarily to ethics codes and other tools of appearance ethics to repair what's broken in American businesses.

Codes and Culture

The most prevalent response by American businesses to public concerns about business ethics *has been* to adopt a company ethics code. A very high percentage (more than 90 percent) of America's largest companies now have written codes of ethics.[24] About two-thirds of these codes were introduced during the 1970s and 1980s.[25] More than a third of the codes were revised in 1992,[26] after Congress enacted the federal sentencing guidelines for corporations, which were "designed so that the sanctions imposed upon organizations and their agents, taken together, will provide just punishment, adequate deterrence, and incentives for organizations to maintain internal mechanisms for preventing, detecting, and reporting criminal conduct."[27]

The federal sentencing guidelines more or less compel companies to adopt "compliance" programs—that is, an "effective program to prevent and detect violations of law." This means having, among other things, "established written policies defining the standards and procedures to be followed by [an organization's] employees and other agents."[28] One way to show "compliance" is to publish a code that expresses commitment not only to law but to high ethical standards. As one business professor puts it, "[I]n an era of highly visible demands for improved business ethics, who wants to admit that one's organization has no code?"[29]

So one might say that the most recent wave of codes is largely an appearance maneuver to ward off the feds. Yet the prevailing opinion is that, even if couched in platitudes, business ethics codes do have value. If nothing else, they are a source of authority. And they *can* be used effectively to *reinforce* a healthy corporate culture.[30] At their best, they also reflect Americans' desire to "live and work in a reasonably just and decent world."[31] Because the average employee now works the equivalent of an additional month more than was worked in 1970, this aspiration for a decent workplace has assumed increasing importance.[32] And so it should.

Problems arise, however, when it becomes seductively cheap and easy for organizations to use these codes to give merely the *appearance* of improving an organization's ethical culture. Thus, many companies are now simply installing "off-the-shelf ethics programs," modeled on federal law, which may or may not match a company's individual needs.[33] A 1987 survey showed that while 92 percent of business executives believed their company's code of ethics was achieving its objective, only 20 percent had developed any means for assessing the code's effectiveness.[34] Moreover, public confidence in the ethics of business leaders has continued to fall despite code proliferation—proving yet again that public relations approaches to ethical problems don't even give you good p.r.

By all accounts Texaco had exemplary policy manuals and glossy ethics brochures long before it found itself in a public relations/legal nightmare in the fall of 1996 for racial discrimination. The legal case against Texaco had been building for some time, but the final explosion occurred when the media got hold of tape recordings (yes, tapes) of conversations secretly recorded in 1994 among senior company executives. The tapes revealed the executives making disparaging racial remarks while plotting to destroy documents demanded in the discrimination suit and discussing other cover-up activities. All of this transpired despite Texaco's proclamation—in a booklet called *Texaco's Vision and Values*—that "Our employees are our most important resource" and that "Each person deserves to be treated with respect and dignity in appropriate work environments, without regard to race, religion, sex, age, national origin, disability or position in the company. Each employee has the responsibility to demonstrate respect for others."[35] The docuuments filed in the racial discrimination suit (which Texaco agreed to settle for $176 million) reflect a different, decidedly unglossy picture of Texaco's corporate culture—involving "backstage" discrimination and intimidation against blacks and other minority groups.[36]

One rather obvious drawback in relying too much on ethics codes like Texaco's is that, generally speaking, codes don't dictate how people actually behave in business organizations. Professor Robert Jackall describes in his book *Moral Mazes* how managers in two major industrial firms and a large public relations agency *actually* made decisions involving moral judgment.[37] Professor Jackall calls the governing principles "the moral rules-in-use," which he argues have been inadequately studied by the "new industry that one might call Ethics, Inc." The central conclusion from Jackall's five-year study:

> As a former vice-president of a large firm says: "What is right in the corporation is not what is right in a man's home or in his church. *What is right in the corporation is what the guy above you wants from you.* That's what morality is in the corporation."[38]

It's not the code; it's the culture.

Professor Jackall uncovered numerous instances where the "guy above" wanted some clearly illegal or improper action undertaken (such as cooking the books or burying pesticides improperly). Amid all the varying circumstances surrounding such pressure, Jackall discovered one relative constant: an excessive attention to appearances. The misconduct he describes occurs in "a world where appearances—in the broadest sense—mean everything," a world in which "the wise and ambitious manager learns to cultivate assiduously the proper, prescribed modes of appearing."[39]

Professor Jackall found particularly destructive an intense pressure to maintain "the appearance of buoyant optimism."[40] This pressure leads managers to maintain an official record of proper conduct and "buoyant optimism," while at the same time making key decisions for reasons that never appear in corporate records.[41] It's the corporate equivalent of the "government by post-it-note" that Suzanne Garment describes in post-Watergate Washington. Becoming associated with a problem on one's watch can ruin a career. So the safest and wisest career paths involve dexterity with symbols and avoidance of real accountability. These bureaucratic pressures overwhelm the fine points of company business codes:

> Bureaucracy transforms all moral issues into immediately practical concerns. A moral judgment based on a professional ethic makes little sense in a world where the etiquette for protecting and covering one's boss, one's network, and oneself supersedes all other considerations and where nonaccountability for action is the norm. As a matter of survival, not to mention advancement, corporate managers have to keep their eye fixed not on abstract principles but on the social framework of their world and its requirement.[42]

In similar vein, in 1995, Harvard business ethics professor Joseph Badaracco conducted in-depth interviews with thirty recent graduates of the Harvard MBA program to get what he called "a view from the trenches," rather than the usual executive or middle-manager perspective.[43] The interviewees had indeed seen the *visible* effects of the latest surge in business ethics. ("After the whole Drexel Burnham thing exploded," one graduate commented, "there was a push to codify ethics. A big-ass policy book came out. No one read it.") The interviews, however, revealed several disturbing patterns in the reality beneath these appearance reforms:

> First, in many cases, young managers received explicit instructions from their middle-manager bosses or felt strong organizational pressures to do things that they believed were sleazy, unethical, or sometimes illegal. Second, corporate ethics programs, codes of conduct, mission statements, hot lines and the like provided little help. Third, many of the young managers believed that their company's executives were out-of-touch on ethical issues, either because they were too busy or because they sought to avoid responsibility. Fourth, the young managers resolved the dilemmas they faced largely on the basis of personal reflection and individual values, not through reliance on corporate credos, company loyalty, the exhortations of senior executives, philosophical principles, or religious reflection.[44]

None of this should be particularly surprising to people who have felt such institutional pressures. Wall Street isn't Main Street, but most readers readily understood what Michael Lewis was saying when he wrote in *Liar's Poker* about his experience at Salomon Brothers during the 1980s: "As a Salomon Brothers trainee, of course, you didn't worry too much about ethics. You were just trying to stay alive. You felt flattered to be on the same team with the people who kicked everyone's ass all the time."[45] The bottom line is the bottom line. And when young trainees see the directional signs to a fat bottom line pointing due east, and the arrows to acting "ethically" pointing west, no one needs advance scouts to predict the stampede east.

The Bottom Line

If the multitude of articles, programs, courses, and books churned out of the business ethics factories over the past decades make anything clear, it is that it apparently requires a mammoth undertaking in America today (a billion-dollar undertaking) to convince our nation's best and brightest that it really isn't stupid or soft-headed to behave decently. Indeed, the core message of just about every *good* new business ethics program is that, contrary to what everyone might think, behaving ethically is not only the right thing to do, it's the smart thing to do. That is, it's actually good for the bottom line.

If it is essential that this lesson be taught (and you'll get no quarrel from us), then it is also essential that business audiences find this lesson to be not merely credible, but compelling. The likelihood that these generally skeptical bottom-liners will find compelling ethics programs packaged by people who describe themselves as specialists in "business ethics" and who discuss such things as Kant's deontology, Mill's utilitarianism, and relativism versus universalism—all subjects of Wharton's post-Milken *Ethics Study Guide* for business executives—is, one may conjecture, somewhat low.

These consultants aren't "the guys above." Nor are they part of the organization's "backstage" culture where people discuss how the guys above *really* want them to act. Shortly after ITT Corporation adopted its code of conduct, the general counsel was pulled aside by one of his friends, the managing director of one of ITT's major companies. The director asked whether the code's provisions were "for real."[46] In other words, what did the guys above really want? An outside consultant may be able to knock some sense into the guys above. But the consultant can't answer the question of what the guys above really want. And when the consultant is part of a staged appearance ethics show in which the guys above have no roles, the message is that this is cover-your-ass theater, not organizational reality.

Moreover, as business strategist Peter Drucker has argued, the very treatment of "business ethics" as a specialized subject creates its own problems. It flies in the face of the uniform belief among Western moral philosophers that "[t]here is only one ethics, one set of rules of morality, one code—that of individual behavior in which the same rules apply to everyone else."[47] Marching in a group of "business ethics" consultants just reinforces the destructive notion that lawyers, doctors, journalists, and business leaders are not bound by normal standards of decency but rather by some complicated "craft ethics."

This can be a very dangerous idea. Readers doubting this point should read the powerful opening scene in James Fallows' *Breaking the News*. The scene shows CBS's Mike Wallace and ABC's Peter Jennings stating in a televised panel discussion on "Ethics in America" that they would not warn American soldiers about a hypothetical attack from North Kosanese soldiers (with whom the journalists supposedly were traveling) if the act of warning the Americans would have gotten in the way of the journalists' filming the attack. Wallace and Jennings carefully rationalized their judgment in terms of some theoretical specialized journalistic ethic. Other panelists were stunned.[48]

Messages about "the bottom line"—to be truly convincing—need to be delivered by people whose specialization *is* "the bottom line." As it turns out, such people do exist: They are managing America's best-run businesses. Forced by intense competitive pressures, these managers have rediscovered that there are clear long-term advantages in acting decently toward one's customers, employees, and shareholders. In Thomas Peters and Robert Waterman's now-famous conclusion in *In Search of Excellence,* these enlightened business leaders have hit upon "the obvious, that the individual human being still counts."[49] In Hedrick Smith's words in *Rethinking America,* they have found that "hardware is less important than human software."[50]

In *In Search of Excellence* and *Rethinking America,* technical treatises on the productivity of manufacturing plants, charts demonstrating the terrific long-term stock performances of America's most "ethical" companies, and analyses of the successful strategies of America's elite high-tech companies,[51] the most astute, hardheaded, feet-on-the-ground business strategists are teaching business leaders today, as a matter of corporate survival, the practical advantages of the Golden Rule—something tough-minded economist and moral philosopher Adam Smith (in *The Theory of Moral Sentiments*) and successful lawyer-judge Henry Fielding were trying to hammer home to the rising business class two centuries ago.

Today, the cutting-edge management strategy is to treat customers, employees, shareholders, and community neighbors as they themselves would like to be treated when purchasing a car, completing an assignment for a superior, investing time or money in a project, or living near a factory. Thus, to take one of a thousand examples, GM learned from a joint venture with Toyota that Toyota achieves its outstanding quality record for assembly-line production not from merely telling employees to "think quality" or rewarding quality work, but rather by drilling into them that they should think of their customers not as unknown buyers in a distant city or country but as the very next worker down the assembly line. As a GM executive put it, "Don't pass a defective car on to your buddy. It was a powerful idea."[52] Toyota treats employees and shareholders with the same solicitude, GM also learned—on GM's way to rebounding from the devastating competitive defeats of the previous decades.

The Tylenol Parable

The number one example of the "good ethics equal good business" principle is Johnson & Johnson's response in 1982 to the startling news that people were dying from Tylenol capsules laced with cyanide. Wharton's ethics program recites this story, as do most business ethics texts and scores of articles. In fact, the repeated telling of this particular parable may be as interesting as the tale itself.

After Johnson & Johnson began receiving reports of Tylenol-related deaths (seven people ultimately died), the company recalled all of its Tylenol capsules nationwide, even though the poisoning had occurred only in the Chicago area. Subsequent cost estimates range from $50 million (after tax) to $100 million (pretax). However calculated, the recall cost Johnson & Johnson many millions of dollars for product tampering that had occurred outside Johnson & Johnson's premises and therefore wasn't the company's fault. The company's swift and conscientious response earned the nation's respect. It also was responsible for the salvation of one of Johnson & Johnson's all-time leading products (as well as the introduction of industry-standard tamper-proof packaging).[53]

Johnson & Johnson merits continuing praise for its handling of the Tylenol problem, as well as for running what by all accounts is an exceptionally humane and profitable business (annual sales: $20 billion). The Tylenol story should be taught, as indeed it is, as "the case example of the decade on how to do it right."[54] Yet isn't there something a little odd in our repeating again and again in such heroic terms a company's decision to spend money—even a *lot* of money—so as to ensure that scores of its customers wouldn't be poisoned to death? (Seventy-five other contaminated capsules were turned up in the recall effort.[55]) Aren't we being a tad defensive? It's as if, rocked by business decisions in recent years that have needlessly cost lives (as in the Ford Pinto case), we all suspect deep-down that most business leaders confronted with a Tylenol-type problem would hunker down in a no-recall strategy that would emphasize the company's compliance with governing statutes and regulations. Even if that alternate strategy did not end up costing lives, it surely would irreparably damage a key business line and lead to all sorts of legal entanglements.

If we are correct about this suspicion, it is almost certainly because a credibility gap exists today in corporate offices between what are commonly perceived to be romantic tales of "ethical" behavior and actual, hardheaded approaches to "real world" problems. Sure, lots of nice guys *do* finish last, just as lots of creeps *have* made a killing ripping other people off. But when one surveys the littered landscape of the last decades and sees how many otherwise exceptional leaders in government and business have *unnecessarily* destroyed their careers by acting improperly in one way or another, and how many once dynamic and profitable businesses have self-destructed in substantial part due to corrupted corporate cultures, it is more than passing strange that the business ethics establishment has had such difficulty getting "the bottom line" message across.

Professor Robert Jackall's study suggests one way out of the moral maze: capitalize on the fact that almost no business executive "wants to appear stodgy before one's peers nor to have one's firm defined in managerial networks, and perhaps thence to Wall Street, as 'slow on the uptake.'"[56] If the latest trends in business management really do make business managers believe they must encourage the reporting of the full range of problems that a business regularly encounters and deal with those problems straight-up with an eye toward the best interests of the company's customers, employees, and shareholders, then it is more likely that the managers will institutionalize those principles. And businesses will inevitably be more "ethical." Those business executives who head in another direction do so at their peril, entering a world not only of lower productivity, but also of increased lawsuits and enhanced likelihood of government scrutiny—made more likely today by the post-Watergate institutionalization of whistle-blowing.

Whistle While We Work

Hollywood knows a trend when it sees one. In the 1990s film version of the 1950s TV series "The Fugitive," the one-armed man who murdered Dr. Richard Kimbel's wife metamorphoses into a hit man hired by a multinational pharmaceutical company to prevent whistle-blowing about the ill side effects of one of its drugs. In the 1996 film *Eraser*, Arnold Schwarzenegger protects a defense contractor whistle-blower played by Vanessa Williams. The 1994 movie *Quiz Show* brings back Herbert Stempel, who blew the whistle on NBC and "The $64,000 Question." Just as exposing government corruption sold tickets in previous years to such movies as *Serpico* (Al Pacino as Knapp Commission informant), *All the President's Men* (Hal Holbrook as Deep Throat), *Three Days of the Condor* (Robert Redford as a CIA whistle-blower), and *Marie* (discussed in Chapter 5), whistle-blowing in the corporate world is now boffo at the box office—even without the cataclysmic concerns of nuclear disaster that underlay the 1980s whistle-blower films *Silkwood* and *The China Syndrome*.

This change in script writing didn't occur without a corresponding shift in cultural winds. We have now had decades of whistle-blown scandals in such diverse areas as the auto industry, the chemical industry, the pharmaceutical industry, Wall Street trading, the defense industry, the news business, the tobacco industry, the movie industry, the egg fertilization business, the nursing-home industry, and—reaching rock bottom—in Morton Thiokol's response to reports on problems in O-ring seals used in the Space Shuttle *Challenger*.

The whistle-blowers themselves have ranged from heros (like actor Cliff Robertson, who blew the whistle on embezzlement at Columbia Pictures only to become a pariah among Hollywood's producers of whistle-blowing films) to half-hero/half-villains to villains (like the team of Stewart and Feder, discussed in the following chapter). The seemingly infinite variety of scandals and whistle-blowers tends to muddy debate over the appropriate degree of legal protection (and, indeed, reward) whistle-blowers should receive.

If there were only one type of corporate whistle-blower—the virtuous and self-sacrificing employee—then it might make sense to support laws that not only protect whistle-blowers from retaliation (as most state laws now do), but that also give them large financial rewards (now the case under certain federal laws discussed below). And there is a long line of Americans who have suffered greatly for merely trying to right wrongs in the workplace—from researchers who have tried in vain to get superiors to focus upon serious dangers in a company's product (an exploding gas tank or a defective O-ring), to middle-level managers whose accurate warnings about acts of racial discrimination have been met with cold silence from the guys above, to accountants who have reported clearly fraudulent accounting practices, and so on.[57] Unfortunately, these are not the only types of whistle-blowers. There are also bad whistle-blowers, persons bent on advancing selfish interests that may be directly contrary to the public interest. These whistle-blowers frequently distort facts or make frivolous allegations.

A few of the many examples of this latter type include the anonymous whistle-blower in Colorado who, holding a grudge against certain local farmers, falsely reported them to federal authorities for federal erosion violations, thereby triggering a costly, mandatory investigation;[58] employees who have accused their superiors in federal employment litigation of such things as throwing stones at a railroad car,[59] using an office telephone for personal calls,[60] wasting federal funds by sending *two* scientists to a conference in Portugal,[61] or "sabotaging" the results of the accuser's amino acid analysis[62]; persons providing false reports to the SEC about others' supposed insider trading ("It's a good way of trying to make life miserable for your worst enemies," then-SEC enforcement director Gary Lynch observed about the spate of spurious calls); and disgruntled employees manufacturing charges of serious wrongdoing in order to exact revenge or to cash in by threatening "disclosure."

What is clear is that protections for the infinite variety of whistle-blowers have never been greater: In the past decade, the number of states with laws protecting whistle-blowers from retaliation by employers has jumped from six to forty-five.[63] Federal procedures and protections are likewise at an all-time high—with anonymous hot lines, a specially established Office of Special Counsel to which one may "whistle," statutory protection against retaliation, financial rewards in certain cases, and so on.

The wholesale adoption of formalized whistle-blowing procedures can cause serious problems in a company, however. The best-run—and most "ethical"—corporations generally depend upon organizational trust and informal systems of communication.[64] Formalized whistle-blowing procedures tend to undermine both. Corporate hot lines, for example, may be a good way to demonstrate "compliance," yet as Barbara Toffler observes, they inevitably create an environment of mistrust.[65] The ensuing investigations are based on anonymous accusations, "which deny people what the legal system allows them: the ability to stand face-to-face with their accusers."[66] Not surprisingly, corporate hot lines are especially despised in Germany and other countries with totalitarian pasts.[67] Anyone wondering whether the institutionalization of whistle-blowing can have adverse effects on an organization should consider what life would be like at home if, instead of being discouraged from "tattling," children were financially rewarded for it.

In any event, a corporation that has to decide how best to handle a stack of anonymous whistle-blower complaints is a company already in trouble. It has forfeited the extraordinary benefits of having in place an informal communications mechanism that employees trust to convey grievances or to call attention to product or service problems.[68] At well-run companies employees can whistle *while* they work, and still climb higher and higher up the corporate ladder. Even Ralph Nader calls whistle-blowing "the last line of defense."[69]

The threat to internal trust is exacerbated by external whistle-blower reward systems, like the federal False Claims Act[70] and similar government programs.[71] The False Claims Act now gives government-contractor whistle-blowers large financial incentives for turning their company in for overcharging the government. The Act's bounty provisions have produced the perverse result in a number of cases of rewarding employees who keep silent for years while gathering evidence for a federal suit. This inaction allows the government's damages to pile up and, as a result, increases the amount of the whistle-blower's bounty.

Many whistle-blowers have suffered tremendous hardships for merely trying to do the right thing—losing a job, enduring false personal attacks, and so forth. But this is not necessarily so with the new whistle-blowing entrepreneur, who may see the employer's errors as a way to build a war chest with which to enter the same market,[72] or to enjoy a life most people only dream about, with a $23 million bounty and a three-level home on the California coast.[73] When these moral entrepreneurs search the Web for whistle-blowing sites, they quickly hit upon law firm advertisements explaining how the employee can become wealthy. A typical Web page, entitled "The Reward," is emblazoned with a large sack of money with a big dollar sign on it.[74] Paul Biddle, the man who blew the whistle on accounting practices at Stanford University, spoke for this new bounty-hunter breed when he declared: "I intend to be a rich man if at all possible."[75]

Exactly *what* Biddle blew his whistle on took four years to resolve, however, and really deserves its own chapter (if not book). In a nutshell, the controversy concerned how Stanford had calculated the indirect costs of research it had passed along to the federal government under various research grants. Stanford defended its accounting practices by pointing to more than a hundred written memoranda of understanding—so-called "MOUs"—it had entered into with the Department of Navy over the years. The MOUs let Stanford liberally define its overhead costs. As *Science* magazine later reported, all of this resulted in an "arcane system for reimbursement—an accounting maze so complex that no outsider [could] easily check it."[76]

Because overhead costs at a university include such things as library acquisitions, it is easy (as the *New York Times* pointed out at the time) for critics of such a system to ask

> why taxpayers are paying 25 percent of the cost of "The Catcher in the Rye" just as they question why taxpayers help furnish the President's house. But they forget that taxpayers avoid picking up 75 percent of the cost of advanced physics journals.
>
> If the system works right, taxpayers pay a fair share. Unfortunately, the system is ripe for abuse because it is hard to draw lines between legitimate overhead and extravagance. If a $1,200 commode is too lavish to include for cost recovery, is $500 also too steep? The regulations don't say.[77]

Paul Biddle arrived at Stanford in 1988 as the Office of Naval Research's campus auditor. He quickly reached two conclusions. One, some of Stanford's overhead charges seemed over the line. And, two, under the False Claims Act he could stand to receive 30 percent of whatever money the government recovered for overcharges—an amount that some initially thought could exceed $200 million. Biddle became quite proactive.

Soon Congressman John Dingell's ubiquitous investigators were on the scene. Leaks from the investigators led to sensational camera shots of a seventy-two-foot Stanford yacht and expensive flowers, charged in part to Uncle Sam. Like exciting teasers to a soon-to-be-released movie, this footage built audience anticipation for the inevitable day when Congressman Dingell's Investigations Subcommittee of the Committee on Government Operations would flip its klieg lights on and Stanford's president would be blasted on television for outrageous billing practices. After the lights were turned off, however, and the cameras shut down, the government made a small settlement with Stanford ($1.2 million); and the Office of Naval Research declared that Stanford had not engaged in any "fraud, misrepresentation, or other wrongdoing." Stanford president Donald Kennedy nonetheless resigned.

Stanford may be filled with all sorts of geniuses. But even these brainiacs never quite puzzled through how terrible their billing practices would appear if exposed to the light of day, much less how a government worker such as Biddle could potentially become "a rich man" as a result of auditing work done at taxpayers' expense.[78] Stanford officials at one point complained to the Office of Government Ethics about the morality of Biddle's conduct. Biddle, after all, had a *huge* (real, not just apparent) conflict of interest. Stanford took particular exception to Biddle's calling Stanford administrators "two-legged rodents" and accusing university trustees of a cover-up.[79] The university's protest didn't prevent Biddle from receiving the Navy's Meritorious Civilian Service Award, nor (after resigning from his position) from using his notoriety as a springboard for a run for Congress.

Looking back on Stanford's troubles with the wisdom gained as cofounder of Hewlett-Packard Co. and as former deputy secretary of defense, David Packard, a longtime Stanford booster, observed that Stanford's president and trustees had made one important mistake: "They should have considered the propriety of these things as well as the legality."[80] A hardheaded observation from one of the most successful and respected businessmen of twentieth-century America. The comment calls to mind Squire Allworthy's advice to Tom Jones that attention to such propriety "is indeed the duty which we owe to ourselves; and if we will be so much our own Enemies as to neglect it," we are laying "the Foundation of [our] own Ruin," upon which "others will, I am afraid, be too apt to build."

Yet the larger lesson is that a bounty system by design encourages the very worst sorts of whistle-blowers, the purely self-interested ones. And it encourages them in a particularly bad way—to communicate their concerns not through informal channels, which may not make them rich, but rather through the device of formal court litigation, which can make them wealthy even if the case is settled for a relatively small sum. (A third of the Stanford settlement is $400,000.)

This reward system may result in increased exposure of corruption in the short term. But to think it won't create havoc in the long run is to ignore experience—both with systems that offer big bucks to the Biddles and Blifils of the world to "turn others in," and with the huge costs, inefficiencies, and delays of complex federal court litigation. Sure, the defense industry in particular has been guilty of terrible overcharge practices in the past. Yet is the remedy really a system of oversight by extraordinarily complex whistle-blower litigation? This is just what we've had in the past several years alone with respect to the AH-64 Apache attack helicopter, the MX missile guidance system, the Lockheed C-5B cargo jet, and the F-15 and F-14 fighter programs. Such a system may give the appearance of balanced, disinterested oversight, but that's hardly the reality.

Playing for the Long Term

It would seem, in any event, that we have lost something when we reward whistle-blowers so handsomely—whether under the False Claims Act, or on the talk show circuit, or in the selling of rights to a TV movie that will retell their story over popcorn. Vincent Canby of the *New York Times* once praised the 1954 film *On the Waterfront* as the "unashamed classic" of the whistle-blower genre.[81] Marlon Brando, readers will recall, places his life on the line in the film to testify before a government committee investigating corruption on the New Jersey waterfront. Unlike Tom Cruise in *The Firm,* who sails off with a big sack of government reward money even without fingering his firm's mob clients, Brando simply wants to preserve his own self-respect and to continue working his arduous waterfront job. He gets beaten to a pulp in the process. "It's one of the few movies about a whistle-blower in which the witness' ordeal is comprehensible and his ultimate decision triumphant," Canby wrote. Precisely.

Values like these obviously require inculcation at an earlier level than

America's professional schools. In the old days, they were taught by families and elementary schools. Today, it ain't necessarily so. "We have had for two generations an educational system that has eschewed the teaching of value systems," said the Ethics Resource Center's then-executive director, Gary Edwards, in 1987.[82] With the decline in the traditional family structure and religious institution, "we have had entering the workforce for several years a generation of people whose moral development has been arrested." No wonder Harvard's business professors, when pressed into ethical service after the Drexel Burnham scandal, felt uncomfortable; "saw ethics as a 'soft,' idealistic, abstract, and even nebulous subject"; and didn't want the responsibility for teaching it.[83] They weren't alone.

Parents, teachers, and professors must all get back to ethical basics. Perhaps the Harvard professors' concern was that *real* business ethics would involve them in advancing the thesis that, despite the long-term congruence between doing good and doing well, building up a firm's long-term reputation often requires short-term sacrifices and a lot of hard, unglamorous work. It is no doubt easier to settle for off-the-shelf ethics programs or quick-fix hot lines. But that's not what the great leaders of American business, like David Packard, have done. Nor is it what the new enlightened American Innovators (Hedrick Smith's term) are doing while playing for the long term. The sooner *their* portraits replace the quick-buck dealmakers of the '80s in our collective Halls of Fame, the sooner corporate culture will change for the better.

7

Weird Science

It is the chief characteristic of the religion of science, that it works.
—Isaac Asimov[1]

As the previous chapters have illustrated, there are real problems with appearance ethics in the political sphere. These problems would be serious enough if the emphasis on appearances, and the general mentality produced by appearance ethics, were confined to the political sphere. Unfortunately, both have spread far beyond the world that produced them, surfacing in almost every part of American society.

Perhaps the most surprising arena in which to find appearance ethics and Blifil Paradoxes is the field of science. Science, after all, functioned for years as an almost autonomous part of American society. The protections surrounding scientists and their work are formidable. Religious interference with scientific research is barred by the First Amendment,[2] and by Enlightenment traditions created in response to the persecution by churchmen of scientists like Galileo and Copernicus. Scientific expression (and, some legal scholars have argued, even scientific research) is also protected by the First Amendment, and by general social values favoring free speech and inquiry.[3] Then there is the protection provided by the subject matter of science itself. Politicians and other authorities are often afraid of becoming too involved in scientific issues because most know little about science, and thus run a very real risk of making fools of themselves. And the established practices of science, including peer review of research and academic self-governance, have produced enormous technological progress and wealth. When whole industries, like semiconductors and biotechnology, can be created by knowledge gained in scientists' laboratories, there is great reluctance to interfere with the goose that can lay such golden eggs. The result, as Georgetown Law School professor Steven Goldberg says, is that science has come to occupy a "privileged status" in American society: not exactly above the law, but in many ways outside it.[4]

As a result, for a long time discussions of scientific ethics had little to do with appearances. Instead, questions of right or wrong turned on two kinds of questions: whether scientists should engage in particular kinds of research at all,[5] and how some kinds of research should be performed to ensure the best interests of research subjects.[6] The questions of whether some research should be performed or not stemmed from a fear that it might produce knowledge or technologies that would have bad consequences for the rest of us: atomic or biological weapons, an inappropriate focus on racial characteristics, and so on. Questions on protecting research subjects, on the other hand, had to do with informed consent where the subjects were human and humane treatment where the subjects were animals.

These were (and are) important subjects. But lying behind all of the discussion of these topics was faith that any research that was performed would be performed properly. That is, whether or not the science was a good idea, or whether its experimentation was ethical, it would be "good science" in the sense that it would produce meaningful data that could be relied upon by other researchers. Scientists might or might not be good people, it was thought, but because they were motivated by a desire to know the truth they would be good scientists. In fact, even the archetypical evil scientist, the "mad scientist" of horror film and literary clichédom, was always motivated by the search for truth. He (it was always a he) might ignore all of the standard ethical prescriptions about informed consent, dangerous experimentation, or even murder, but nonetheless the mad scientist was still a *scientist,* typically justifying his excesses in the name of the higher law of truth. His flaws came from taking the search for knowledge too seriously, not the other way around.

Such a view of science also fit the conventional wisdom about how science works. In the conventional view of science, researchers worked diligently to develop new building blocks of knowledge. Each block of knowledge was stacked upon the blocks that had come before. If earlier research or theory was flawed, research based upon its conclusions would come out wrong. When it did, scientists would revisit the earlier work and correct it until the resulting edifice of knowledge and theory was once again solid. Furthermore, the processes of peer review and refereeing, in which research plans and articles submitted for publication were scrutinized by panels of experts in the field, meant that claims that were outrageous or unlikely faced additional scrutiny. As a result, most scientists (and others) believed that the system of science was self-correcting and thus very resistant to fraud or mistake.

Like most conventional wisdom, this view contained a good deal of truth, but also like most conventional wisdom, it was by no means the whole story. Despite the allegedly self-correcting nature of science, the system had never been perfect. Fraud was not unknown: The infamous Piltdown Man, a cobbled-together fake fossil probably originally intended as a joke, had fooled scientists for years. Even famous ancients, like the astronomer Claudius Ptolemy, were believed to have faked observations. And clouds of uncertainty hung around the works of other greats, from Galileo to Newton: suspicions not of saying things were true that were not, but of selectively reporting data to make their experiments look more conclusive than they really were.

Still, these classic cases were seen as aberrations (in the case of Piltdown Man) or as unimportant: Ptolemy, Galileo, and Newton, after all, were eventually proved right or wrong by the work of other scientists. (Disproving Ptolemy, it was sometimes admitted, took many centuries, but he really predated the scientific age.) Whatever the occasional misguided individual might do, any fraud that was significant would be discovered by the system; fraud that wasn't significant enough to be relied on by other scientists, and thus discovered by the self-correcting nature of the system, wasn't significant enough to matter anyway.

A central assumption of this conventional wisdom, of course, was that scientists and their research were primarily aimed at discovering new truths. In the pre–World War II era, this was almost universally the case, not least because the other rewards of science were so scant.[7] After the war, everything changed. In a way, it was corruption by politics: Where previously only one research dollar in six had come from the federal government, after the war only one dollar in six came from anywhere else. And, of course, the amounts increased dramatically. "Big science," the child of the Manhattan Project, was expensive: As a character in *The Right Stuff* famously remarks, "no bucks, no Buck Rogers." And those who paid the bills naturally wanted results to match.[8]

It has been proposed as a universal law that every successful system attracts parasites, and postwar science, especially in America, became one of the most successful systems in human history. It should have come as no surprise that once huge amounts of money began flowing into the scientific enterprise, its character would change. Nor did everyone miss the point: By 1958, Cornell physicist Robert Wilson was expressing nostalgia for "the quiet times when physics was a pleasant, intellectual subject, not unlike the study of Medieval French in its popular interest."[9] But Medieval French is not studied to the tune of billions of dollars per year, and if it were its character might change, too.

Still, like a middle-aged athlete who denies the effects of time, the scientific community for the most part did not acknowledge the changes in its world except when forced to do so. In the case of scientific fraud, what forced the acknowledgment was a series of well-publicized misdeeds.[10] These cases began to capture the public imagination, and the attention of journalists.

Perhaps the most famous such case was the 1974 Summerlin Mouse case, in which a skin-transplant researcher, William Summerlin, claimed impressive scientific results that turned out, upon closer examination, to have been achieved with a felt-tip pen. Summerlin had claimed to have developed a revolutionary method for transplanting skin and corneas without rejection. Other researchers had doubts about his ability and were unable to reproduce his work. With his research under fire, Summerlin tried to bolster his results by inking in black patches on white mice, then claiming that the black patches had actually been transplanted from black mice.[11]

A few years later, a famous cancer researcher at Boston University, Marc Straus, faced charges from lab workers, charges denied by Strauss, that he had ordered them to falsify data in clinical tests to make his experimental cancer treatments look better than they were.[12] And a young researcher at Cornell University, Mark Spector, developed a unified theory of how cells became cancerous, known as the "kinase cascade," that was supported by almost unbelievably good experimental data—data that turned out to be so good because they were faked.[13]

These cases garnered enough publicity to produce congressional hearings, chaired by then Congressman Albert Gore, Jr., concerning scientific fraud and deception.[14] Those hearings did little to dispel the sense of some journalists and politicians that the scientific community was doing little to police its own ranks. As Gore remarked during the event, "I cannot avoid the conclusion that one reason for the persistence of this type of problem is the reluctance of people high in the science field to take these matters very seriously."[15]

Gore's feelings appeared to have some basis. During the hearings, witness after witness from the top ranks of the scientific world testified that there was no real problem: Reports of science fraud were, they said, "grossly exaggerated," and the self-correcting nature of science meant that serious fraud would always be discovered and corrected. Furthermore, the witnesses seemed to spend a great deal of time lecturing the committee on how its members knew little about science and should simply leave scientific matters to those who understood them, an attitude that Congressman Robert Walker characterized as "arrogance."[16] Even after the hearings, many in the scientific community downplayed the problem. Despite claims by leading science journalists William Broad and Nicholas Wade that for every major fraud case that became public, there were a hundred thousand cases of fraud that did not,[17] the institutions of organized science continued to maintain otherwise. In an editorial in *Science,* the prestigious journal of the American Association for the Advancement of Science, editor-in-chief Daniel Koshland opined that fewer than one scientific paper in a million was fraudulent.[18]

In an earlier age, when the authority of science—and of institutions in general—was better established, such an approach might have worked. But by the early 1980s, after Vietnam, Watergate, and a variety of other scandals, institutions were in bad repute. Scientists still stood higher in public esteem than politicians or business leaders, but their reputation had been stained by the arguments over nuclear weapons and energy, by the revelation of unethical experiments like the Tuskegee Syphilis Experiment (in which a group of black men were given a false diagnosis of "bad blood" so that their syphilis would remain untreated to allow study of its development),[19] and by the failure of projects like the War on Cancer or fusion energy research to live up to the promises of their promoters. Furthermore, while congressmen and journalists may not have known much about science, they knew a good deal about people and organizations and had considerable doubts that any institution made up of people could function as perfectly as the scientists maintained theirs did.

These doubts were reinforced over the next several years, as additional cases involving claims of misconduct arose. Some involved such eminent figures as Nobel prize winner David Baltimore and AIDS researcher Robert Gallo.[20] Others involved less eminent figures, but demonstrated what some considered a lackadaisical approach to investigation on the part of authorities, and even a tendency to stigmatize or punish whistle-blowers. Some worried that if fraud cases continued to surface, there would be an appearance problem, and the public would no longer support generous funding for science: "No matter how small the percentage of scientists who might be fakers of data, it required only one case to surface every few months or so for the public credibility of science to be severely damaged."[21] It seemed clear even to supporters of science that something had to be done.

The ultimate result was the creation of a formal apparatus to investigate claims of scientific fraud and misconduct: a scientific Ethics Establishment. Unfortunately, the history of this establishment illustrates the very real perils of the post-Watergate approach to ethics. In the end, the scientists may turn out to have been wiser, if less politically astute, than their critics.

For a variety of reasons, the biological and medical sciences seem more prone to research fraud than do other areas. Their subject matter is less mathematical and precise than that of the so-called "hard sciences," they attract a more eclectic community of researchers, and their methods of operation may be less resistant to fakery than other fields. Perhaps because of these factors, or perhaps simply because most of the well-publicized fraud cases dealt with biomedical subjects, this was the field that saw the first serious effort to institutionalize the response to scientific fraud.

Because so much biomedical research is funded by the federal National Institutes of Health, that organization took the lead by creating an Office of Scientific Integrity (later the Office of Research Integrity) within the Public Health Service whose sole function was to investigate claims of scientific fraud.[22] The first question was how to define scientific fraud. Although few would fail to condemn the kinds of conduct involved in cases like Summerlin's, the creation of a new bureaucracy raised more difficult questions. What sort of conduct should be covered? What should be excluded? What standards and procedures should govern?

These problems were daunting, but all questions were initially resolved in favor of making sure that fraud did not go unpunished because of technicalities. First, the term itself was broadened: No longer was the target just fraud, but a new species of wrongdoing named "scientific misconduct." According to the NIH, scientific misconduct consists of "fabrication, falsification, plagiarism, or other practices that seriously deviate from those that are commonly accepted within the scientific community for proposing, conducting, or reporting research."[23] This expansion of jurisdiction generated some criticism within the government,[24] but not enough to derail it, given the great deal of public attention that the subject had received.

Once the Office was established, it set to work with the energy and dedication displayed by most brand-new bureaucracies. Unfortunately, the results left a great deal to be desired, so much so that one journalist who studied the process described it as "the fraud fraud," concluding that "up close, the alleged sins of scientists look minor."[25] One could not always say the same of those investigating scientific misconduct, however, as some of ORI's major cases illustrate.

One of ORI's best publicized cases involved Rameshwar Sharma, a researcher at the Cleveland Clinic Foundation.[26] Sharma applied for a 1.1 million dollar federal grant, which was never funded, for work involving protein research. Two proteins in particular matter here. One, $alpha_{2A}$, was relatively simple: Sharma had already performed a great deal of work on it. Another protein, $alpha_{2GC}$, was considerably more complex, and Sharma had not yet completed work on it.

Even today, most word processors are unfriendly to writers using subscripts, and that was even more true a few years ago. Since he had to type the symbols for these proteins 130 times in the forty-six pages of his grant application, Sharma got around this problem by programming two "macro" keys with the two symbols. The two keys were next to each other on his keyboard, and at one point in his grant application Sharma (or his sometime-typist wife) hit the wrong one without noticing while typing page twenty-one of his application, calling $alpha_{2A}$ $alpha_{2GC}$. Sharma then sent in the application, which went through the ordinary "peer review" process before being denied.

No one on the NIH panel that reviewed the grant application was misled: They all knew the difference between the two proteins and recognized that if Sharma had performed experiments on $alpha_{2GC}$, as the typo seemed to indicate, he would have made much more of the fact. Furthermore, all the data following the typo had to do with $alpha_{2A}$.

Unfortunately for Sharma, however, an anonymous accuser steered ORI toward his application. ORI officials looked at it and concluded that Sharma was guilty of scientific misconduct by misrepresenting his research in order to get a federal grant—in essence, of pretending that he had done more research than he actually had to make his grant application look better. This began a three-and-a-half-year nightmare for Sharma.

Sharma's life was made worse by the fact that his boss at the Cleveland Clinic Foundation, Dr. Bernadine Healy, had gone on to head the National Institutes of Health and, in that capacity, to clash with Representative John Dingell (D-Mich.), then chair of the powerful Investigations Subcommittee of the Committee on Government Operations. Dingell's subcommittee had taken a major role in investigating scientific misconduct, including charges (later dropped) against Dr. Robert Gallo and Nobel prize winner Dr. David Baltimore. (One staffer had boasted to Healy that "we have taken out the two biggest names in science."[27])

In response, Healy criticized Dingell's investigations, maintaining that scientists accused of misconduct should have due process rights, including the right to confront accusers and a right of appeal. Known for his aggressive response to critics, Dingell responded by singling out the Sharma case as evidence that Healy had done a bad job of dealing with scientific misconduct at the Cleveland Clinic.[28] In a speech reprinted in the *New England Journal of Medicine*,[29] Dingell said that Healy had mishandled the investigation of the Sharma case, and that Sharma "was ultimately found to have falsified his grant applications."

This wasn't true—Sharma's case was still under appeal, so there had been no "ultimate" finding—but according to Sharma it had a "devastating effect" on his reputation, and his career. His lab at the Cleveland Clinic had been shut down as a result of the federal investigations, and he wound up in an unsalaried position at an optometry college in Pennsylvania, living in a dormitory. His financial problems were so severe that he was unable to keep his two children in college, or to fly to India for the funeral of his father.[30] Ironically, Dingell was guilty of the same thing he blamed scientists for: Making a statement that was not true, seemingly based on his own self-interested assessment of the subject. There were two differences, though. Sharma's statement was the result of a typo, while Dingell's statement was intentional and false. And Sharma's life and career suffered enormous repercussions, while Dingell's did not.

Despite Dingell's efforts, Sharma was eventually vindicated by an appeals panel that concluded: "ORI's findings are not supported and the proposed administrative actions are not justified." According to the panel, Sharma's typo "was the result of a careless error," not a case of misconduct. Rather than apologizing in the face of contrary data, however, Dingell's office continued to take the offensive. "Is this an admission that the falsification of a grant application is okay?" one anonymous Dingell staffer was quoted as asking the *Washington Post.*[31]

The Sharma case might be forgiven if it were an isolated incident, but in fact the leading cases brought by ORI all suffered from similar problems. Another researcher, Margit Hamosh at Georgetown University, was similarly charged with "anticipatory research" because of a single statement in one 20,000-word grant application. The statement in question, which had to do with a minor part of a much larger study, read, "Last, but not least, we are presently using the newborn rabbit as an animal model for total parenteral nutrition (TPN). . . ." This statement was open to interpretation. While Hamosh was using the rabbit as a model, her experiments were not actually in progress when the grant application was written. She had completed all of the necessary preliminaries: demonstrating the validity of the model, getting the necessary funding, purchasing the equipment, collecting preliminary data on the rabbits, and so on. In short, the rabbit experiments were getting off the ground, but were not yet fully underway.

Although the statement was open to interpretation, ORI insisted on interpreting it as meaning "we are at this moment doing the important part of the rabbit experiments," rather than the equally reasonable "we are in the process of performing the rabbit experiments." It thus concluded that she had lied on her grant application and found her guilty of scientific misconduct. When she appealed, ORI dismissed the charges.[32]

The Sharma and Hamosh cases, however, were small potatoes compared to ORI's next two cases, the Mika Popovic and Robert Gallo cases, cases that had also attracted the attention of John Dingell. Popovic and Gallo were collaborators, working on the AIDS virus. Popovic performed the experiments that led to the modern AIDS test. ORI accused him of fraud based on a 1984 paper.[33] The key charge was that Popovic had misrepresented the degree of his success in growing different strains of HIV, the virus that is implicated in AIDS. Among the dozens of entries on the charts, eight have entries of "ND." On the chart, ND is said to stand for "not done." Popovic's lab notebooks, however, make clear that he did in fact perform the experiments, but did not write down the results.

As Malcolm Gladwell of the *Washington Post* puts it, "ORI never came up with a motive. But under its rules, it didn't need one. He was guilty."[34] But, as Gladwell goes on to note, Popovic didn't write the part of the chart identifying ND as "not done." "He's a recent Czech emigre," Gladwell notes, "and his English is so bad that others did the bulk of the editing."[35] According to Popovic, he used ND to mean "not determinable," a common abbreviation among virologists meaning that the experiment's results were either unreadable or not conclusive enough to merit inclusion. ORI never indicated how Popovic benefited from the action it challenged, or whether it somehow made the results of his work less useful or accurate. Nonetheless, ORI found him guilty of misconduct.

On appeal, he was exonerated, but ORI was not. As the appeals board put it, "One might expect that from all this evidence, after all the sound and fury, there would be at least a residue of palpable wrongdoing. That is not the case."[36]

Popovic did not suffer the fate of Rameshwar Sharma, but his career certainly was not helped by the investigation, and one can only speculate as to what other discoveries he might have made during this period had he not been coping with ORI. One can also only speculate as to the effect on other researchers' morale and willingness to take risks.

Popovic's fellow researcher, Robert Gallo, was also investigated by ORI. Gallo was charged with, in essence, stealing the credit for discovering the AIDS virus from French researcher Luc Montagnier of the Pasteur Institute. After 7,000 hours of deliberations and interviews, and a careful review of Gallo's lab notebooks (which piled together reached thirteen feet),[37] ORI's claim against Gallo boiled down to the following sentence on the difference between Montagnier's virus cultures (which the French called LAV) and Gallo's own. Gallo wrote that the two viruses looked quite different, but "it is possible that this is due to insufficient characterization of LAV because the virus has not yet been transmitted to a permanently growing cell line for true isolation and therefore has been difficult to obtain in quantity." According to Gallo, this statement meant that the two viruses might be the same, but that it was hard to tell because the French had not been able to culture LAV as thoroughly as Gallo had cultured the virus that he was studying. According to ORI, Gallo was saying that no one had cultured LAV and that was not true because Gallo himself had.

Once again, it is not clear what Gallo might have hoped to achieve by this statement, even if he meant it to say what ORI claimed. Eventually, ORI dropped the charges against Gallo. "Presumably," Gladwell writes, "Gallo will avoid compound sentence structures in the future."

Undoubtedly the most famous science fraud case of all, however, was that involving Nobel laureate David Baltimore and his collaborator, Thereza Imanishi-Kari. Even by the standards of science fraud investigations, this was a complex and muddled case. But the following outline will make clear its importance for our purposes.

David Baltimore, a 1975 winner of the Nobel prize in medicine, collaborated with Thereza Imanishi-Kari on some important research involving antibody production, culminating in a paper published in the prestigious scientific journal *Cell*. In short, the research had to do with antibody production, and with experiments that seemed to show that implanting foreign genes for antibody production also stimulated already-present genes for producing the same antibodies. An assistant to Dr. Imanishi-Kari, Margot O'Toole, found it impossible to reproduce some of Imanishi-Kari's work. Imanishi-Kari told her that it was because her laboratory technique was poor; O'Toole became convinced that it was because Imanishi-Kari was faking experimental results.

O'Toole complained to her superiors, who investigated and found a few minor errors, but nothing of significance. She continued to complain, until she struck an alliance with Charles Maplethorpe, an unhappy former graduate student of Imanishi-Kari's, who conveyed her accusations to two self-styled "fraudbusters" at the National Institutes of Health, Walter Stewart and Ned Feder. After undistinguished work researching the nervous systems of snails, Stewart and Feder had begun to carve out a niche for themselves as investigators of science fraud.

Stewart and Feder found no difficulty believing O'Toole's accusations and began circulating accusations to scientists around the nation. At this point, the ubiquitous Congressman Dingell entered the scene once more.

The relationship between Stewart and Feder, on the one hand, and Congressman Dingell's office, on the other, was extremely close. Stewart and Feder appeared to have ghostwritten letters from Dingell to their boss, Dr. Bernadine Healy,[38] and at one point even claimed that their activities were protected by the same kind of immunity granted to members of Congress under the Constitution's Speech and Debate Clause. (Though entirely spurious, this claim seems to have intimidated their superiors at NIH.) Dingell seized on this opportunity to score political points against Healy, and to further demonstrate his unfettered power to investigate whomever he pleased.

Dingell held hearings, at which Baltimore strongly defended Imanishi-Kari, and refused to back down. As Daniel Kevles writes,

> Dingell was in any case interested only in the fact that the paper contained errors. He seemed not to know that errors vary in their scientific significance, that evaluating their meaning involves critical judgment, and that discrimination in the use of data is a feature of scientific inquiry.[39]

There followed more hearings, a Secret Service review of Imanishi-Kari's lab records and notebooks, and extensive politicking. Dingell's office, and NIH officials, leaked damaging (and sometimes false) information about Imanishi-Kari and Baltimore.

Although Baltimore was never accused of any wrongdoing himself, he began to suffer severe consequences for his unstinting defense of Imanishi-Kari: He was forced to resign the presidency of Rockefeller University and was denounced by a number of his fellow scientists. Instead of admiring Baltimore for sticking by a subordinate in trouble (which in days gone by might have been seen as an admirable sign of character), many of Baltimore's colleagues thought he should have thrown Imanishi-Kari to the wolves for the sake of appearances. Indeed, in this supposedly truth-oriented field, there were a surprising number who felt that it was more important to maintain the appearance that scientists could discipline their own than to seek the truth. As Maxine Singer notes, "The self-serving reason given for all this was concern that unless the scientific community was seen as policing itself, the flow of federal research funds would be in jeopardy."[40] Thus scientists, committed to truth, succumbed to pressure to put appearances first. The result, not surprisingly, was disaster.

Imanishi-Kari, not being a Nobel laureate, suffered more than Baltimore. She was relieved from her teaching position at Tufts and suffered enormous damage to her scientific reputation. And although she was represented *pro bono* by Crowell & Moring, a major Washington law firm, that firm ran up hundreds of thousands of dollars in costs doing so.[41]

At Dingell's insistence, the Office of Scientific Integrity (as it was then called) became involved. As in other cases, its investigation seemed designed to ensure conviction, rather than fairness: Complex forensic data were presented to the accused only in oral form, making responses difficult, many aspects of accusations were not shared with the accused at all, and a draft copy of OSI's report was leaked to the press without Baltimore or Imanishi-Kari being given a chance to respond.

Meanwhile, a number of scientists were confirming Imanishi-Kari's experimental results. And her accusers were never able to come up with a convincing motive for the alleged falsifications: The data in question simply weren't the sort that a fabricator would fabricate. But, as in earlier cases, motive didn't matter, and Imanishi-Kari was found guilty.

She immediately appealed, and once again the result was complete exoneration. Indeed, it was more than that: It was a stunning rebuke to ORI. Not only did the appeals board find that her accusers had completely failed to state their case, it noted that ORI itself had misrepresented the results of forensic investigations, such that it claimed they supported its accusations when in fact they supported Imanishi-Kari's story. The fraudbusters, in short, were themselves guilty of fraud.

In the end, a system set up—and manipulated—to preserve appearances turned out to produce the greatest set of humiliations for American science in this century. Though ultimately those who deserved it the most—John Dingell, Stewart and Feder, and the cowardly scientists who called for Baltimore's resignation—were also the most humiliated, that result is cold comfort. Who knows what scientific discoveries might have been made, had not so many first-rate minds been tied up in a decade-long scandal without basis?

Strangely enough, one group emerged from this affair with its reputation improved—lawyers. Although scientists usually regard lawyers with cordial dislike, many found a new appreciation for the ways of law. "If it wasn't for the lawyers," said Gallo after it was all over, "we'd all be dead. Where would we be if we left it to the politicians, and, if you'll pardon me, the media, and, if I'll pardon myself, the scientists among us?"[42] And Bernadine Healy recounted that "I came full circle to thinking that an adversarial system was necessary. It had become obvious that this was a totally polluted system where these scientists got behind closed doors and worked out their venom, taking down their colleagues. It was a Star Chamber, a hideous travesty of justice."[43] Lawyers, it should be noted, have consistently opposed efforts to bring their own profession under an appearance standard.

This set of cases leaves a frustrating situation. Science fraud is, at least in some ways, a very real problem. But the political and legal system's effort to deal with it in the standard way, by setting up an ethics bureaucracy and promulgating formal rules based on appearances, has been an abject failure. According to Gladwell, "ORI's concern really wasn't with science fraud as it is popularly understood. It wasn't chasing con men. It was after something substantially more abstract and elusive. ORI wanted scientists to be perfect."[44]

Gladwell is right, but there is more to the story. ORI didn't just want scientists to be perfect, it wanted them to be perfect in a particular way. It wanted them to be perfect in a way that left a paper trail; it wanted them to be perfect not only in the truth of their results, but in the neatness of their process of getting there. In short, it wanted them to be perfect after the fashion of lawyers, rather than scientists. Yet, strangely enough, ORI (and Dingell) didn't want to meet such standards themselves. They wanted scientists to work like lawyers, but they did not want to conduct their own investigations in a lawyerly fashion. As a result, they got the worst of both worlds: the pickiness of lawyers, and the disregard for procedures of scientists. It made a poor combination.

The Clash of Cultures

In writing about the difference between lawyers and scientists, Steven Goldberg has drawn an important distinction between the culture of lawyers and the culture of scientists. Both, of course, tend to be well-educated and to possess a fair amount of social status. They may live in the same neighborhoods and drive the same cars. But the fundamental purposes of their professions are quite different.

Science, says Goldberg, is more than anything else about the pursuit of truth. That is, it is about making and testing hypotheses about how the universe works and building upon previous knowledge. The real test of a scientist, then, is whether he or she contributes toward this process. The end justifies the means, not in the sense of excusing immoral conduct, but in the sense that in science the collateral things don't count for much: There are no extra points for penmanship or conduct. The most meticulous research, by the most pleasant and well-mannered scientist, counts for nothing if it produces no new knowledge. On the other hand, a scientist who can produce new and useful insights will be forgiven virtually any human flaw. And many of the best scientists have been prone to use shortcuts: Rather than "showing their work" after the fashion of junior high school mathematics classes, they found ways of solving problems that successfully avoided many intermediate steps. Richard Feynman, the Nobel prize–winning physicist, was famous for finding original shortcuts that allowed him to solve in a few minutes or a few hours problems that took months or years to solve using conventional "brute force" mathematics. Other scientists did not despise him for this—they envied him. The test, after all, was not the meticulousness or conventionality of his procedures, but the accuracy and usefulness of his results. Similarly, Feynman's off-hours were filled with exploits, from womanizing to safe-cracking, that could hardly be called proper. Other scientists may not have thought more of him as an individual for these activities, but they considered them irrelevant to his character as a scientist.[45]

For lawyers, on the other hand, things are very different. Scientists may be interested in consensus and truth, but as Goldberg says, with law, "the scientists' emphasis on progress is replaced by the lawyers' emphasis on process. Rather than seeking greater knowledge of the natural world, the law seeks the peaceful resolution of human disputes."[46] Indeed, many of the subjects that law deals with *have* no "right" answer. Lawyers are constantly having to deal with questions about what sort of behavior is "reasonable" or which of two individuals' perceptions of an event in the past is to be trusted. Galileo's famous posttrial statement that "nonetheless, it still moves" expressed a scientist's faith in truth over process. Pilate's question "What is truth?" expresses a typical litigator's (or judge's) response.[47]

Because the law deals with areas where determining the truth is often difficult or impossible, and because its ultimate goal is the peaceful resolution of social problems rather than knowledge *per se,* law tends to stress procedures over outcomes. We may be unable to tell whether a defendant is guilty or not, so we concentrate on being able to say that he got a fair trial; we may be unable to attest to the authenticity of a piece of evidence, but we require that the "chain of custody" be uninterrupted and documentable.[48]

Unfortunately, applying these lawyerly methods—entirely appropriate in their place—to the process of *doing* science produces bad outcomes. In a legal document, a single misplaced comma can be disastrous, meaning that such documents are carefully scrutinized for typographical errors. In a grant application, what matters to the scientist is that the reviewers understand what he or she is trying to do; details aren't as important because the reviewers are expected to know enough about the field to fill in the gaps themselves. Lab notebooks are for keeping track of experiments; it is expected that once the results are published other scientists will rely on the published material, not the underlying unpublished notebooks. They are records, not evidence.

Of course, legal norms are all right in their place. Other lawyerly traits, such as an emphasis on cross-examination and fair procedure, have turned out to prevent serious miscarriages of justice in the science fraud context. Systems that involve accusation and punishment are peculiarly vulnerable to Grand and Petty Blifil, to political manipulation, and to outright lynch-mob justice, without these norms. ORI's failure to recognize this led to its downfall. But expecting working scientists to treat their notebooks the way practicing lawyers treat multimillion-dollar contracts is silly, and prosecutions based on such an expectation are repugnant.

But when an ethics bureaucracy is created, the norms of lawyers—or, far worse, of scientists playing at being lawyers—soon take over, with unfortunate results. Many scientists worry that too much attention is being paid to things like laboratory notebooks, conflicts of interest, or piddling misstatements in grant applications, perhaps because those are easier for investigators to understand than the underlying substance. Soon ethical matters become more a question of convenience for the Ethics Establishment than of underlying right or wrong; the focus shifts to appearances instead of substance. As the cases discussed in this chapter illustrate, the results often have little to do with ethics.

8

A Plague of Originality

Plagiarism Book Is Plagiarized

Stanford University said today it had learned that its teaching assistant's handbook section on plagiarism had been plagiarized by the University of Oregon. Stanford issued a release saying Oregon officials conceded that the plagiarism section and other parts of its handbook were identical with the Stanford guidebook. Oregon officials apologized and said they would revise their guidebook.[1]

If the Temple of Science can be desecrated by the Watergate Syndrome, then it should not be surprising that *any* field of intellectual inquiry could be similarly imperiled. Indeed, many have suffered such incursions. But one problem can be used to typify many similar issues in academia today, since it touches on most disciplines. The problem is originality.

There would seem to be no ethical standard more obvious or generally accepted than the rule that one should not steal the written work of others. Yet matters here seem far from clear, despite the frenzied efforts of self-appointed overseers. On the one hand, formal rules against plagiarism grow ever more abundant and ever more stringent (even if no more original), and op-ed columnists wax furious in their condemnation of alleged plagiarism by public officials. On the other hand, many op-ed columns are written by individuals other than the one whose name appears on the byline, and for that matter many newspaper stories are more or less verbatim versions of press releases sent out by political organizations, trade associations, or other interest groups. Hardly anyone believes that politicians write their own speeches anymore, and few among the *cognoscenti* in the legal community believe that Supreme Court justices author their own opinions in more than a supervisory sense.

Under these circumstances, it is not surprising that some individuals find the subject of plagiarism confusing. Nor is it surprising that some experts have stepped in to say, "Sure, you'd never *purposely* plagiarize someone else's work, but here's how to avoid even the *appearance* that you did."[2] Yet the application of appearance rules to plagiarism turns out to raise problems of its own.

A Short History of Plagiarism

Even before the development of written language, poets and bards raided one another's work. As Alexander Lindey notes, Homer based the *Iliad* and the *Odyssey* on oral traditions that dated back centuries or more; Aesop's fables were not the work of Aesop, if indeed there ever really was an Aesop. And even after written language became well established, originality was not at a premium: Aristotle, Socrates, Aristophanes, and Plato borrowed heavily from earlier works.[3]

Some of this borrowing went beyond ideas and influence: "Aristotle," Lindey reports, "lifted whole pages from Democritus."[4] And Virgil's *Aeneid* is lifted heavily from Homer: "If Homer gives a catalogue of an army . . . Virgil draws up his forces in the same order."[5] And Pliny the Elder reported that "I have discovered that some of the most eminent writers have transcribed, word for word, from other works, without acknowledgment."[6]

But although unacknowledged transcription was always disfavored, the classical view of what constituted plagiarism was far different from the modern view. In classical times, originality was not favored. Writing was thought hard enough, and risky enough, that too much striving for originality simply seemed too dangerous—a shortcut to near-certain failure. Instead writers strove, even consciously, to imitate earlier great works. This should not be confused with simple copying. Simple copying was regarded as wrong: The term "plagiarism" came from the word *plagiarius,* which literally meant "kidnapper." It was first used by the poet Martial regarding someone who had "kidnapped" some of his poems by copying them whole and circulating them under the copier's name.[7] But while copying so as to take credit for another's work was wrong, use of another's work to create something of one's own was not. The goal was to take an idea that someone else might have had first, but to improve on it, or its execution.

That a work had obvious parallels with an early work—even similar passages or phrases—was a mark of pride, not plagiarism, so long as the overall work could stand on its own. Classical writers were not opposed to originality, they simply had a different (and perhaps more realistic) idea of what constituted originality than do many moderns. Attacks on this kind of imitation were generally dismissed as motivated by jealousy, pedantry, and propaganda. Imitation was bad only when it was disguised, or a symptom of laziness. It was not denounced simply on grounds of being "unoriginal."[8]

Although grumblers always raised claims of plagiarism,[9] this classical view remained pretty much the standard until fairly recent times. Shakespeare's *King Lear* was based on a rather similar predecessor, *King Leir,* but it was not plagiarized. Many of Shakespeare's contemporaries knew the source of his inspiration, but he was (and is) judged by what he produced rather than what he drew from. Turning the forgotten *King Leir* into the unforgettable *King Lear* was an act of creation, even if by modern standards not an entirely original one.[10]

The Romantic Era saw a much greater emphasis on "originality" as a virtue—originality not merely in the sense of avoiding plagiarism, but in the sense of creating something utterly unlike anything ever created before.[11] No longer was a writer supposed to build on top of the structures left by earlier figures. Now he or she was supposed to sweep the ground clear and build from scratch.

Unfortunately, this turned out to be difficult. Even the ancients had complained that all of the good ideas had already been used. By the late eighteenth and early nineteenth century, things had not improved. But there was another source of pressure—economics. The development of printing and binding technology, and of copyright law, meant that there was money at stake. As Thomas Mallon notes, "One thing is clear: plagiarism didn't become a truly sore point with writers until they thought of writing as their trade."[12] Once money was involved, people became more vigilant for copying, whether real or imagined.

Still, as recently as 1952, the classical view had not been entirely abandoned. That was the year in which Alexander Lindey wrote his *Plagiarism and Originality,* still in many ways the leading work on the subject. Lindey defined plagiarism this way:

> Plagiarism is literary—or artistic or musical—theft. It is the false assumption of authorship: the wrongful act of taking the product of another person's mind, and presenting it as one's own. Copying someone else's story or play or song, intact or with inconsequential changes, and adding one's name to the result constitute a simple illustration of plagiarism.[13]

But Lindey also warned that "We must be careful, too . . . not to confuse borrowing with theft. There is a world of difference between the winnowings of a Dante and the outright looting of a Stendhal."[14] And, he cautioned, "every instance of borrowing must be assessed in its time and place. The laws of conscience," he pointed out, "derive from custom." What might be theft in some circumstances might well be permissible borrowing in others. Only a careful review of what was used, how it was used, and what the expectations of the community were can answer the question of plagiarism.

In particular, Lindey warned against a narrow focus on the appearance of similarity between two works, without paying attention to the substantive issues. To assess plagiarism, one must compare the forest, not similarities between the trees.

Employed with probity and intelligence, parallels can be of help—limited help. . . . But the narrow nature of their function must never be lost sight of. They must not be allowed to becloud or eclipse the paramount canon that the crucial test of plagiarism is and must be a reading of the rival works themselves in their entirety.[15]

Although Lindey's view looks more modern than that of, say, Horace, it nonetheless respects many classical notions: that the focus should be on what the alleged plagiarizer has created, as much as on what he or she has taken, and that such issues cannot be resolved by a narrow focus on similarities in language, plot, or structure.

Contrast this with the Modern Language Association's 1975 definition, adopted as the Big Bang was in full explosion. Although that definition starts with the Lindey quote above, it continues in a very different vein:

Plagiarism may take the form of repeating another's sentences as your own, adopting a particularly apt phrase as your own, paraphrasing someone else's argument as your own or even presenting someone else's line of thinking in the development of a thesis as though it were your own. In short, to plagiarize is to give the impression that you have written or thought something that you have in fact borrowed from another. Though a writer may use other person's words and thoughts, they must be acknowledged as such.[16]

Like Nixon's concern about the appearance of a cover-up, this standard reduces a matter of substance to one of appearances. Despite the Lindey quote, it involves doing exactly what Lindey warned against: comparing isolated similarities rather than comparing whole works. As K.R. St. Onge comments: "For a term derived from *kidnapped* and a definition that is supposedly drawing on Lindey's legal experience, the MLA definition extends its application of the term to phrases and thought processes as if a kidnapper could abduct portions of its victim or notions in the victim's head."[17]

The MLA standard might be defended on the ground that it is aimed primarily at students, who are expected not simply to make literary contributions but to demonstrate skills for evaluation. As Lindey said, one must take time and place into account. But the MLA rule seems as much as anything to be a post–Big Bang application of appearance standards; its adoption in 1975, just after Watergate, may not be coincidental. The MLA standard says that rather than undertaking the hard work of deciding whether a piece is plagiarized based on the kind of substantive evaluation urged by Lindey, we should instead just look for similarities and, if we find them, pronounce guilt.

If it were limited to the clumsy efforts of undergraduate copyists, the MLA standard might be harmless and ultimately unimportant. But on further examination it appears to have marked yet another step away from substance and toward appearances—a step with impact reaching far beyond the academy, among other places, back into politics to impact (perhaps) the presidency itself.

Senator Biden's Tale

Plagiarism charges are a staple of entertainment news, of literary litigation, and of academic scandal. The issue of plagiarism seemed to hit a modern high point, however, with Senator Joseph Biden's rather free use of language from a speech by British politician Neil Kinnock. Biden began a speech in Iowa by saying:

> I was thinking as I was coming over here, why is it that Joe Biden is the first in his family ever to go to a university? Why is it that my wife who is sitting out there in the audience is the first in her family to ever go to college? Is it because our fathers and mothers were not bright? Is it because I'm the first Biden in a thousand generations to get a college and a graduate degree that I was smarter than the rest? . . . Those same people who read poetry and wrote poetry and taught me to sing verse? Is it that they didn't work very hard, my ancestors who worked in the

coal mines of Northeast Pennsylvania and would come up after 12 hours and play football for four hours?

These lines were very close to those of British Labor Party politician Neil Kinnock, who had said:

Why am I the first Kinnock in a thousand generations to be able to get to University? Why is Glenys [Kinnock's wife] the first woman in her family in a thousand generations to get to university? Was it because all our predecessors were thick? . . . Those people who could sing and play and recite and write poetry? Those people who could make wonderful, beautiful things with their hands? Those people who could dream dreams, see visions? Why didn't they get it? Was it because they were weak? Those people who could work eight hours underground and then come up and play football?[18]

Although Biden at first said that he saw nothing wrong with his use of Kinnock's phrases, the scandal forced him to withdraw from the 1988 presidential race shortly thereafter.

Although one commentator described it as "modest paraphrasing,"[19] Biden's use of Kinnock's language was certainly nontrivial, even by the rather loose standards of political campaigning. Columnist William Safire described it as "heavy lifting," but noted that it was hardly unusual in political speech. Safire went on to note that his first reaction to the speech was its clumsiness. "Focused on this particular tree," he said, "I missed the forest of moral outrage that sprang up" in response to Biden's borrowing.

Maybe my familiarity with rhetorical borrowing has left me insensitive to the shock of recognition. I remember listening to John F. Kennedy's inaugural, with its stirring line "In your hands, my fellow citizens, more than mine, will rest the final success or failure of our course." I had to admire the way Ted Sorensen evoked the rhythm of the line in the Lincoln first inaugural: "In your hands, my dissatisfied fellow-countrymen, and not in mine, is the momentous issue of civil war." (Kennedy subtly corrected Lincoln's redundancy of fellow-countrymen; that was especially astute.) What's wrong with such evocation? Winston Churchill, writing his ringing 1940 speech about defending his island by fighting on the beaches, in the streets, etc., recalled Georges Clemenceau's defiance in 1918: "I shall fight in front of Paris, within Paris, behind Paris." (Clemenceau, in turn, was paraphrasing marshal Ferdinand Foch on Amiens.) That sort of boosting—a less pejorative term than lifting and certainly far from plagiarizing, rooted in the Latin for "kidnaping"—is done all the time.

Safire went on to confess that in 1968, as a speechwriter for Richard Nixon, he had lifted a phrase from John F. Kennedy that Kennedy had adapted from Adlai Stevenson, and that Stevenson had taken from FDR. "After that speech," he reported, "I felt a little pang of guilt," and so called up the author of FDR's speech to apologize. The author, Samuel Rosenman, told him that the line came from Robert Ingersoll's 1876 speech nominating James Blaine for President. Concluded Safire, "I never credited Sam Rosenman, and Rosenman never credited the guy who wrote it for Ingersoll; why should the Biden speechwriter give a public pat on the back to the hack who pounds away for Kinnock? The answer is that times have changed; you can't get away with borrowing anything these days."[20]

Times *had* changed, and the treatment of Biden made that clear. Although there was much hand-wringing over the wrongfulness of Biden's actions, many news stories stressed that the real problem was appearances. Politicians might have stolen from each other since ancient Greece but, as Safire said, times had changed. The real problem with Biden, we were told "is not the alleged sin but the obvious stupidity."[21] Biden hadn't harmed Kinnock by his borrowing, nor was Kinnock's commercial all that original itself. As one observer noted, the Kinnock commercial from which Biden took the language was itself rife with images lifted from John F. Kennedy, and even the "thousand generations" language was said to have come from George Lucas's *Star Wars.*[22] Nor had Biden deceived his audience: Few listeners believe that politicians write their own speeches anyway. At worst, said one expert, "Biden purloined piffle."[23] Yet somehow Senator Biden, alone among politicians who had done the same kind of thing, became widely known as a plagiarist because he borrowed the Kinnock language.

As Professor K.R. St. Onge says, "It is typical of plagiarism charges that often the significance of *what* was used is totally ignored in favor of the fact that it *was* used."[24] Plagiarism charges call for careful analysis and involve substantive issues of propriety, of honesty, and of law. Yet the Biden affair suggests (once again) that the Ethics Establishment is poorly suited for such judgments:

> The Biden case is a painful and dreadfully pointed reminder of the state of ethics of the educated elite. It had no uneducated participants. The case was addressed only on the grounds of superficial propriety; no deeper ethical concerns intruded. . . . It is a precise measure of our ethics, our notions of plagiarism, and our rationality, that the *New York Times* would lend dignity to such charges and that the media would so sedulously attend to appearances to the total exclusion of content and significance.[25]

The Biden "standard"—to the extent that any principle emerged—was this: Do not say anything that anyone has said before, unless what you say is so colorless and unoriginal that no one will think it worth stealing. It is no surprise that our political speech has become so uninspiring, or our electorate so uninspired, under such a standard. Candidates now may be original mostly via gimmicks: a national sales tax, "three strikes" criminal legislation, the death penalty for "drug kingpins," or similar twaddle. So long as you repeat over and over again, "The one hope for America is adopting my frozen-yogurt tax credit," you can be sure of avoiding plagiarism. Or candidates may adopt standard politicianspeak, using clichés so dead that everyone (or at least everyone able to remain conscious) knows they are in the public domain.

In none of these cases is the public interest served. It is bad enough when philosophy departments focus on linguistic rules rather than

ethics, or when teaching students how to write a research paper has de-
volved into teaching footnoting at the expense of the quality of students'
arguments. Outside the academic realm, the effects are worse still.
When politicians are talking about gimmicks, they are not talking about
substantive issues. And politicianspeak doesn't just put voters to sleep: It
causes them to disengage from the political process, leaving things all
the more open to control by special-interest groups whose selfishness
provides them enough reason to stay awake. Voters stayed home in
droves for the 1996 presidential election, with less than half the electorate bothering to turn out. Given the pablum being spooned out by
the two leading candidates, perhaps in part because of the Biden "rule,"
that low turnout is not difficult to understand. Moral and ethical standards are supposed to serve the broader interests of the community. It is
hard to see how the lessons of the Biden affair have done that.

Computer-Aided Absurdity

The Biden standard has, however, quietly metastasized beyond politics
into a new academic form. Although many works on plagiarism warn
about the danger of simply matching text against text—G.K. Chester-
ton warned that "to see the similarities, without seeing the differences,
seems . . . a dangerous game"[26]—such matching became the favored
test. Fittingly enough, it fell to the two self-styled scientific "fraudbusters," Walter Stewart and Ned Feder, to carry this to its *ad absurdum*
conclusion.

After their not-entirely-successful effort at policing science fraud,
Stewart and Feder branched out into a new business—policing plagiarism. The method they developed was simple—a computerized text-
comparison system. Books, journal articles, dissertations, and so forth
were scanned and loaded into a database that then compared strings of
text until it found matches. Some of these matches were obviously
meaningless—phrases like "on the other hand" or "make haste slowly."
For others, however, the meaning was largely in the eye of the beholder.
Not surprisingly, Stewart and Feder beheld plagiarism. (Given their ap-

parent involvement with ghostwriting letters for members of Congress, one would have expected more modesty in this context, but the ability of accusers to see motes in others' eyes while ignoring beams in their own is well documented.)[27] In particular, they became interested in the case of a historian and Abraham Lincoln biographer, Stephen Oates. After scanning in three of Oates' books, they decided to complain to the American History Association, stating that Oates "repeatedly plagiarized the work of other writers," in particular Lincoln biographer Benjamin P. Thomas.[28]

At one level, their argument seemed well founded: it had come from the dispassionate comparison of texts by a computer, after all, leaving no room for human prejudices. Of course, that comparison also left no room for human judgment. According to one news account:

> As an example of what Stewart calls their "*fantastically* strong" case against Oates, for instance, they cite his sentence: "The two Presidents said little to one another as the carriage bumped over the cobblestones of Pennsylvania Avenue, part of a gala parade." They compare that with the earlier work by Benjamin P. Thomas: "As the open carriage jounced over the cobblestones of Pennsylvania Avenue, Lincoln looked into the faces of the crowd that jammed the sidewalks."[29]

The overlap in language is there, but it is not great. The overlap in ideas is great, but the idea is trivial: a carriage ride. Is this plagiarism? Stewart and Feder, of course, thought so. Others disagreed. Oates responded that the repetition of short phrases does not constitute plagiarism and pointed out that a 1987 article by Stewart and Feder in *Nature* repeated phrases from other works in a similar fashion. Oates quoted Lindey: "Parallels are too readily susceptible of manipulation. Superficial resemblances may be made to appear as of the essence."[30]

Although Oates was not a member of the American Historical Association, that association's Professional Division nonetheless reviewed the charges and produced a report that said Oates' work was "derivative to a degree requiring greater acknowledgement" but that did not find him guilty of plagiarism. Historians who spoke publicly on the subject were divided. According to one, Professor John Simon of Southern Illinois University, Oates was treated unfairly. "He wrote popular biographies, interpretative biographies in which, so far as I know, the claims to scholarship were modest enough." Another historian, Robert Bruce at Boston University, said, "It sounds to me as if it's plagiarism, but they decided not to call it that." Still another, James McPherson of Princeton, said "I would say the weight of it lies toward an exoneration of Oates."[31] Afterward, Oates complained to Congress and to Stewart and Feder's employer, the National Institutes of Health, arguing that government employees should not be paid to undertake free-lance investigations of citizens. Stewart and Feder were reassigned other duties of a largely clerical nature.[32]

Was Oates guilty of plagiarism? Probably not. As Lindey notes, in parallelism cases, "the technique for the presentation of findings is fairly standard. . . . You take excerpts from the supposedly offending work, and corresponding ones from the alleged source, and you put them one below the other, or—more effective still—side by side. You see to it that both the selection and the arrangement underscore the resemblances. You make no mention of any differences unless you have to."[33] This is, of course, exactly what the Stewart/Feder plagiarism computer was programmed to do. The problem, however, is that "[t]he technique makes a weak case look strong"[34] because "[m]ost parallels rest on the assumption that if two successive things are similar, the second one was copied from the first. This assumption disregards all the other possible causes of similarity."[35] Stewart and Feder had taken the MLA definition to its logical extreme, virtually eliminating judgment and reflection from the process. Not surprisingly, the results were poor. This was the Biden standard writ large. It was, in essence, an appearance standard, sharing all the vices of appearance standards in general.

In fact, the standard applied to Biden embodies both of the Blifil Paradoxes. Petty Blifil was triggered by John Sasso, the Dukakis campaign manager who sent the "attack video" containing both the Kinnock commercial and the Biden speech to several news organizations.[36] Sasso's goal was to destroy Biden's candidacy in order to further that of his boss, Massachusetts Governor Michael Dukakis. A shrewd political operative, Sasso knew that the press and the commentators would focus on appearances rather than substance. He was right. A standard that can be manipulated in such a fashion, for such self-serving reasons, embodies Petty Blifil.

But the Biden furor also illustrated Grand Blifil, for the standard applied to Biden was one that left room for many things that debase the political process far more than the impropriety it forbids. Not everyone missed that point at the time. As columnist Edwin Yoder wrote:

> The Biden plagiarism affair might serve a cleansing purpose in politics if Biden's habit were seen as the latest manifestation of a deepening rot in our public discourse. The public figures who still write for themselves seem to be a shrinking minority. The *New York Times* Book Review recently carried a fascinating account of how Lee Iacocca's best-selling book was proposed, designed and manufactured for him by publishers and a ghostwriter (who went on to write a book signed by former speaker Tip O'Neill). Similarly, political oratory has become little more than a tawdry process of passing shopworn phrases from mouth to mouth, like a sort of communal toothbrush—or, to alter the metaphor, like rancid wine in a new goatskin—every four years.

As Yoder noted, the decay of political discourse meant that not only could voters no longer rely on political figures' words being their own, they could no longer even be certain that the words reflected the candidates' views. Instead, "all this hand-me-down stuff is no more a reflection of the speaker's character than a play script is of an actor's. It is calculated to sound the clichés of the hour, to create an effect, to manipulate emotions. . . . Far from being inspiring, it is not far short of political decadence."[37] Yoder wrote before the largely idea-free 1996 presidential campaign, but his words have only gained in force with the passage of time.

Ironically, just as Stewart and Feder's computer, coupled with an astonishing lack of backbone among the academic committees who became involved, was establishing far too high a standard for originality in the academic world, commercial book publishing was going the other way. The commercial world was routinely suppressing the author credit on behalf of a different appearance ethic. Take a stroll through the nonfiction section of your neighborhood bookstore and see how many of the books display the photo of a celebrity author on the front. Few of these books were authored by the individual on the cover. They were instead written by ghostwriters who receive little or no credit.

Who is being deceived by this? Not the publisher, of course. And not the (real) author. Just the reader, who may actually believe that he or she has purchased a book that offers a glimpse into the mind of the putative author. Yet books ranging from Lee Iacocca's best-selling autobiography, to the campaign memoirs of Robert and Elizabeth Dole were the product of unacknowledged ghostwriters. As Charles Krauthammer writes, "If lying about authorship is now a hanging offense, there are not enough lampposts in Washington to handle the volume."[38] A strange legacy of the Biden affair.

Motes and Beams

Yet in fact the problem goes beyond the worlds of celebrity book publishing and political ghostwriting that Yoder and Krauthammer describe. Those who followed the uproar of Senator Biden's speech, or for that matter the more recent flap over Joe Klein's false *denial* of authorship with regard to the novel *Primary Colors,* might have been surprised to know how little of the content in their daily newspaper or newscast actually originated with the producers and editors.

News stories, to a degree seldom appreciated by the general public, are often the product of press releases generated by trade associations and interest groups. Often those releases are converted into news stories by the simple expedient of placing a reporter's byline on top. Television news stories (especially those appearing on local stations) are often supplied fully produced, with blank spots left for the local news reporter to insert commentary that makes the story appear his or her own. Opinion columns are often "placed" by businesses or interest groups to support a particular point of view—often, they are even written by those groups and then run with the byline of distinguished individuals, or even regular commentators, who have barely read the piece, much less written it. Indeed, the Sasso "attack video" was something of this sort, for the journalists who broke the Biden/Kinnock story did not at first disclose their source.

Most readers and viewers have small appreciation of how little of what they see on television or read in newspapers and magazines is original with the reporters, editors, and producers involved. Yet, in fact, news organizations are highly dependent on predigested information from public relations firms, government officials, and advocacy groups, information that is often passed on to their readers and viewers with no indication that it is not original. That problem is not new, but it has gotten worse in recent years.

Thirty-five years ago Daniel Boorstin wrote of what he called "pseudo-events" and noted that much of what passes for news is actually made up of items manufactured by public relations flacks and distributed to the public by way of news organizations. The news organizations, he wrote, go along with this sort of thing out of a need for material, and out of laziness: It's just easier to take predigested material and reprint it than it is to come up with real news. In tones of dismay, Boorstin reported that the National Press Club in Washington was equipped with racks holding the handouts from press conferences throughout the capital, in order to save the reporters the trouble of actually attending.[39] As Boorstin went on to note:

> We begin to be puzzled about what is really the "original" of an event. The authentic news record of what "happens" or is said comes increasingly to seem to be what is given out in advance. More and more news events become dramatic performances in which "men in the news" simply act out more or less well their prepared script. The story

prepared "for future release" acquires an authenticity that competes with that of the actual occurrences on the scheduled date.[40]

The practice Boorstin described has not gone away: It has expanded into new frontiers. Technology in the early 1960s was primitive and favored live or minimally produced television news; as a result, that medium acquired a reputation for realism and immediacy that print reporting lacked. A print story could be made up, but an image on television was *real.* But nowadays, when many high schools have network-quality television studios, and when videotape is sold at convenience stores, that has changed. Although a "video news release" is still more expensive to produce than a standard paper press release, they have become much more common. According to a recent poll, 75 percent of TV news directors reported using video news releases at least once per day.[41]

These releases, with their high-quality images and slick production, are produced by companies and groups who want to get their message across, but don't want simply to purchase advertising time. They are designed so that television producers at local stations or (less often) major networks can simply intersperse shots of their own reporters or anchors (often reading scripted lines provided with the release) to give the impression that the story is their own. Their use has been the subject of considerable controversy within the journalistic profession, although some commentators have claimed that they are used no more often, or misleadingly, than written press releases are used by the print media.[42]

A recent scandal in Britain involved network use of a video news release produced by the group Greenpeace that some considered misleading.[43] But, of course, for every video news release, or VNR as they are called in the trade, that comes from an environmental group there are hundreds that come from businesses or government organizations. Though a keen eye can usually spot a VNR (hint: the subject matter wouldn't otherwise be news, and it usually involves experts and locales far from the station that airs it), most viewers probably believe that today's story on cell-phone safety or miracle bras is just another product of the news program's producers—and hence, implicitly backed by the news people's public commitment to objective journalism. The truth, however, is different.

It is fair to say that the wholesale use of others' work is a major part of modern journalism. But news officials are quick to distinguish that from plagiarism. In a mini-scandal at the *San Diego Tribune,* a reporter's story was canceled when editors noticed that it looked very much like a story that had already appeared elsewhere. At first, presumably, it was thought that the story had been plagiarized from the other publication. Then it turned out that both stories were simply near-verbatim versions of a press release. According to the *Tribune's* deputy editor, *that* wasn't plagiarism. "If you look up the definition of plagiarism, it is the unauthorized use of someone's material. When someone sends you a press packet, you're entitled to use everything in there."[44]

Certainly this statement seems to capture the attitude of many in the journalistic professions. One public-relations handbook explains it this way:

> Most reporters aren't scoop-hungry investigators. They're wage earners who want to please their editors with as little effort as possible, and they're happy to let you provide them with ideas and facts for publishable stories. That is why most publicity is positive for people and their businesses.
>
> You're still not convinced? Go to the library and glance through a few days' issues of several newspapers, including the *Wall Street Journal, USA Today,* and some local papers. You'll discover that the same stories appear over and over again. That's because they were initiated by the companies being covered, not by an eager young reporter looking for a scoop.[45]

An experiment by a group of journalism students at the University of Tennessee demonstrates just how willing reporters can be to accept facts and story ideas that involve little work. The students concocted a fictitious press release from a group opposing "political correctness" and mailed it to a number of newspapers. Most did not run it, but quite a few did—and none checked the details one way or another. One newspaper even embellished the story with additional details that were not included in the original press release. When word of the experiment got out, journalists were predictably outraged, with one even saying that it violated the bond of trust (!) between journalists and public-relations professionals.[46] A more likely explanation for the outrage is that the experiment uncovered a pattern of shoddy work that its practitioners would have preferred to keep unexposed. Not plagiarism, perhaps, but something that in many ways is worse.

In Oates' case, all of his similarly worded passages were trivial. Readers may not have had any idea of the similarity, but the "deception," if it can be called that, was of no account. In Biden's case, obviously self-interested political speech turned out not to be original. Again, voters were not deceived in any meaningful way. But in the cases described above, self-interested speech masquerades—sometimes with the active connivance of journalists and editorial-page editors—as neutral reportage or independent commentary. Which is more likely to deceive its audience? Obviously the latter. Yet the same investigative journalists and pundits who pilloried Senator Biden have little to say about offenses this close to home. Grand Blifil indeed.

There is something wrong with this picture. From the world of science to the world of politics, there has been an eagerness to address ethical issues in terms of appearances. And across the board the results have been poor. Appearance standards are readily manipulated by the unscrupulous, as in the Baltimore and Biden cases, or by the self-important, as in the Oates case. And although adopted in the name of increased sensitivity to ethics, they tend to draw attention away from sins worse than they condemn. The end result is seldom increased public respect, even though the need to maintain such respect is always given as a justification for judging by appearances.

In fact, appearance ethics not only fails to foster better behavior in those it governs, it also undermines the behavior of those who apply it. One of the chief appeals of appearance ethics to its enforcers (who include the corps of press and commentators) is that—much like reprinting press releases as news—judging appearances requires little knowledge of substance, allowing one to discuss the issues without the need for bothersome research or thought. Classical thinkers on ethical matters had a term for this tendency to avoid hard work. It was called *laziness,* and it was not considered a virtue. Another appeal of appearance ethics is that it provides something to talk about: When appearance ethics is the rule, even an unsubstantiated accusation can be said to create a bad appearance. Thus, even an unsubstantiated accusation provides grist for the mill of news flashes, op-eds, and talking-head shows. The classical term for this sort of behavior was *malicious gossip,* and it, too, was not considered a virtue. This powerful appetite for accusations based on appearances itself encourages bad behavior: When the prevailing attitude is "where there's smoke there's fire," we should not be surprised to find a brisk trade in smudge pots. This was known as *temptation.* That all of these human characteristics exist should come as no surprise. That they exist, by design, in an area dedicated to the improvement of ethics would have surprised classical thinkers. We should be concerned that such a situation goes unremarked today.

9

Crime Follies

Attempt no more good than people can bear.

—Thomas Jefferson

Time was, people understood what would be criminally wrong about a defendant's alleged misconduct in a high-profile prosecution. This is no longer so. From Iran-contra to Whitewater, from the celebrated prosecutions of sports agents in Chicago and a lobbyist in Massachusetts, to the trials of a local Republican Party chairman in New York and Democratic Party officials in Kentucky, people are left confused, not enlightened. Too often cases lack coherence. And any positive message that might be communicated is frequently drowned out by charges that the prosecution does not represent the rule of law, but rather mere politics disguised as law. ("Don't your mommy and daddy know I'm a convicted felon?" one subject of a recent corruption case asked a friendly high-school student. The not atypical reply: "My folks don't care. They said it's just politics.")[1]

One might have thought that the increased civil regulation of ethics (and greater attention to the "ethics" of public officials) would have made it less necessary to use *criminal* laws to enforce *ethical* behavior. In fact, the opposite has proved true. The increase in federal prosecutions for breaches of ethical standards after the Big Bang is commonly described as "an explosion," accompanied by "a period of inflation" in the definition of conduct prosecutable as a federal crime.[2] Inflation, of course, involves the devaluing of a currency even as its supply is increased. This chapter discusses how, by so expanding the universe of federal crimes, we have dissipated one of our most precious resources for moral instruction.

At the same time, perhaps trying to get more educational bang for our diminishing bucks, we have increasingly used the criminal law for symbolic gestures (making flag burning a crime or enacting a mandatory death sentence for killing a federal poultry inspector). These pronouncements are calculated to give the appearance of toughness on crime. But what they've done is further devalue the criminal law's moral currency, as well as divert us from seeking hard solutions to difficult social problems. Moreover, as we've become more accustomed to approaching problems from the standpoint of how they *appear*, we've tended to develop appearance-oriented solutions, like the War on Drugs, which eschew cost-effective and achievable goals in favor of imagery and special effects.

Setting the Stage

Public-corruption prosecutions "exploded" soon after Watergate, when newly installed President Gerald Ford directed federal prosecutors to target political corruption at the state and local levels,[3] and the Justice Department established its Public Integrity Section. Jimmy Carter nonetheless attacked Ford during the 1976 presidential debates for not adequately addressing white-collar crime.[4] Once elected, President Carter intensified the federal effort to prosecute government officials.

In 1970, before Watergate, federal prosecutors indicted forty-five federal, state, and local officials. By 1980, when President Carter left office, this annual figure had increased about tenfold (to 442); by 1990, more than twentyfold (to 968).[5] The concentrated federal digging into official misconduct initially uncovered activities (such as bribery and extortion) rich in criminality. It became increasingly difficult over time, however, to extract pure criminal ore from the mine. The prosecutorial machinery nonetheless continued to drill, justifying the cost of deeper exploration with more exotic criminal theories for assaying various samples of unethical behavior.

We began expending our criminal resources in this profligate way just as social research was underscoring the need for frugality. People obey the criminal law largely because of its moral legitimacy.[6] Since the power to stigmatize and concentrate public blame is a scarce resource, Columbia University law professor John Coffee and others have argued that the criminal law must use that power sparingly if it is to perform its socializing role as a system for moral education. Unfortunately, the more complicated and detailed our civil regulation of ethics has become, the more we have delegitimized civil ethics rules and diluted their educational benefits, and the more we have felt we needed the criminal law to teach right from wrong. The criminal law, we learned in Watergate, can be a powerful moral stimulant. But, like true stimulants, its effects too have been diminishing with overuse.

By the end of the 1970s, federal courts had recognized the Hobbs Act (an extortion statute),[7] the federal mail and wire fraud statutes,[8] and the Racketeer Influenced and Corrupt Organizations Act (RICO)[9] as major weapons against various types of unethical behavior.[10] Each statute has its own separate, but parallel, story of expansion. The following discussion selects mail fraud, largely because of its enormous popularity with federal prosecutors. The discussion then pulls back and widens the focus to provide a more panoramic view of the pervasiveness of federal criminal laws. From there it is rather easy to see why today's strategy of appointing an independent investigator to explore whether a particular person committed a crime is so problematic. We conclude with a few observations about the election-year practice of passing criminal laws that merely give the appearance of coming to grips with problems confronting America.

Mail-Fraud Fraud

When Tom Cruise decides to help the FBI bring down the corrupt Mafia law firm of Bendini, Lambert & Locke in the film version of John Grisham's novel *The Firm,* the federal crime he settles upon is mail fraud. This might seem like a strange way to go after lawyers who had engaged in criminal money laundering, blackmail, and (at least as accessories) murder. And indeed it is. (In the book the Tom Cruise character furnishes the FBI with proof of hard-core criminality, but this was a messy ending from Hollywood's perspective because it left Cruise exposed to possible Mafia retaliation.) Still, the legal theory underlying the film's mail fraud ending is entirely plausible. If the Bendini, Lambert lawyers had deliberately overbilled their clients in invoices sent through the mail, the lawyers indeed would have been using the postal service "for the purpose of executing" a "scheme or artifice to defraud" in violation of the federal mail fraud statute, 18 United States Code § 1341. Old-fashioned, run-of-the-mill mail fraud.

Today, mail fraud is no longer old-fashioned or run-of-the-mill. In an effort to root out public corruption, we've traveled quite a distance in the past two decades from this prototypical case. To illustrate just how far, consider what *The Firm* would have looked like if Tom Cruise, a young lawyer in the Bendini, Lambert firm, had pursued the sort of expansive mail fraud prosecution one sees in public-corruption cases today.

As the film now runs, Cruise apologizes to the wide-eyed Mafia clients (the Moroltos) for his firm's overbilling in a comical hotel room scene near the end of the movie. Cruise then explains how use of the mail transformed this overbilling into a federal crime (of which the Moroltos were the victims). The point of the scene is to allow Cruise to assure the Moroltos that he hasn't turned *them* in (nor will he if they leave *him* alone); he has simply fingered his old law firm. And he fingered the firm for mail fraud on the conceit that the Bendini, Lambert lawyers had overbilled the Moroltos through the mail.

A revised ending could have had Cruise discover, however, that the firm had failed its clients in other ways. For example, Cruise might have found out that the firm had not disclosed to its clients important information concerning conflicts of interests—such as the firm's surreptitiously representing an off-shore bank in tax matters while also representing the Moroltos in large transactions with the same bank. But what would audiences or critics have done with a revised hotel room scene in which Cruise goes over the detailed ethical rules governing lawyer conflicts of interest, then explains to the Moroltos how the firm's failure to disclose its work for the off-shore bank violated these rules, then tells the Moroltos how the firm's ethical lapses can be stretched into a "scheme or artifice to defraud," and then elucidates how the sending of (accurate, not padded) invoices could be sufficiently connected to the "scheme" to constitute "mailings" so as to complete the ingredients for a federal felony?

Americans are willing to suspend disbelief to allow a cow to come spinning by within fifteen feet of tornado watchers in *Twister,* a parachuteless James Bond to defy laws of gravity so as to catch up to a falling plane in midair in *GoldenEye,* aliens to invade in *Independence Day,* or the partners and associates in a prestigious Memphis law firm to conspire with mobsters for years in *The Firm* while the FBI looks on helplessly, apparently without subpoena power. But there *are* limits. No employable screenwriter would have dared lay the Cruise film open to the charges of gimmickry, unreality, and confusion that would have followed from Tom Cruise's concocting such a far-fetched federal crime. After the Big Bang, however, federal prosecutors dare to go where screenwriters fear to tread.

Believe it or not, the revised ending would find support in the so-called "intangible rights" theory of mail fraud. The "scheme or artifice to defraud" of mail fraud now can be invoked if someone "deprive[s] another of the intangible right of honest services."[11] The theory has been used primarily to prosecute fiduciaries, persons who are in a position of trust and therefore owe special legal and ethical duties to others. Corporate officers owe such duties to shareholders, lawyers to clients, trustees to beneficiaries, employees to employers. The enforcement of such duties has traditionally been a matter of civil law, with money damages as the remedy. Prosecuting these persons *criminally* based upon their obligation to provide "honest services" creates problems, however. The civil law traditionally has described a fiduciary's responsibility in the loftiest terms. The private fiduciary becomes responsible for any injury to a beneficiary that is caused by the fiduciary's failure to live up to these high standards. Importing these standards into *criminal* prosecutions, in which there is no requirement (as there is in a civil case) that the fiduciary's misconduct must actually cause economic injury to some identifiable beneficiary, has us expending precious criminal resources in cases that a civil judge would dismiss for going too far.

Early troubling sounds could be heard in cases like the 1975 prosecution of then Maryland Governor Marvin Mandel on mail fraud and racketeering charges. The evidence against Governor Mandel revolved around support he had provided to racetrack legislation benefiting various associates who had given him gifts and financial favors. The mail fraud counts charged the Governor with bribery, but the government retreated from this theory at trial, and the jury was not required to find bribery. They were only asked to decide if the Governor had deliberately failed to disclose his relationships and gifts to legislators who were considering the racetrack bill. Thus, what machine politicians once practiced with abandon—pushing for legislation to benefit friends and supporters—became criminal as soon as it formally became unethical, so long as not publicly disclosed. This nondisclosure was criminal, the federal appeals court later concluded, because it was "contrary to public policy and [in] conflict[] with accepted standards of moral uprightness, fundamental honesty, fair play and right dealing."[12]

The prosecutor went so far as to introduce into evidence portions of the Maryland Code of Ethics. The Code admonished state officers to avoid not only impropriety, but the appearance of it.[13] The Code did not apply to the Governor, only to his subordinates. Nor did the Code create *criminal* liability under Maryland law even for those persons who were covered. The federal prosecutor nevertheless used the Code to cross-examine Governor Mandel and made sure jurors could refer to it in their deliberations. "Read it when you are in the jury room, take a look at it and see what it says," he directed in his closing statement.[14] Presumably they did, before convicting Governor Mandel and his associates on fifteen of twenty mail fraud counts.

In 1990, shortly after the appeals court decision in *Mandel,* federal prosecutors in New York brought a mail fraud prosecution against Jack E. Bronston, a New York lawyer and state senator.[15] Bronston had secretly helped a company that was bidding for a bus-stop-shelter franchise while other partners of his law firm were representing minority investors in a rival company that was seeking renewal of the franchise. Bronston clearly violated the rules of professional ethics—working clandestinely for one client against the interests of another. He just as clearly deserved censure (including disbarment). The case troubled legal commentators, however, because it transformed civil wrongs into criminal conduct in a way that provided little guidance for future cases.

This problem was compounded by the trial court's instructing the jury with language from civil cases discussing the high ethical standards for fiduciaries: "[M]any forms of conduct permissible in a work a day [*sic*] world for those acting at arm's length are forbidden to those bound by fiduciary ties. A fiduciary is in a position of trust and is held to something stricter than the morals of the marketplace."[16] These words were taken from a famous passage in a common law decision by Benjamin Cardozo.[17] It is a terrific statement of what we should expect from lawyers, trustees, public officials, and other fiduciaries.[18] Yet it is hardly a guidepost for determining whether a *federal crime* has been committed.

While legal observers were trying to keep up with the latest expansions in mail fraud doctrine, federal prosecutors in New York made "another quantum leap in the extension of the statute"[19] by applying the "intangible rights" doctrine to a local Republican Party chairman, Joseph Margiotta. Margiotta did not work for any government. He was instrumental, however, in making certain that local government jobs went to friends and supporters.[20] The U.S. Court of Appeals for the Second Circuit affirmed Margiotta's mail fraud conviction on the theory that he had participated enough in the operation of government to become a "de facto" public official and therefore owed a fiduciary duty to the general citizenry of the town of Hempstead and Nassau County, the breach of which could lay the predicate for a criminal mail fraud case.

In 1987, in *McNally v. United States*,[21] the Supreme Court tried to bring the curtain down on "intangible rights" prosecutions—only to have Congress promptly reopen the show. The Supreme Court held in a 7-to-2 decision involving Kentucky Democratic Party leaders that the mail fraud statute did not create a crime for cheating someone out of intangible rights like "good government." The Court's logic was simple: The century-old mail fraud statute clearly protected property rights, but did not refer to the intangible right to good government and should not be construed "in a manner that leaves its outer boundaries ambiguous and involves the Federal Government in setting standards of disclosure and good government for local and state officials" without a clear statement from Congress. "If Congress desires to go further," the Court stated, "it must speak more clearly than it has."[22]

The Supreme Court's conclusion in *McNally* rests upon the bedrock "rule of law" principle that criminal laws should give persons clear and definite notice of the types of misbehavior that rise to the level of a crime. Not because we expect the Moroltos to run to the statute books to see how well they are complying with the blinding array of criminal statutes. But rather primarily because we want *prosecutors* and *judges* and *jurors*—the instruments of criminal punishment, one of the most awesome powers of government—to know what is criminal and what is not. One of the most tangible "intangible rights" we have as citizens is the right to have this fundamental governmental power exercised on a principled, nondiscriminatory basis.[23]

In cases like *Mandel*, courts lavishly describe the obligation of public officials to act in accordance "with accepted standards of moral uprightness, fundamental honesty, fair play and right dealing."[24] Yet that is precisely what we mean by insisting upon the rule of law in criminal cases. Granting prosecutors the largely unreviewable power to make up federal crimes more or less as they go along is to abandon standards of fair play and right dealing where they matter most.

Can there be any doubt, for example, as to which is a worse advertisement for the abuses of governmental power (and therefore greater reason to distrust government and public officials): favoring political friends, disfavoring political enemies, and targeting unpopular groups and certain minorities in the exercise of the state's criminal prosecution powers, or engaging in similarly unethical behavior in the awarding of a $15,000 municipal insurance contract? Even if the question were close, it would obviously make no sense to invite the former abuses in an effort to stem the latter. Yet we plainly do.

McNally triggered an outcry that the Supreme Court was somehow shackling federal prosecutors in their efforts to eradicate corruption.[25] And so, on the last day of the 100th Congress, buried among thirty unrelated provisions that were added to the Omnibus Drug Bill lay a provision (now law) stating that for purposes of the federal mail and wire fraud statutes, "the term 'scheme or artifice to defraud' includes a scheme or artifice to deprive another of the intangible right of honest services."[26] No one in Congress bothered to explain what this means, other than a return to the uncertainty before *McNally*.

Since many of the ethical rules in "intangible rights" cases address mere appearances of corruption,[27] it was inevitable that defense lawyers would attack the paradoxes of appearance ethics. And so they did. A great example occurred in the 1989 Chicago mail fraud prosecution of sports agents Norby Walters and Lloyd Bloom.

Walters and Bloom (who were by numerous accounts disreputable men) had secretly signed scores of college athletes while the athletes were still playing college football and before NCAA rules allowed the players to hire an agent. These signings made the athletes ineligible under NCAA rules. The students kept the deals quiet, however, and continued to play.

The NCAA has many eligibility rules, just as it has many finely tuned rules regulating such things as the provision of various modes of transportation to recruits during campus visits.[28] The *academic* eligibility rules require that each student-athlete be admitted as a degree-seeking student according to published entrance requirements, be in good academic standing in accordance with standards applied to all students, and be enrolled as a full-time student and making satisfactory progress toward a degree.[29] The rules are designed, among other things, to maintain the transparently false appearance that the athletes are normal college kids, treated just like other students, in good academic standing and "making satisfactory progress toward a degree."

The mail fraud case against Walters and Bloom was premised on the notion that the two agents had flimflammed four Big Ten colleges—Michigan, Michigan State, Purdue, and Iowa—by prematurely signing some of their football players. These signings made the players ineligible and had the further consequence (here comes the mail) of causing the schools to send letters to the NCAA erroneously confirming the players' continued eligibility.

The trial ended in convictions on some of the mail fraud counts. The forewoman of the jury, University of Chicago administrator Marjorie Benson, conceded that the jury had to do "some stretching" to find that Walters and Bloom had anticipated the subsequent misuse of the mail.[30] But that's par for the mail fraud course. More interesting was Benson's explanation as to why the jury had convicted Walters and Bloom of defrauding Michigan and Purdue but not Michigan State and Iowa. Federal prosecutors, after all, had carefully selected these particular colleges as relative exemplars. When the smoke cleared, however, despite restrictions on the defendants' ability to obtain and present evidence of the schools' own NCAA violations,[31] defense cross-examination of Iowa and Michigan State officials convinced the jury that those colleges were themselves far too enmeshed in NCAA rule violations to have been cheated out of anything by Walters and Bloom.

For example, in a scene reporters described as "painful,"

the Assistant Athletic Director at the University of Iowa who had earlier praised the school's academic vigilance read through the transcripts of players Ronnie Harmon and Devon Mitchell. By the end of his junior year, Harmon had taken only one class toward his computer science major and was put on academic probation for poor academic performance. Each semester his grade point average was below a "C." He was enrolled in many "slide" courses [including teaching gym, officiating football, coaching basketball, bowling, billiards, and watercolor painting]. Despite this record, the University of Iowa certified him as academically eligible—that is, that he was in good academic standing and making satisfactory progress toward his degree. . . . Devon Mitchell's academic record was similar. . . .

Mitchell's curriculum included karate, billiards, bowling, jogging, tennis, ancient athletics, recreational leisure, and advanced slow-pitch softball. . . . Neither Harmon nor Mitchell returned to school after his academic eligibility expired.[32]

On the government's theory of the case, it is hard to see why University of Iowa officials weren't committing mail fraud themselves when certifying these players' academic eligibility in letters to the NCAA. Unless, of course, the NCAA itself didn't really care. In which event the entire case would have collapsed. No one seriously suggested prosecuting Big Ten officials, however, or any of the other 109 colleges and universities that violated NCAA rules during the 1980s.[33]

Defense attorney Dan Webb argued to the jury that it can't be a federal crime to violate NCAA rules any more than it can be a federal crime to violate the rules of a local Elks Club—mail or no mail. But jury interviews suggested that the jury was swayed by testimony (irrelevant to the mail fraud counts) concerning some violent threats by Walters and Bloom and possible connections to organized crime. Government prosecutors, NCAA officials, Big Ten administrators, and jurors were right to be worried about the influence of professional gambling on college athletics. A number of NCAA officials and sportswriters already fear that college point shaving is more common than imagined—especially in basketball, where it is relatively easy to maintain the mere appearance of trying to score. Officials are terrified of what a major scandal—involving, say, the wildly successful "Road to the Final Four"—could do to college sports.

All of the ingredients of a major scandal are there: The athlete sees that colleges have trivialized the governing rules and circumvented them when it suits their ends. He knows his college is making a fortune on his efforts while he's not allowed to make a dime. He feels exploited and anxious about life after college. And then he catches sight of a gambler waiting in the wings offering money now. No one in Chicago wants another Black Sox scandal. But when disillusioned and embittered athletes start thinking that they should grab what they can while they can, the clock turns back to 1919.

Regardless which combination of substantive reform proposals might work best—whether or not it involves paying the athletes something for their labors (a current hot issue)—plainly something needs to be done. And that something isn't the quick—apparent—fix of a mail fraud prosecution that leaves sportswriters, legal commentators, jurors, and sports fans scratching their heads. "We felt there were no innocent bystanders," forewoman Benson commented after the Walters-Bloom trial. "What was the crime Walters and Bloom committed?" asked the *New York Times.*[34]

Where mail fraud law will end is anybody's guess. In the meantime, we can empathize with Torrance, the FBI agent in *The Firm.* At a point in the novel when FBI investigators cannot locate Tom Cruise and suspect he has double-crossed them, Torrance puzzles over criminal charges the FBI has drafted to justify a warrant for Cruise's arrest. "Torrance was not sure where the mail fraud fit, but he worked for the FBI and had never seen a case that did not include mail fraud."

300,000 Reasons for Caution

The federal mail fraud statute is only one weapon in the federal arsenal. Incredibly powerful, perhaps, like wire fraud, the Hobbs Act, and RICO, but still only one weapon. The number of additional arms we have stockpiled in the federal war against crime is truly staggering: It has been estimated that more than 300,000 regulations at the federal level are criminally enforceable.[35] And there's the high-megaton federal conspiracy statute,[36] which criminalizes agreements to violate federal civil provisions, and the federal false-statement statute (discussed below), which reaches oral and unsworn false statements in any matter within the jurisdiction of any executive department or regulatory agency.

When state criminal laws are considered, there is more truth than humor in the observation that we have achieved "the criminalization of nearly everything."[37] Indeed, several years ago two *Wall Street Journal* reporters tried to prove that in one sense or another nearly every American is a criminal.[38] The journalists selected twenty-five rather common crimes (petty larceny, possessing illegal drugs, drinking in public, and so forth). The authors themselves admitted, between them, to having committed sixteen crimes on their list. Most of the dozens of people interviewed had committed eight or more crimes. An Episcopal priest confessed to twelve crimes. Today, Diogenes could wear out his sandals looking not for an honest man, but merely for an unindictable one.

We are all saved from some sort of Kafkaesque prosecutorial hell because prosecutors generally exercise common sense and, moreover, can't possibly chase all of us down. They have other fish to fry. A Los Angeles architect who was interviewed for the *Journal* article (and who confessed to a large number of crimes) captured the prevailing attitude. He wasn't overly concerned he'd be prosecuted because "I'm a good guy, and I look honest." But what if he appeared crooked? Or came from Watts? Or what if he were nominated for city council and a political enemy circulated rumors about his possible lawlessness, prompting an inquiry by an independent prosecutor who has no other fish to fry?

Cover-Ups, Lies, and Independent Counsel

In the old days, we would refrain from ringing up the cops until *after* there was fairly clear evidence of a crime, such as Professor Plum lying in a pool of blood in the conservatory. Off everyone would go looking for clues, with the concrete fact of Professor Plum's corpse to focus their energies. Today, though, we frequently summon our sophisticated investigative technicians *before* there is evidence of a crime. We run to the phone as soon as someone suggests Colonel Mustard might have committed some impropriety. We then try to solve the mystery of whether this or some other past indiscretion of Colonel Mustard just might constitute a crime.

Nowadays, it is more remarkable when the ethics crime laboratory cannot come up with a viable theory of criminality than when it can. Using today's sophisticated equipment, investigators are usually able to tease several potential crimes out of the fibers of a prominent person's life—like mail fraud for violations of certain ethical rules coupled with a few "mailings." This reality gives rise to one of the central problems with using "independent" investigators, such as the Ethics in Government Act's Independent Counsel, to produce the appearance of even-handed justice.

The greatest clash between executive-branch deception and the Office of Independent Counsel occurred in Iran-contra. We grew so weary of Iran-contra that it's hard to recall how it loomed over the nation. The various disclosures—the downing of the Hasenfus flight over Nicaragua, the secret U.S. arms sales to Iran, press reports on a "shredding party" at the White House, the "diversion" of profits from the Iranian arms sales to contra bank accounts, and so on—and the assorted investigations— the Tower Board, the individual Senate and House committee hearings, the joint congressional hearings, the Independent Counsel inquiry— *dominated* the national news for more than a year. And continued to generate stories for years thereafter.

Few people thought the Independent Counsel's work ended satisfactorily. As the *New York Times* commented after President Bush, decrying the "criminalization of policy differences," pardoned six Iran-contra figures in December 1992:

> Many might dispute that dismissive characterization. But few people, even those who most strongly supported the Iran-contra prosecutions and who now deplore the pardons, would argue that the legal process of a criminal investigation has shed light on the affair.[39]

Most Americans seemed to agree that much of the underlying conduct was wrong. But it was difficult to understand what was criminal or what should be. And the wrongfulness of behavior was obscured by a fog of technical legal arguments surrounding the criminal cases.

As the months passed, more and more people began calculating the costs of the whole investigative enterprise—not merely in raw dollars ($47 million for only the criminal inquiry), but in lost opportunities. As James Fallows observes in *Breaking the News,* during the first year's investigation,

> the federal government went another $200 billion into debt. The crack cocaine epidemic got under way. The savings and loan industry was about to suck incalculable sums from the national treasury. The United States spent nearly a billion dollars a day on the military, and added a billion dollars a week to its trade deficit with Japan. If all the citizens, politicians, journalists, and scholars in the country were working together, they might not have been able to solve any of those problems in a year. But by spending a year goggling at Oliver North, they guaranteed that they could avoid dealing with the issues that really threatened the country.[40]

In many ways Iran-contra became the test "rule of law" case for the Office of Independent Counsel. Everyone seemed to talk about the "rule of law." Columnists wrote about it. Senators talked about it. The authors of the congressional report on Iran-contra devoted a chapter to it. One of the crystallizing moments of the televised congressional hearings occurred when Oliver North's NSC secretary, Fawn Hall, blurted out, "Sometimes you have to go above the written law." There were gasps all around.

It would have seemed under the circumstances, particularly in light of the congressional mandate to promote the appearance of nonpartisan justice, that the Independent Counsel should have used the federal criminal laws so as to maximize their power to teach the importance of the rule of law and to clarify the differences between criminality and immorality. In January 1987, at the beginning of the Iran-contra investigations, Harvard Law School professor (and future Clinton administration Deputy Attorney General) Philip Heymann noted Americans' increasing tendency to confuse the two concepts. This confusion leads to "social acceptance of whatever behavior is not forbidden criminally." "I am not a crook" becomes an ethical defense. Professor Heymann ruminated that the Independent Counsel's greatest service in the Iran-contra cases "might be to remind us of the limits of his charge, to speak explicitly of the limits of the criminal law itself as a device for coming to grips with issues of propriety, morality, and wisdom that are central to the nation."41 Three years later, however, Independent Counsel Lawrence Walsh was offering, as the core justification for his office's work, having *extended* federal criminal law by establishing for the first time in the nation's history the criminality of unsworn lies to Congress by members of the executive branch.42

The vehicle for this extension was the federal false-statement statute, 18 United States Code § 1001,43 discussed in the next paragraph. For more than fifty years, until Iran-contra, no prosecutor had ever applied the false-statement statute to the executive-legislative dialogue. And its scope in traditional cases (lying to federal regulators) had widened to such a degree that no one could possibly have known which categories of false statements by an executive-branch official to a congressman were covered and which were not. In this respect, the false-statement provision stood in marked contrast to the much more clearly defined federal perjury, obstruction, and contempt statutes, which for more than fifty years indisputably had protected Congress's right to receive truthful information from executive-branch officials. Yet these statutes didn't go far enough for the Independent Counsel, who felt that nonperjurious, nonobstructive, noncontemptuous false statements by executive officials should also be criminal.

The false-statement statute criminalizes the concealment of material facts (cover-ups) and the making of unsworn false statements (lies) in any matter within the jurisdiction of any federal "department" or "agency." The statute has existed in its current form since 1934,44 when it was enacted to cure a problem federal regulators were experiencing in policing New Deal programs. Existing criminal law only protected the government when people tried to cheat it out of money or property. New Deal legislation, however, required executive departments and regulatory agencies to police all sorts of things (like crude-oil production and timber use) in which the government itself had no direct pecuniary interest. The false-statement statute filled this regulatory gap.

Like the mail fraud statute, the false-statement statute became a darling of federal prosecutors. By 1984, both liberal Supreme Court Justice William Brennan and conservative Justice William Rehnquist were lamenting that the statute had been so extravagantly interpreted that a person's casual misstatement to a neighbor would be criminal if the neighbor, unbeknownst to the speaker, subsequently used that statement in connection with his work for a federal agency.[45] Justices Rehnquist and Brennan were not alone. Law reform groups had long criticized the statute's overbreadth in its traditional application to false statements made *to* executive and regulatory officials.

If false-statement law applied to declarations *by* executive officials, then everything from false statements at presidential news conferences, to misrepresentations in a telephone conversation between a White House aide and a congressional staffer, to misstatements in the presidential budget would constitute felonies. Asking an Independent Counsel under these rules of engagement to see if a law has been broken would be like asking a referee at a professional hockey game to blow his whistle if he spots any player contact. FDR, Eisenhower, Kennedy, Johnson, Reagan, Bush, Clinton—they'd all be felons.[46] Maybe we've shown less than perfect judgment in the Presidents we've elected, but still . . . all felons?

Thankfully, the Supreme Court reined in these excesses in 1995— long after the charges and countercharges over Iran-contra had subsided—in a case that involved false statements to a bankruptcy court. The Supreme Court held that, despite contrary language in a 1955 case, the false-statement statute does not cover false statements made to the courts or to Congress.[47] The Court thereby restored the rule of law to what otherwise would have been a hopelessly confused and undefined crime of political deception delivered to us by an institution that was supposed to reaffirm the rule of law, not undermine it. In 1996, Congress enacted a narrowed amendment to the statute, which created a crime for false statements made to Congress in the course of an official "investigation" or "review."[48]

There has been no question that the false-statement statute applies to statements an executive official makes before entering federal service. Thus, an Independent Counsel investigates HUD Secretary Henry Cisneros for allegedly lying to the FBI about the *level* (not the fact) of payments he made to a former mistress. The FBI questioning was part of its background check of Cisneros before he came to Washington. Cisneros was clearly wrong to lie, if he did. But isn't something also a bit wrong with a system that demands complete and accurate answers to such intimate questions by federal authorities upon threat of jail?

Federal investigators and agency employees ask Americans about virtually everything these days. And virtually everything we say in response (sworn and unsworn, oral and written) is subject to federal criminal law. We remain relatively secure, however, because, again, federal prosecutors can't be bothered with prosecuting us—any more than they can be troubled with prosecuting each other for lying about such things as prior drug use on personal information forms completed during their office's initial hiring background check. Furnishing false answers on these forms constitutes a felony committed by literally hundreds of Assistant U.S. Attorneys during the last ten to fifteen years. Yet the prosecutors are (and, under the circumstances, should be) safe from prosecution—unless they amble a little further into the public spotlight, questions are raised, and someone demands an independent investigation in order to dispel any appearance of special treatment.

From the Recreational to the Hallucinogenic

The legislative measures supporting this expansion of federal criminal laws have typically been passed as part of Congress's biennial ritual of chest thumping over crime.[49] (As one of us has proposed elsewhere,

Congress would do us all a great favor if it would henceforth pass crime bills only in odd-numbered years.[50]) So, for example, somewhere among the death-penalty and enhanced-sentencing sections of the Violent Crime Control and Law Enforcement Act of 1994—the Crime Bill—lies a provision further broadening "intangible rights" mail fraud to reach not only items sent through the federal mail, but also any "matter or thing whatever to be sent or delivered by any private or commercial interstate carrier" (such as Federal Express, Atlas Van Lines, or Greyhound).

These sorts of provisions are intended to give the appearance of toughness on crime. Yet, as shown above, far too often they weaken the law's effectiveness. Since these provisions are part of larger crime packages aimed at the problem of violent crime, one might wonder whether the crime packages themselves have been crafted primarily to give the *appearance* of solving the violent crime problem. This would be Grand Blifil on a decidedly grand scale. Unfortunately, it turns out to be the case.

There is nothing new about using criminal laws symbolically, of course. We have long had unenforced laws criminalizing a variety of sexual activities, including sexual intercourse between unmarried adults.[51] These old laws, however wrongheaded, are not a grave national problem. But what *is* a national problem is Congress's resort to similarly symbolic criminal measures, like the Flag Protection Act of 1989[52] (the flag-burning crime), which purposefully create "wedge" issues to divide Americans and divert public attention from more pressing problems. Moreover, when such laws *are* directed toward real-world problems—like drugs and crime—they can have staggeringly bad consequences while giving the illusion that we have developed and are implementing a well-thought-out battle plan. And the transparently self-serving character of the congressional sponsorship of these laws undermines the criminal law's claim to moral legitimacy. It's "just politics."

Congress's passage of the self-evidently symbolic flag-burning law reveals much about the forces at work when the stakes are larger. In a nutshell, it shows members of Congress throwing proportionality out the window, often against their better judgment, to gain voter respect by appearing morally pure on the issue of patriotism and morally tough on the issue of crime. Like other mere public relations efforts to gain voter confidence, however, the whole effort paradoxically, but predictably, lowered respect for members of Congress in most voters' eyes. Yet again, an appearance-based approach proved to be not even good p.r.

Whatever one's views about the merits of the slippery crime of "flag desecration," it would take a Darrow to defend the proportionality of the congressional response in 1989 to the Supreme Court's decision in *Texas v. Johnson*.[53] This Rehnquist Court decision overturned, on First Amendment grounds, the conviction of Gregory Lee Johnson under a Texas statute criminalizing the desecration of venerated objects. Johnson had set fire to the American flag outside of the Republican National Convention in Dallas in August 1984. The *New York Times* had reported on only one other flag-burning incident in the five years preceding Johnson's display[54]; and in the five years following the great "flag-burning" debate (from 1990 to 1995), the ACLU counted only two.[55] The flag issue nevertheless was analyzed in lengthy congressional hearings, newspaper columns, talk shows, and the presidential campaign (for instance, by President Bush while visiting a flag factory). Why all the fuss? Cartoonists identified one reason: legislators running for cover under a flag-burning umbrella from a pounding rain of difficult national problems. Historians have noted that lawmakers increasingly resort to such symbolic gestures when reality, like violent crime, gets too hard to handle.[56]

Despite reservations, lawmakers fell over one another to pass something they thought would be aesthetically pleasing on a moral level to most Americans. Congressmen repeatedly went off the record to express opposition to a given proposal while simultaneously complaining, "Who can vote against something like this?"[57] Even on-the-record comments were unusually revealing. After former Reagan administration Solicitor General Charles Fried had testified before a House Judiciary subcommittee in opposition to a constitutional amendment, subcommittee chair Don Edwards allowed, "Your point of view is the correct point of view, but it's such a loser."[58] Then–Senate Minority Leader Bob Dole opined that a vote against a constitutional amendment "would make a pretty good 30-second spot" during the 1990 elections.[59]

The objective may have been to bolster public confidence in Congress's responsiveness to the problems of the day, but over time the pandering had an opposite effect. Sure, Americans might still say they thought flag burners should be flogged, but increasingly they thought the same of members of Congress. The lampoons, cartoons, and Jay Leno jokes seemed to take their toll. As *Time*'s Barbara Ehrenreich counseled House members in the summer of 1995, when they decided to return to the "weighty" subject of flag burning, the legislators "should realize that just because someone does not douse them in kerosene and hold a match to their pants cuffs is no reason to think they are held in respect."[60]

If one credits the public with the modicum of common sense necessary to separate symbolic opportunism from substantive accomplishment, this loss of credibility was eminently predictable. After all, as Medal of Honor recipient Senator Bob Kerrey pointed out at the time:

> When you're all done arguing, what have you got? Have you built a house? Have you helped somebody? Have you created a better world? Have you fought a battle worth fighting? Or are you banging into shadows on the wall of a cave? It seems to me there's nothing produced for it and you've divided the nation.[61]

It is bad enough to use this sort of symbolic legislation recreationally to express moral disapproval while retreating from other problems. But, as they say, casual use can lead to the hard stuff. And here the "gateway drug" of governing ethics according to appearances has led to the more serious vice of attempting to govern the *country* according to appearances. In this case, the hard stuff is socially expensive symbolic legislation on deadly serious subjects, like drugs and crime.

Thoughtful experts hold a wide range of conflicting opinions on how best to tackle violent crime in America. Yet most experts share the belief that the decades-long War on Drugs has been far too long on imagery and special effects and far too short on trying to find cost-effective and achievable ways to address the complex of problems. There is, of course, no greater special effect, in Hollywood or Washington, than an ersatz war. Even if you knew nothing about how to tackle violent crime in America or discourage drug abuse, a "War on Drugs" should make you nervous, just as it has made our post-Vietnam military leaders nervous when they've been asked to involve branches of the service.

Those favoring drug decriminalization (who now include conservative William F. Buckley) and those opposing it (such as Professor James Q. Wilson, who is about as expert on the subject of drugs and crime as anyone can be) have targeted their criticism on the official war metaphor not because it is easy to make fun of a pretend war, but rather because such symbolism has distorted the entire effort. As Professor Wilson has noted, this problem begins with the declaration of war itself:

> I have watched several "wars on drugs" declared over the last three decades. The wars typically begin with the statement that the time for studies is past and the time for action has come. "We know what to do; let's get on with it." In fact, we do not know what to do in any comprehensive way, and the need for research is never more urgent than at the beginning of a "war." That is because every past war has led, after brief gains, to final defeat. And so we condemn another generation to risk.[62]

Professor Wilson recommends that we withdraw with honor from the war and begin an array of "frankly experimental" programs to see what works and what doesn't.[63]

Instead, we are knee deep in the Big Muddy. And because there can never be a decisive victory (there will always be drug use and violent crime), the war necessarily devolves into "a series of gestures—a drug bust, the capture of a cocaine shipment, an invasion of Panama—all highly publicized, all with clear-cut good and bad guys, and all triumphs for the good."[64] We measure success by such things as "street value" ("It is for the War on Drugs what the body count was for the Vietnam War; and it has been about as accurate a predictor of success."[65]) or "kilos seized or destroyed" ("Helicopters suddenly appeared over the hills and hundreds of men in fatigues began sliding down ropes into the fields below as part of a DEA slash-and-burn campaign. Oklahoma narcotics agents reported that they were told to exaggerate the amount of marijuana they eradicated in order to boost federal funding for the state drug war."[66]) The head of the federal Bureau of Prisons discusses acquiring college campuses and religious seminaries and converting them into minimum-security facilities[67]—the Drug War's strategic hamlets. And the President, when concerned that he's not appearing steely enough on the drug problem, casts a four-star retired Army general, Barry McCaffrey (ironically, a Vietnam veteran), to manage the war effort.

The foot soldiers in this war are the local narcotics commanders. They are often as skeptical as the war's harshest critics:

> [T]heir recurrent metaphor is the war in Vietnam; as one of them put it, "the country has to learn that another division, and another division, doesn't win the war." "Can I guarantee you another 21,000 quality felony narcotics busts? Yes. Can I tell you that will do anything about drug dealing? No," says one senior official of the [New York] narcotics division. [Francis C. Hall, the division's retired commander] is equally frank: "People expect us to eliminate drugs. Some of them use expressions like drug-free zones, drug-free communities. Unrealistic! Totally unrealistic. It's certainly not going to happen in my lifetime."[68]

So New York City's Tactical Narcotics Team does its counterinsurgency best, penetrating an area at street level with special teams that drive overt drug dealing to other neighborhoods until the troops leave and life returns to normal.[69] We may have progressed since G. Gordon Liddy's Operation Intercept, but it's not particularly clear how.

One aspect of this war effort that is not for show is its cost. The Drug War has placed extraordinary burdens on police, prosecutors, judges, and prison officials; diverted resources away from violent crimes toward crimes of drug possession and low-level street dealing; and exacted often terrible social costs in our inner cities. Yet the greatest costs are just beginning to come due: those produced by already overcrowded prisons receiving swelling numbers of additional inmates on a long-term basis— the result of ever-increasing mandatory sentences imposed under tough-appearing federal antidrug laws. Placing to one side the human costs of imposing severe mandatory prison sentences on even relatively minor (and predominantly minority) possession offenders—sentences that are now "horrifying" even the most conservative Reagan-appointed judges[70]—the financial burden is staggering.

America already leads the world in percentage of its population in prison.[71] As of 1993, forty-two states were under court order to reduce prison overcrowding, requiring the states either to let violent offenders go free or to build more prisons.[72] Florida initially chose the former course, releasing 130,000 felons early, many of whom went on a violent crime spree.[73] California is adding more prisons:

> California has more people locked up in prison than any other state. . . . This spring [1996], 146,290 inmates are crammed into 32 adult prisons and 10,500 are in facilities for juveniles.

> By 2001, according to California's Department of Corrections, the state will have 250,000 felons beating at the doors and will need 50 prisons to hold them.
>
> Money is tight. California's corrections budget is growing by 11% a year, while state revenue is increasing by only 5.3%. . . . Five years from now, officials predict that the cost of housing prisoners may be close to $5 billion.
>
> The prisoner-bulge is often attributed to the 1994 "three-strikes" law, which specifies that offenders convicted of a felony for a third time must serve 25 years to life without parole. But the "three-strikes" convicts are just reaching the prison system. . . . The flood is expected in two or three years' time.[74]

The principal reason for the overcrowding is severe and mandatory sentencing, which is born of legislators' fear of seeming soft on crime.

One congressional opponent of tougher sentencing laws observed, "When you call for more incarceration, you do not have to explain yourself; when you argue for effective alternatives, you do. And in politics, when you start explaining, you've lost."[75] "But," as columnist Stuart Taylor has asked, "how tough is it to be wasting scarce police, prosecutors, judges, and prison cells going after petty drug offenders instead of killers and robbers?"[76]

This mismatch between crime problem and crime solution calls to mind the scene from Kingsley Amis's novel *Lucky Jim* in which Jim observes from the window of a passing car as a big fat man looks with furtive lust at two rather pretty girls. As the car speeds along, Jim's attention shifts to a cricket match in which the batsman, another big fat man, is violently hit in the stomach by the ball and doubles over in pain. Jim wonders whether "this pair of *vignettes* was designed to illustrate the swiftness of divine retribution or its tendency to mistake its target."

We may wonder likewise about government responses to Americans' justified anxieties about violent crime and the nation's moral climate. Swiftness in response there is, be the triggering event a Supreme Court decision (mail fraud or flag burning), a scandal (politics or college athletics), or fear of an uncontrolled outbreak (church burnings or drug abuse). Yet, especially when we declare "war" on problems and attack them with all our weapons indiscriminately, we have a costly tendency to mistake the target and even to find ourselves casualties of friendly fire.

Moreover, in "war" truth is the first casualty. And so it has been here. It is rather hard to develop solutions for problems one hasn't accurately defined, as Professor Wilson observed. Yet leaping over the first step of trying to ascertain the true state of affairs is increasingly becoming the norm. Congressional leaders (spurred by appeals from the President) began drafting new federal antiterrorism legislation in response to the bombing in Atlanta's Centennial Olympic Park and the explosion on TWA Flight 800, for example, almost immediately after the incidents occurred—before it was possible to form any reasonably accurate understanding of what had transpired, and despite hard statistical evidence that domestic acts of terrorism are way down.[77]

Similarly, journalists who took the trouble to investigate the facts surrounding the recent church-burning hysteria found no support for the proposition that church arson is a dangerously escalating race problem. For instance, James Glassman in the *Washington Post*—stipulating that church arson is evil, and doubly so if motivated by racial animus—uncovered statistics from the National Fire Protection Association and the Bureau of Alcohol, Tobacco, and Firearms indicating that arson is no more a problem for black churches than for white churches.[78] Longtime civil rights leader Roy Innis agreed. He further observed that church burnings nationwide have been steadily declining—from 1,430 reported in 1980 to 520 in 1994. Innis called "for a backing off of the hysteria."

Enacting legislative measures under such circumstances is a bit like purchasing policies of "appearance" insurance. At exceptionally low premiums (some modest staff time and a few legislative hearings), the measures protect legislators from future "appearance" mishaps (such as negative campaign attacks for appearing insensitive on issues of drugs, terrorism, racism, and so forth). And these particular insurance policies begin paying dividends right away. Legislators can appear "tough" and "responsive" to late-breaking problems *and*, by so widely diffusing responsibility for addressing whatever the problem is, assure that no one is actually held responsible for the problem's subsequent worsening or for the costs of the legislative effort. No wonder the policies are so popular. Unfortunately, *we* are saddled with the continuing premiums for years to come—in lost dollars, lost liberties, lost opportunities, and lost political accountability.

10

The End of Accountability

A typical company has just enough resources to do one of the following:
1. Accomplish something.
2. Prepare elaborate presentations that lie about how much is being accomplished.

The rational employee will divert all available resources away from accomplishing things and toward the more highly compensated process of lying about accomplishments. It's the same amount of work, but only one has a payoff.

—Scott Adams[1]

A half-serious maxim among military historians contends that you can determine which army is more effective by looking at their uniforms. The best-dressed army is generally the least effective.

—James Dunnigan[2]

One reason why even reformers have been willing to settle for the appearance of ethical behavior is that the reality has become so much harder to enforce. Throughout our society, from government, to industry, to the nonprofit sector, to the media, holding people responsible for their actions has become more and more difficult. Since holding some individual accountable for his or her actions is one of the most important ways of enforcing genuine ethical behavior, in its absence we have had to settle instead for appearances.

One reason may be size: Everything is bigger than it used to be. When the framers of our Constitution met in Philadelphia, the nation was small enough that everyone of consequence knew practically everyone else. The government was small, too. When John Adams commissioned his "midnight judges" just before turning over the presidency to Thomas Jefferson, the commissions (even those for mere justices of the peace) were hand-delivered by the Secretary of State, John Marshall. And there were no colossal business conglomerates; the rise of the corporation as an important form of doing business was still almost a century away.

But size isn't everything. Even large organizations can maintain accountability if responsibilities are clear and if there is a culture that encourages individuals to own up to their actions. Inversely, where such clarity and encouragement are not present, even small organizations will have problems. The trouble is, there are many human tendencies that encourage the demise of accountability.

In short, as a brilliant essay in the *Economist* noted some years ago, the most effective systems are "crunchy"—that is, systems in which poor performance is immediately noticeable. But the natural tendency of systems is to become "soggy" over time—to break the connection between performance and reward (or punishment), to run things for the day-to-day convenience of those in charge.

> Crunchy systems are those in which small changes have big effects—leaving those affected by them in no doubt whether they are up or down, rich or broke, winning or losing, dead or alive. The going was crunchy for Captain Scott as he plodded southwards across the sastrugi. He was either on top of the snow crust or floundering thigh-deep. The farther south he marched the crunchier his predicament became.
>
> Sogginess is comfortable uncertainty. The modern Scott is unsure

how deeply he is in it. He can radio for an airlift, or drop in on an American early-warning station for a hot toddy. The richer a society becomes, the soggier its systems get. . . . Intelligent questions replace the church's absolute faith. Seat belts are worn. Words (like these) are not written down, but processed endlessly. Exam papers are no longer passed or failed but graded, with no one quite sure what grade is needed for what.

Some of these softnesses are the welcome accompaniments of wealth. But lurking beyond sogginess lies moral hazard and systemic drama. . . . A crunchy policy is not necessarily right, only more certain than a soggy one to deliver the results that it deserves. Run your country, or your company, or your life as you think fit. But whatever you decide, keep things crunchy.[3]

This is a widely recognized issue within the military, as one commentator observes:

Human nature being what it is, most leaders, military or otherwise, seek the easy way out. Unless feedback corrects ineffective actions, the wrong procedures become standard. On ships and in aircraft, mistakes are painfully apparent. Pilots and sailors tend to get buried with their mistakes. Therefore, air force and navy leaders are forced to get to know their subordinates' strengths and weaknesses. Army leaders must rock the boat to gain the same knowledge. Making a commotion is dangerous in any large organization. Most military leaders are cowards when faced with peacetime administrative danger, while the same men would be fearless in the face of wartime danger. It's a case of the pen, indeed, being mightier than the sword.[4]

In wartime, of course, the enemy provides a painfully effective learning tool. But in peacetime, appearances tend to rule:

Hardware is often viewed in a different light than the software of training experience, and general effectiveness of the troops themselves. Hardware you can see and feel. The troops? The goal is often to

have the troops smartly turned out. Never mind that the most effective ones often look like a bunch of bandits. Perfectly aligned and
garbed formations of soldiers are easier to perceive than their ability
efficiently to inflict mayhem upon the enemy.[5]

Military forces that seek to be effective devote a lot of effort to coun-
tering these tendencies, through the development of intense training
regimes, strong military traditions, and so on.[6] Indeed, the U.S. military
devoted a great deal of time and energy to remedying the problems
growing out of the Vietnam War, with considerable success. Its performance in the Gulf War was excellent, and (despite some problems) it is
now one of the most-respected institutions in America, having been one
of the least-respected after Vietnam.

But even in Vietnam the excessive focus on appearances was an accident, the product of poor management, not deliberate design. In the
post–Big Bang ethics world, on the other hand, the focus on appearances is deliberately fostered. It is no surprise that the result has been its
own kind of Vietnam: a massive misallocation of resources, producing
substantial human suffering while failing to yield the promised results.
And, like the U.S. military after Vietnam, it is time that we consider an
approach based more on fundamentals, and less on appearances.

The body-count approach taken in Vietnam was designed for the
convenience of the establishment running the war. It produced a measure that appeared clear and clean, and it obviated the need for the kind
of careful, in-depth analysis that would otherwise have been required to
measure the progress of the war. Similarly, the appearance standard primarily benefits the establishment running the political process, including the Ethics Establishment. It provides a seemingly clear and exacting
standard: Don't do anything that even *looks* wrong. And it allows those
invoking it to avoid the unpleasant work of careful, in-depth analysis
(and the personal responsibility that accompanies making substantive
accusations) by intentionally focusing on appearances: "We don't have
to decide if what Senator X did *was* wrong, because we know that it creates an appearance of impropriety." Simultaneously, it provides a super-

ficial cloak of propriety for activities—essentially vote buying by special interests—that everyone knows, or should know, *are* wrong.

Another vice of the appearance approach parallels that of the body-count approach in Vietnam: It encourages misapplication of efforts. When the measure of success was Vietcong killed, it hardly mattered when, where, or how (in fact, it didn't matter much if they were really Vietcong), so strategy was replaced by butchery. When the measure of success was tons of bombs dropped, it didn't matter much *where* they were dropped—in fact, using this measure distracted from the fact that truly vital enemy targets were deliberately left untouched.

Similarly, the appearance standard makes little distinction between incorrectly filled-out forms and truly wrongful behavior. As in Vietnam, the result is misapplication of effort: Minor affairs get more attention than they deserve, while truly awful behavior gets less. This problem has spread beyond the ethics field. As mentioned earlier, 65 percent of Americans feel that national leaders are only interested in appearing to solve national problems, not in actually solving them. It is easy to see why: We have had an endless succession of "crime" bills (inevitably passed in election years) that do little about crime, "terrorism" bills that have little to do with terrorism, tax "reform" bills that are riddled with loopholes for special interests, spending "cuts" that are merely reductions in the rate of spending growth, and so on. The reason is that national government leaders are less accountable than they have ever been, even as the public demands more accountability. Though the move to appearance standards has exacerbated this problem, it is itself more a symptom than a cause.

One need only look at the changes in government since the Framers' day to see how accountability has been lessened. The original plan of government outlined in the Constitution was designed to promote accountability. The federal government was one whose powers were, in James Madison's words, "few and defined"—making it inherently easy for voters to see how it was discharging its responsibilities.[7] And within the federal government, powers were separated into legislative, executive, and judicial, making it relatively clear who was doing (or supposed to be doing) what. This was particularly true because the main responsibilities of the federal government—such as the national defense, the mails, roads, and protection of civil rights—were relatively easy to monitor. The responsibilities of states were broader and less well defined, but their discharge took place closer to voters, making it easier to determine who was doing what.

Now, of course, everything is different. Where once the federal government's powers were few and defined, now it seems involved in everything. Even today, when we have been assured that the era of Big Government is over, politicians seem unable to avoid overstepping their bounds: The last presidential election included an effort by both Clinton and Dole to position themselves on such previously local questions as mandatory school uniforms and the enforcement of truancy laws. Nor are things better as one moves lower in the hierarchy. As the quotation from Michael Blumenthal in Chapter 2 illustrates, even at the level of cabinet secretaries, the jobs are so complex, and involve so many variables, that performance is judged almost entirely by appearances.

As Peter Pitts points out, this itself is a major reason for the loss of faith in government in recent decades. Far more Americans trusted the government in 1964 than do today. One reason may be the change in the government they were trusting. "[B]ack in 1964," Pitts observes, "the federal government did fewer things than it does today—but did them better—with a higher degree of responsibility." In short, he says, "it's easier to 'trust' the government when it's in the business of building roads and defending our national security" than when it's engaged in amorphous projects of uncertain value. One reason is that roads and national defense are "crunchy"—it is easy to see when the government is doing a good or bad job, making "trust" a very different proposition in such cases than it is with regard to things like promoting "family values" or "social justice" (to pick favorite slogans of the right and left), where the outputs are soggy and uncertain.[8]

This expansion of federal responsibilities is a relatively recent phenomenon. Prior to the New Deal, federal responsibilities remained largely limited to those spelled out in the Constitution, and the

Supreme Court enforced constitutional limits on federal authority rather vigorously. After the New Deal, the Court began interpreting Congress's authority to regulate "commerce among the several states" so as to allow legislation reaching many kinds of conduct previously considered beyond federal jurisdiction, a tendency that expanded during the Great Society years of the 1960s.[9]

Strangely enough, however, it was not Democrat LBJ but Republican Richard Nixon who presided over the greatest-ever expansion of federal authority. Among scholars of administrative law, the early 1970s are known as the years of "regulatory explosion." Nixon imposed wage and price controls. New agencies, such as the Environmental Protection Agency and the Occupational Safety and Health Administration, were created. And federal authority was extended to all sorts of activity that even the most hard-boiled New Dealer would have considered purely local.

Interestingly, this "regulatory explosion" was almost perfectly simultaneous with the "ethics explosion." One difference, of course, is that the regulatory explosion really did deliver more regulation, while it is a matter for debate whether the ethics explosion actually produced more ethics. But both had lasting impacts on American life.

The massive expansion of federal authority that took place during the regulatory explosion had enormous impact not only on those being regulated, but on the culture of Washington. Before the 1970s, Washington was a backwater, famously derided by JFK as a city of northern charm and southern efficiency. Outside regulated industries like railroads, aviation, and broadcasting, few in the business world paid it much attention. And although there were Washington journalists and trade associations, they were not, for the most part, terribly important. Compared to other major cities like New York, Los Angeles, or Chicago, Washington just didn't matter that much. It was a city of hard-working bureaucrats and mediocre but inexpensive restaurants, not a place that catered to the life styles of the rich and famous.

All of that changed after the regulatory explosion. In some ways, these changes were more important than the changes in the government itself. As Fred Barnes writes in the *New Republic,* the regulatory explosion produced what he calls a "parasite culture" of lobbyists, trade associations, journalists, and similar government hangers-on. After the regulatory explosion, says Barnes,

> Soon the city was thick with "public interest" outfits pressing for strict enforcement. To combat them and cope with the new regulations, corporations hired more and more Washington lawyers. In the late 1970s, the era of deregulation began, and demand for lawyers should have leveled off. It didn't. . . . Membership in the District of Columbia Bar Association more than doubled between 1975 and 1986, from 20,311 to 44,394.[10]

By 1996, that number had grown to 66,448.[11] And lawyers, of course, are only the tip of the iceberg: Washington also became a magnet for lobbyists, trade associations, industry newsletters (with names like *Candy Industry* or *Satellite Week*) that advise their readers on regulatory developments, and so on. And, as Barnes also notes, the city became flooded with the kind of money that such interests bring, sprouting luxury car dealerships, expensive restaurants, upscale shops, and five-star hotels until it had more in common with Rodeo Drive than with the Washington of previous years.

The growth of federal power increased the role of special interests because it made lobbying the federal government vastly more attractive. A government that can regulate wages attracts the attention of lobbyists for trade unions and manufacturers; a government that can pass "crime" bills attracts the attention of police unions, local governments, gun-control activists and opponents, and so on. And a government that is the target of so much lobbying looks less trustworthy. This should come as no surprise, but many commentators have so far failed to make the connection. But not all. According to Jonathan Rauch's insightful book *Demosclerosis,*[12] one reason why more special interests are lobbying the federal government is that there is more money involved. As Rauch notes, the federal budget was about 3 percent of the American economy in 1929, and only about 10 percent at the peak of the New Deal. Now it is over 25 percent.[13] And with it raining federal soup, it is no surprise that interest groups have rushed out with buckets. But each new program creates a new lobby:

> Indeed, a built-in side effect of new government programs is their tendency to summon into being new constituencies—which, in turn, often lobby for yet other new programs, keeping the whole cycle going. Fifty years ago the elderly were a demographic category. Today they are a lobby.[14]

Or as George Will puts it, "Intervention in economic and social relations does not merely propitiate interest groups, it creates them. This is supply-side government, whereby government supplies a program, increasing the groups making demands."[15] So the abandonment of limitations on federal power has led to greater special-interest pressure in no small part simply because it has made the federal government more attractive to lobby. And the prevalence of such special-interest pressure has caused many Americans to fear, rightly, that many federal programs are simply disguised ways for the well-connected to pick their pockets, or otherwise push them around. This is a problem that no appearance ethic can remedy, but the problem goes beyond that.

A federal government with more powers and responsibilities is also under increasing pressure to delegate decision making to the bureaucracy. Such delegation moves decision making from elected lawmakers, subject to voter supervision, to unelected bureaucrats (or congressional staff), who are much more insulated and unaccountable. It is not surprising that people trust such a government far less than they trusted a government in which decisions were made by accountable legislators on topics producing measurable outputs. A constitutional doctrine known as the antidelegation principle formerly prevented such moves, but when the Supreme Court effectively stopped enforcing the doctrine during the New Deal, that check was lost.[16]

Thus, an important reason why the special-interest problem has grown worse in our society in recent decades is that the safeguards that the Framers put in place have largely been removed. With those safeguards removed, it is no surprise that the tendencies they guarded against have grown, any more than it is a surprise when someone whose immune system has been suppressed develops infections. In both cases, parasites quickly appear to take advantage of the new opportunities that open up. And, in both cases, the best hope for long-term survival is to reestablish the necessary immunity. In the political sphere, we might do that by restoring the very constitutional safeguards whose removal has led to the current problem, and by holding the federal government to a narrower, easier to supervise set of responsibilities. Attending to appearances, on the other hand, actually undermines accountability and may increase the very distrust it is intended to address.

Finally, of course, there is the question of fear. A federal government that focused on the responsibilities spelled out in the Constitution was unlikely to intrude directly in the lives of very many citizens. Thus, the worst threat was that the government would waste tax money—and back when the federal government's responsibilities were limited, federal taxes for most Americans were quite low. But (as the previous chapter makes clear) the increasing reach of federal criminal law, and of a regulatory bureaucracy that increasingly makes use of criminal law to enforce its rules, means that today no American can realistically consider himself or herself to be outside the concern of federal prosecutors. One demands far more trustworthiness of someone who holds a gun to one's head than of someone seen as largely peripheral to one's life. Thus, paradoxically, as the federal government became more powerful, less accountable, and more subject to corruption, people began to be more and more demanding with regard to ethics. Yet the response to those demands, appearance ethics, was manifestly inadequate. This is a recipe for distrust.

Back when the federal government's tasks were "few and defined," it was relatively easy to allocate credit or blame. But once the federal government overflowed its constitutional limits, anyone who could get a working majority in Congress, or influence a sufficient part of the executive branch, could get what he or she wanted. Courts were unlikely to block such actions on constitutional grounds, unless they violated the Bill of Rights. And, as our discussion of the Drug War illustrates, maybe not even then. As the number of cooks multiplied, responsibility for the broth became steadily more diffuse, with predictable results.

It may be that the nearly simultaneous growth of appearance ethics stemmed from this diffusion of responsibility. With no one obviously responsible for results, appearances became more important. Or, more cynically, with results harder to monitor, the maintenance of appearances became more appealing.

Unfortunately, the consequence was not increased confidence. The reality, visible to anyone who paid attention, was that Washington had become the focus of more concentrated special-interest attention than at the worst heights of the Gilded Age. As Jonathan Rauch says, "Never before has organizing groups to lobby for benefits been as potentially lucrative as it is today; never have the sums available been as large or the paths to them as plentiful."[17] Nor was the appeal merely mercenary: Lobbying efforts were devoted as much to fending off *other* groups' lobbying as to gaining a spot at the public trough in the first place. As Rauch notes:

> In the economy, as in nature, a parasite is set apart from a mere freeloader by its ability to force its target to fend it off. This is the sense in which transfer-seekers are, not so loosely speaking, parasitic: they are not only unproductive themselves, *they also force other people to be unproductive.*[18]

Thus, even someone who felt lobbying the government to be wrong might well wind up doing so, merely out of self-defense. This "arms race" was lucrative for lawyers and lobbyists, but bad for society as a whole.

How bad? Well, now that it is well established, we have seen the appearance of numerous books like Rauch's, with titles like *Demosclerosis, Tragedies of Our Own Making, Why Government Doesn't Work,* and *Lost Rights*. In different ways, they all ring the same theme: Special-interest power has made it hard for government to do the right thing, and all too easy for it to do the wrong thing.

Even those who don't read such books, however, can see the more obvious signs of trouble. Things don't work as well as they used to. We lurch from one crisis to another—oil embargoes, the savings and loan debacle, the looming bankruptcy of Social Security, the growth of a colossal federal deficit. Often, government fails to act in time. Even more often, it makes things worse. Yet at the same time, those in power seem to be doing better. Washington fills with limousines and expensive restaurants to a degree unimagined during the allegedly glamorous days of JFK; politicians and staffers who leave office, even in defeat or disgrace, wind up in new jobs with fat salaries, and even convicted felons become bestselling authors. Like corporate CEOs whose compensation goes up and up even as their corporations do badly in the marketplace, the Washington establishment seems immune to the consequences of its actions.

Indeed, as the CEO example illustrates, this immunity seems to have spread well beyond government. The breakdown of accountability in the corporate world, what even conservative columnist George Will calls the "looting" of corporations by management whose pay has nothing to do with performance,[19] has been made famous in everything from books like *Barbarians at the Gate* to comic strips like "Dilbert." Nor are things better in what the *New Republic* calls the "backslapping world of professional activism,"[20] where poor performance records seldom harm careers, or among other kinds of nonprofit organizations. As David Samuels writes, large grant-making foundations that used to focus on measurable goals (like the elimination of polio), or at least subject their programs to rigorous outside evaluation, now tend to focus on projects without realistically measurable goals, and to conduct their own inhouse evaluations rather than using outsiders. As a result, "the project is evaluated, declared a success, and everyone—the program officer, the trustees and you—can go home happy." Not surprisingly, he says, "it's almost impossible to evaluate what actual good they do."[21]

The Ethics Establishment merely became part of that parasite culture, and it, too, has been largely unaccountable. What are the consequences when a group makes charges against an official that later turn out to be baseless? Or when that group—in fact, pretty much *all* such groups—misses debacles like the savings and loan crisis until it is too late? None.

Average citizens may not keep score, but they can tell how the game is going. The parasite culture has grown, and the Ethics Establishment is visibly part of it. The appearance standard is not a cure for special-interest influence. It is merely a symptom.

11

Now What?

When you find yourself in a hole, the first thing to do is to stop digging.
—Anonymous

The previous chapters have outlined the origins and growth of appearance ethics in politics, the creation of an ethics establishment, and the spread of the ethic and the bureaucracy into various areas of private life. We have also spent a modicum of time looking at the reasons why appearance ethics and the rules that result from such an approach have been powerfully appealing even as they have been socially destructive. After so many accounts of how appearance ethics has become predominant, and of the harm that its spread has done, it seems only fair that we offer some thoughts on what to do about the problem.

We apologize in advance, however, to those readers who expect a simple checklist of statutory and regulatory changes that purport to constitute a solution to the problem. No such quick fixes are available. Indeed, a great deal of our current problem stems from the attempt to provide such quick fixes, or at least the appearance of quick fixes, in statutory and regulatory form. But we have also observed in ourselves a phenomenon that we hope readers will experience as well: Once we started thinking about the explosion of appearance-oriented approaches in one or two contexts, we began to recognize it in many other settings. And once we recognized the problems and prevalence of appearances, we found we were thinking about the underlying issues very differently. If our readers experience the same phenomenon, that itself will be a substantial step toward a solution. With this in mind, here are some more general thoughts on dealing with the problem of appearances.

As the quotation from Henry Fielding at the beginning of Chapter 2 makes clear, an excessive regard for appearances is nothing new. What *is* new is the deliberate creation of systems that promote an excessive regard for appearances. Superficiality as a by-product of human nature is one thing. Superficiality as a deliberate result of human design is quite another.

Systems that work share an important characteristic: They ensure that bad news travels to the top. When we stub our toe, the intervening ganglia don't try to figure out ways to avoid sending the news on to the brain. The result is that we're usually pretty careful about how we walk. Similarly, the North Vietnamese Army placed a premium on accurate reports of bad news by field commanders. Only if the bad news was reported accurately, they reasoned, could they learn how to fight the highly mechanized American forces, something about which they had no experience. American forces, on the other hand, placed a premium on the *appearance* of winning. They rewarded good news, and penalized bad, a practice that grew more pronounced as the war continued. As a result, rational commanders quickly began devoting their resources toward producing the appearances that the system was rewarding, rather than the realities that it needed. Eventually, David sent the well-coiffed Goliath packing.

Similarly, the NASA of the 1960s, under a management system instituted by James Webb, placed a tremendous premium on sound engineering and professional accountability, rewarding managers and contractors for accurately reporting problems and allowing even low-level individuals to call a halt where something was wrong. But in the 1970s, NASA switched to a system known (inaccurately, as it turned out) as "success-oriented management." By the 1980s, NASA became more interested in producing the appearance of a successful program than in the reality. And although large numbers of inspectors and so on were required to "sign off" on the safety of equipment and procedures, that was largely for show: There was a tremendous systemic bias in favor of going ahead anyway. Those who reported bad news, or who suggested that budget and cost projections were unrealistic, were quickly branded as malcontents and punished or ostracized. The result, ultimately, was the *Challenger* explosion, along with a series of budgetary and management problems that plague the agency to this day.[1]

Alas, the Vietnam and *Challenger* examples are not aberrations, but merely emblems. What makes NASA and the military unusual is not that they are more prone to such failures, but that such failures are so visible when they occur. When other agencies, from the Drug Enforcement Agency to the Department of Education, act similarly, the failures are less dramatic, not less important. It is thus entirely possible that the problem is worse elsewhere in the government.[2] The less obvious failures are, the more room there is for appearances. Similarly, the more government operations have expanded beyond the core functions spelled out in the Constitution, the more room there is for agencies and legislators to focus on appearances rather than reality. And often the focus on appearances is a smoke screen for special-interest influence, or sheer incompetence.

Rule One: Accentuate the Negative

As outlined above, if left to themselves organizations will inevitably tend toward the suppression of bad news and the creation of good appearances. The solution to this problem is simple: seek out and encourage the reporting of bad news. Not scandal, or improper appearances, but truly bad news about things that aren't working. It's more important, for example, to find out that highways are in bad shape than that there is cronyism in the awarding of highway repair contracts. It's more important to learn that a drug education program like D.A.R.E. doesn't work than to hear about the political benefits it provides for police and school systems.³ It's more important to find out whether a scientific experiment can be reproduced by other researchers than to examine the credentials and notebooks of the experimenter.

This is hard—not least because journalists, who are the main transmitters of this sort of information, find it easier to report on appearances, and because responsible officials (in or out of government) find it more rewarding to cater to that tendency. But this characteristic can be dealt with, in part, by proper institutional design. Which brings us to the next point.

Rule Two: Keep It Crunchy

Human nature being what it is, no amount of lecturing by pundits will keep people from trying to promote good appearances where they can. But people only do what they can get away with, and some situations make it easier to substitute appearances for reality than others. A simple illustration should suffice.

Imagine that you are the chief executive of a trucking company. You are worried about public fear of big trucks on the highway, and you want both to make your trucks safer and to reassure the public that you care about safety. Consider these two possible approaches: (1) You hire expensive consultants, who organize a series of "safety sensitivity" seminars for your drivers, and you plaster huge signs that say "We care" all over your trucks; or (2) You give each truck a distinguishing number, and plaster that number, plus a toll-free telephone number, all over your trucks.

Guess which approach works. As research proves, truckers drive better when they have the toll-free number on the back. Why? Life has suddenly become crunchier for them. The link between driving discourteously—much less unsafely—and an unpleasant outcome has become much more direct.

Similarly, in almost any setting, organizational structures in which someone has to take responsibility for results, and in which results are obvious, produce better behavior than those in which responsibility is diffused, and results are difficult to measure.

Both characteristics are missing in our current political system. Instead of clear responsibility and obvious outputs, we have appearance ethics and a confusing mass of government agencies and responsibilities. Voters, then, can be forgiven for concluding (as so many have) that the federal government is (1) corrupt, because of the obvious failure of appearance ethics to promote ethical behavior despite all the hoopla, and (2) incompetent, because so little of what the federal government does succeeds, or even produces results. And the two are related: Programs that don't produce results (like roads) that are tangible are more prone to corruption. The awarding of highway contracts may be corrupt, but at least anyone can tell whether the road has been fixed. With many modern government programs, even that level of voter supervision is impossible, making trust that much more difficult. This, of course, does not mean that federal employees are dishonest or inept: In fact, the vast majority are neither, and try hard to do a good job. What is unfortunate is that they are embedded in a setting that systematically promotes counterproductive behavior. Making the system crunchier would do far more good than another layer of restrictions on frequent-flier mileage.

Rule Three: Keep Your Eye on the Ball

This leaves two questions: How do we make sure that people are acting ethically, if we don't use appearance ethics? And, aside from that, how do we make the system crunchier?

With regard to the first problem, the failure of appearance ethics, the solution is not easy, but it is simple: limit appearance ethics to those narrow areas where it is appropriate, sectors involving specialized officials who are supposed to make nonpolitical decisions. Judges, for example, or baseball umpires. In other cases, we need to focus on substance and motive, even if doing so is harder than relying on appearances.

When a politician receives a large contribution from a group whose interests fall under his or her jurisdiction, we needn't look to see whether the check was handed to one aide or another, or delivered before or after a meeting at which legislation was discussed. We need merely ask: Is it more likely that the interest group is trying to buy favor, or that the money is unrelated to the politician's work? Is it more likely that the politician will be influenced by the gift, or that he or she will ignore it? The answers to these questions will seldom be difficult, despite the protestations of those involved.

Ethics rules should be designed to facilitate such inquiries, not obfuscate matters further. Preventive rules should not be based on appearances, or on filling out forms, but on real issues. For example, a rule that members of congressional committees should not be allowed to accept campaign contributions from those under their committees' jurisdiction is infinitely preferable to a rule that says that such contributions can be accepted, but not at the same meeting where legislation is discussed.

With regard to the larger question—the general sogginess of the federal government today—the solution is also simple, but not easy. In fact, it is very hard. The original design produced by the Framers of our Constitution was very crunchy indeed. As James Madison wrote, the powers of the federal government were "few and defined."[4] They were also limited to subjects that were easily evaluated by voters—national defense, post offices and post roads, the coining of money, and so on. But over the years, especially after the New Deal and World War II, the power of the federal government expanded considerably in ways that were, to say the least, constitutionally dubious. An even greater expansion of the regulatory state occurred during the Nixon presidency, taking effect right about the time of the Big Bang. This expansion of federal power increased both the opportunities for corruption and the difficulty for voters of evaluating performance. It is not surprising that there is much less trust in government today than when its tasks were few and easily measured.

It may be impossible to return the federal government to the small size and limited scope that it enjoyed before the New Deal—or even to the size and stature it possessed prior to the Nixonian regulatory explosion. Nor are we necessarily arguing for such a change here. But the problems inherent in federal expansion, and their implications for trust in government, have gone largely unexamined by most who have written on the topic. Any serious proposal for addressing Americans' increasing unhappiness with their government must take such concerns more seriously.

Rule Four: Responsibility Is for Everyone

When we try to judge ethics based on substance, not appearance, motivation is an important factor. Likewise, when an accusation is made, we should expect responsibility from the accusers. A strong ethical system would demand more from accusers, as well as from the accused. This is the flip side of the current system, which is easy on everyone. If we all take responsibility for acting ethically, we must ask not just, was the act in question actually *wrong*? Or, what were its motive and result? We must also ask *ourselves*, why am I making this particular accusation, and at this particular time? What do I stand to gain? And others should ask such questions as well.

As the case of David Baltimore and Thereza Imanishi-Kari illustrates, our contemporary culture tends to uncritically accept the charges of whistle-blowers. We are similarly uncritical when the accusation comes from groups that style themselves as supporters of "good government." Yet, as we have seen, such individuals and groups are no more immune to self-interest, self-absorption, or conflict of interest than are those they target. Such groups are often wrong, and sometimes flat-out dishonest. Their charges should be evaluated in light of their track records and their motivations. And if they turn out to be wrong, or malicious, this should be held against them. Right now, political activism is one of the soggiest of professions—pursued for vague ends, in an opportunistic fashion, with other people's money. Crunchiness should be for everyone.

Rule Five: Don't Call Virtuous People Chumps

One of the most destructive aspects of modern ethical thought is the now-widespread notion that anyone who fails to take advantage when he or she can is, well, a chump. As Richard Brookhiser points out,

George Washington succeeded in large part because of his virtue, not in spite of it. Yet today we are frequently told that it is more important that a leader be tricky—after the fashion of Richard Nixon or Bill Clinton—than honest. It seems unlikely, however, that history will judge Presidents Nixon and Clinton in the same category as Washington.

Many people want to be successful, and even more, apparently, want to do whatever is generally regarded as the smart thing. When we tell people, over and over again, in ways both explicit and implied, that the smart thing to do, the way to get ahead, is to attend to appearances, then we should not be surprised if that is what we get. And if we underscore that message by treating those who do not focus on appearances as chumps, then we should not be surprised if the general tone of our society declines. More on this later.

There is, however, another problem with this approach, one that even the most self-serving and mendacious among us might find compelling: It doesn't work.

Rule Six: If You Focus on Appearances, You Will Fail Even at That

In Vietnam, the American military was hijacked by appearances. The result was the worst military humiliation the nation has ever suffered, and a tremendous loss of confidence in the armed forces. In Watergate, Richard Nixon focused on appearances, and ended up resigning in disgrace. After Watergate, the entire political establishment focused on appearances, and now sees its reputation at the lowest ebb in living memory. The scientific establishment focused on appearances in its treatment of science fraud, and as a consequence has never looked worse. And so on.

It seems to us that there is a lesson in all of this. It was once common advice to "be what you would seem." The thought was that (over the long term) appearances tend to reflect reality. Furthermore, virtues, like anything else, improve with practice. Thus, as George Washington's example illustrates, the best way to promote the appearance of virtue is to practice it regularly. If you want to seem courageous, act courageously. If you want to seem honest, then cultivate honesty. If you want to seem polite, practice courtesy. Such an approach is less fashionable today, but it may be on its way to making a comeback. Since focusing on appearances is not only wrong, but also doesn't work, it ought to collapse under its own weight. The sooner the better.

Rule Seven: Cultivate Virtues, Rather than Appearances

Instead of appearances, we must cultivate virtues. Doing so is unfashionable; as Christina Hoff Summers writes, today we tend to teach "ethics without virtue."[5] Ethics involves rules about what to do. Virtue, on the other hand, is about who we are.

Cultivating virtue does not simply mean trying to do the right thing. It means trying to be the kind of person who does the right thing. Rules of ethics provide instruction on what to do in various situations, but the situations are always more various than the rules can account for. A person who violates an ethical rule can always formulate an excuse. A virtuous person, on the other hand, will feel bad if he or she acts unvirtuously.

In our personal lives, we understand the difference. We would rather buy a used car from someone we trust than from someone shady who nonetheless has a "Used Car Dealer's Code of Ethics" prominently displayed. We know that an honest person will feel bad if he or she cheats us, while a dishonest one will point to the weasel-worded part of the car dealer's code of ethics that makes clear that you cannot sue him for violating it.

Similarly, we generally want to instill such admirable qualities as honesty, integrity, and decency in our children. We spend a great deal of time, most of us, in trying to make clear that not only specific actions, but specific motivations, are wrong. "No one likes a tattletale," we tell four-year-olds, not because we approve of the conduct they are tattling about, but because (as with Master Blifil) we know the motivation for telling is revenge, or self-aggrandizement, and we do not wish to encourage such sentiments. Indeed, since behavior forms character, and the character built by tattling is likely to be poor, we want to discourage it even when the specific outcome is consistent with the rules.

Such an approach makes sense. Character matters more than specific outcomes, though over time a focus on character probably will produce better outcomes as well. Good people may not always do the right thing, but they are more likely to do so than bad people, regardless of the formal rules. And, many of us believe, good people are likely to have happier, and perhaps even more successful, lives overall than bad people. That is what we tell our children, and the way we raise them underscores our belief.

The problem, of course, is that while these common-sense approaches remain popular with parents, they have become almost foreign to the public world, where appearance rules and ethics establishments have almost completely displaced virtue and character as touchstones. Witness, for example, the reaction of many scientists to David Baltimore's courageous defense of Tereza Imanishi-Kari: Instead of admiring his willingness to stand by a colleague he believed was right, many scientists felt he should have attended to appearances, whatever his beliefs. Yet it is a strange sort of "ethics" that makes throwing a colleague to the wolves more admirable than defending that colleague against persecution—and it is hard to believe that such an attitude would, over time, make scientists more trustworthy, or more trusted. It is hard to imagine George Washington endorsing such an approach. If we are to revive popular trust in institutions, we must consider the (unfortunately) now-radical notion that the best way to achieve trust, over the long run, is to be worthy of it, even when doing so has costs in the short run.

Furthermore, if it is true that one of the biggest problems in ethics today is the success self-interest theorists have had convincing us that only "chumps" behave "ethically,"[6] then those seriously interested in ethics reform need to devote more time and energy to teaching about the long-term personal advantages of truly ethical behavior. Fielding said it in the eighteenth century; it bears repeating today.

Our modern-day ethicists should reread Fielding. We must strip bare the lie that a manipulative, selfish approach to one's career, however "un-ethical" it may be, is nonetheless the wisest way to maximize one's career potential. The famous Leo Durocher misquote that "Nice guys finish last" sometimes seems true in the short term; it is seldom true in the long term. As Fielding wrote, virtue is not the "morose" enemy of ambition that some represent her to be: "[S]he will accompany you in cities, in courts, and in camps" and has been known "to raise some of the highest dignities in the State, in the Army, and in the Law."[7]

Perhaps the most damning comment on today's ethics is that this latter proposition now seems to call for proof. One need go no further, however, than Richard Brookhiser's brilliant recent book *Founding Father: Rediscovering George Washington*.[8] *Founding Father* peels away the layers of clichés that over the years have obscured our perception of Washington, thereby revealing the awesome reality of Washington's character and accomplishments. Washington not only was the person most responsible for the birth of America, Brookhiser reminds us, Washington *dominated* this country for a quarter of a century:

> Washington was the most important man in America, whether he was onstage or off, for twenty-four years; for seventeen of those years, he was front and center. It is a record unmatched in our history, scarcely matched in the history of modern democracies.[9]

Washington triumphed not because he was the smartest of the Founding Fathers. He wasn't. Nor because he was the most courageous, though he may have been. It was his towering integrity, displayed in such seemingly small ways as the courtesy he extended to political adversaries. "Courtesy and reputation made it possible for a would-be Roman in the North American boondocks to say to his countrymen, we, and to command a response."[10] Washington believed politeness was the first rule of politics, not because he was foppish about manners, but rather because politeness communicates respect. "It acknowledges the importance of someone else's rights and point of view."[11] This is the principle, after all, upon which American democracy was founded. And, as suggested a bit earlier, Washington developed his virtues through constant practice. He worked hard at developing the character for which he became famous. The result was not accidental, but every bit as much a work of art as a painting or novel.

Washington also paid careful attention to appearances, physical as well as political. But he did not regard appearances as a substitute for virtue. Washington employed his towering figure and military dress, for instance, to *reinforce* messages about leadership, dignity, and pride. Childless like Fielding's Squire Allworthy, Washington nonetheless was the quintessential father, bequeathing to us, as Allworthy did to Tom Jones (and Pericles to Athenians), instruction by example on the indispensability of morals, which "integrated him and held his being together, even as they connected him with his fellow Americans."[12]

In this century, likewise largely by force of moral character, Dwight Eisenhower became "the most successful general of the greatest war ever fought,"[13] commanding the respect of often-feuding generals heading different armies from different countries speaking different languages. No wonder Eisenhower listed integrity, courage, and understanding among the qualities of great men.[14] They were the elements he had forged into the sword of leadership with which he slew one of the most dangerously immoral leaders in world history. It is therefore passing strange that while we appear to be paying so much attention to "ethics" today, too many of us secretly join Nixon in his belief that "virtue is not what lifts great leaders above others."[15] Perhaps not, at least in Nixon's case. But lack of virtue is what cast Nixon down.

Moreover, as Fielding observed:

> [H]ow much more desirable is preferment acquired by virtuous than that obtained by vicious means. The virtuous man, for the most part however, enjoys his preferment with a security of mind, with safety, and with honour. Whereas the man, who by base and dishonest means hath raised himself to power, stands as it were on a pinnacle, exposed to every wind, fearful and disquieted within, hated and pursued without. His power seldom lasting, always uncertain, and generally sure to end in ruin and dishonour.[16]

Richard Nixon, readers will recall, was notably insecure about the position he obtained, continuing to attack his foes and obsessively cultivate appearances even when his reelection was assured. Nor have the careers of other political figures noted for their cleverness rather than their virtue generally contradicted Fielding's observation. If we wish for our children, and our nation, to enjoy the blessings that Fielding describes, we should, at the very least, stop exaggerating the virtues of Nixonian cleverness and downplaying the benefits of Washingtonian virtue.

Instead, we should encourage individuals to be what they would seem. To appear honest, practice *being* honest, in large and small ways. To appear thoughtful, practice courtesy, even toward those who cannot do oneself any good. Then, let those traits show—not as mere appearances, but as accurate portrayals of the character they reflect. That may be difficult when, like the young Tom Jones, people see around them examples of Blifils, Thwackums, and Squares, all thriving (for the moment at least) through the shrewd cultivation of appearances and the callous disregard of substance and motive.

But it may not be as hard as it seems. As Fielding said, "Simplicity, when set on its Guard, is often a match for Cunning."[17] Most citizens already see through the charade of appearances: That, after all, is why distrust in the institutions that have turned to appearances has grown to such dramatic, even dangerous, levels. The Age of Appearances is, one way or another, drawing to a close. Perhaps it will usher in an era not of cynicism, but of trustworthiness.

Appendix

The Whitewater Appearance Wars

How bad have things gotten? Well, the frequency and intensity of our attention to appearance problems—and our resort to the Ethics Establishment to resolve them—have reached the point where "obsession" actually seems a fair characterization. Hyperbole? Take a look at Whitewater. Not at *what* was being investigated but *how* it was being investigated. (Promise to readers: You don't need to know anything about the McDougals or Madison Guaranty Savings & Loan.)

Regularly for more than two years following the initial Whitewater news stories, various parties issued statements of concern about the "appearance of impropriety" created by some action taken or to be taken in connection with the investigation. For a time these appearance questions dominated the news on Whitewater. And just about everyone who had an actual or potential role in the investigation had to dive for cover to avoid the sustained crossfire of appearance accusations. Rather than removing public doubts about the integrity of the process, the heightened attention to ethical appearances spawned them and impeded efforts to understand exactly what was potentially criminal in the past conduct of the President of the United States.

The story begins innocently enough in November 1993, when the U.S. Attorney in Little Rock, Arkansas, withdrew from prosecuting a criminal fraud case against a local lawyer and a former municipal judge, who had begun making allegations involving President Clinton. The U.S. Attorney, Paula Casey, knew President Clinton personally, had worked on his presidential campaign, and owed her job to him. Casey informed U.S. Attorney General Janet Reno that she was removing herself in order to avoid an appearance of impropriety.[1] Fair enough. Attorney General Reno also didn't want to oversee the investigation, however, because she, like Casey, owed her job to Clinton. Reno could not ask federal judges to appoint a statutory Independent Counsel because the original Independent Counsel law had expired and Congress had not yet renewed it. So, on January 31, 1994, expressly to avoid any appearance of impropriety, Reno herself appointed as Independent Counsel Robert B. Fiske, Jr., a longtime Republican and former hard-charging U.S. Attorney in New York.

The use of "appearances" to decide who should participate, and if so how, in some facet of the Whitewater investigation was just beginning, however. Questions in the spring of 1994 about the President's legal team set the tone. In March, news reports disclosed that White House Counsel Bernard Nussbaum had met with Deputy Treasury Secretary Roger C. Altman to discuss the status of the Resolution Trust Corporation's investigation of Madison Guaranty Savings & Loan. After President Clinton publicly joined the chorus of concern that the meetings had created "the appearance of impropriety"—i.e., had allowed a suspicion of improper White House pressure on an ongoing investigation—Nussbaum promptly resigned. ("Just say it was an appearance of impropriety," White House aide George Stephanopolous had counseled Nussbaum.[2]) Explicitly to offset the appearance of impropriety, then–White House chief of staff Thomas F. "Mack" McLarty issued new ethics rules on permissible contacts between White House staffers and Whitewater investigators, and President Clinton appointed respected Washington lawyer Lloyd N. Cutler as new White House Counsel with "full authority to handle appearances of impropriety."

In May 1994, President Clinton hired Washington, D.C. lawyer

Robert Bennett to defend the sexual harassment suit filed by Paula Jones. Bennett was perhaps best known for his prosecution of the "appearance of impropriety" case against the "Keating Five" before the Senate Ethics Committee. Amid speculation that Bennett might also assist in the Whitewater defense effort, however, Bennett himself became a target of appearance charges. An appearance question was raised, for example, about Bennett's simultaneous representation of President Clinton and, on fraud charges, Democratic Representative Dan Rostenkowski: "'It is not a clear-cut conflict,' [said] one lawyer, who ask[ed] not to be named. 'But it gives the appearance of impropriety. It gives the public impression that Rostenkowski might get lenient treatment because his lawyer represents the president.'"[3] Questions followed about the appearance of President Clinton's becoming financially obligated to Bennett's law firm, which, like most large law firms with Washington, D.C. offices, handles all sorts of matters before federal agencies and departments.

At the end of June 1994, two developments induced Robert Fiske's opponents to roll out appearance weaponry to eliminate him as Independent Counsel. First, President Clinton signed new legislation reestablishing the statutory office of Independent Counsel (and the three-judge panel that oversees and appoints Independent Counsel).[4] Although Attorney General Reno promptly asked the federal panel to continue Fiske's role by appointing him as statutory Independent Counsel for Whitewater—arguing that switching counsel after seven months would seriously disrupt the investigation's progress—the judges had the power to name someone else. Second, Fiske announced results favorable to the White House on two matters under investigation. He confirmed that White House aide Vincent Foster had not been the victim of "foul play" but in fact had committed suicide as originally reported. And Fiske found no grounds to pursue a criminal prosecution arising out of meetings between White House and Treasury Department officials on the subject of the RTC's investigation of Madison Guaranty.

Fiske came under public attack for improper appearances promptly after issuing these conclusions. North Carolina's Senator Lauch Faircloth led the charge during nationally televised hearings of the Senate Banking Committee. Typical was Faircloth's allegation that Fiske was unacceptable because he had professional "links" to former White House Counsel Nussbaum and Clinton lawyer Bennett. The "links" were that the men had worked together in the past as private attorneys on a few cases representing different clients. Senator Faircloth also suggested Fiske was tainted because his law firm had represented a company (International Paper) that in the 1980s had sold land to Whitewater Development Corporation. Senator Faircloth did not pause to explain how this connection could have had any significant impact on Fiske's performance as Independent Counsel.

In July 1994, the three-judge panel denied the Attorney General's request to reappoint Fiske and replaced him with former Bush administration Solicitor General Kenneth W. Starr. The panel said a new Independent Counsel was needed to avoid any appearance of impropriety. Fiske owed his position to the Attorney General, who in turn owed hers to President Clinton. Even Democratic Senator John F. Kerry seemed resigned to the outcome: "Once there were any questions whatsoever about appearances regarding Fiske's investigation, then it was very important to take any steps necessary to guarantee nobody was left with any doubts."[5]

In this climate, however, the only guarantee was that substantial doubts about the purity of the investigative process would proliferate. That is just what happened—on two fronts. First came stories about Starr's "links" to Clinton's enemies and conflict-of-interest questions far more germane than those Senator Faircloth had raised about Fiske. Starr, like Fiske, had a reputation for integrity, but he also was very actively involved in Republican politics. He not only had lost his position as Solicitor General because of President Clinton's election, he had considered a run for the U.S. Senate from Virginia—a campaign that presumably would have involved him in attacking the Clinton administration. Starr also had taken a highly visible public stance against President Clinton's claim for immunity while in office from civil suits such as Paula Jones's and allegedly had agreed to donate time to a conservative women's group to prepare a legal brief on the issue.[6]

Then came reports about how Starr had been selected. Capitol Hill sources guided reporters to the discovery that, shortly before Starr's appointment, Senator Faircloth had lunched on Capitol Hill with the presiding judge on the three-judge selection panel, U.S. Court of Appeals Judge David B. Sentelle. Judge Sentelle is a longtime North Carolina Republican and a protégé of Fiske-opponent Senator Jesse Helms (R-N.C.), who also attended the lunch. Helms had sponsored Sentelle for his seats on the federal district and appeals courts in the face of substantial opposition. Judge Sentelle thus owed his job to Helms. In addition, Sentelle apparently had personal reason to dislike Fiske, because Fiske had chaired the American Bar Association's judicial selection committee when leaks from the committee had damaged Sentelle's candidacies.[7]

Judge Sentelle told reporters that he and the senators had merely discussed cowboy boots and prostate exams at their lunch. Judge Sentelle said he could not recall discussing Fiske. Charges of "appearance of impropriety" nonetheless rang out on Capitol Hill and in the nation's newspapers. People who had defended the appearance of the Fiske-Bennett-Nussbaum "links" attacked the appearance of the Starr-Sentelle-Faircloth-Helms "links." And vice versa.

It was only a matter of time before Judge Sentelle came under direct ethical attack. On September 2, 1994, the first of three complaints of misconduct against Judge Sentelle was filed in the U.S. Court of Appeals for the District of Columbia Circuit.[8] The complaints charged the judge with acting improperly in meeting with Senators Faircloth and Helms, and in receiving private correspondence from House Republicans opposed to Fiske's reappointment. The complainants argued, among other things, that Judge Sentelle's "conduct resulted in an appearance of impropriety that was 'prejudicial to the effective and expeditious administration of the business of the courts.'"[9] On September 20, five former presidents of the American Bar Association issued a statement jointly endorsing this view. They argued that the Ethics Act was intended to depoliticize the appointment process, "to insure that the selection would not be influenced by the very sort of political considerations that the Act was adopted to avoid."[10]

In accordance with federal law, the complaints were referred to the Chief Judge of the D.C. Circuit, Harry T. Edwards. Judge Edwards is a Democrat, appointed by Jimmy Carter. When he had not acted on the ethics complaints by mid-October, however, one of the complainants wrote to protest the delay and to question Judge Edwards' own ethical fitness to determine Judge Sentelle's ethical fitness to have weighed the ethical advantages of replacing Fiske with Starr. The complainant urged Judge Edwards to step aside and appoint—what else—an independent investigative committee, which would not be hampered by the appearances created when one federal judge scrutinizes the behavior of one of his colleagues. This device, the complainant argued, would "eliminate any possible criticism that the matter was whitewashed at the preliminary stage."[11]

On November 1, 1994, Judge Edwards rejected the suggestion that he should recuse himself and dismissed the ethical complaints against Judge Sentelle. The complaints failed to allege facts sufficient to show that Judge Sentelle had engaged in conduct "prejudicial to the effective and expeditious administration of the business of the courts."[12] Judge Edwards said the "appearance of impropriety" charge was grounded in a fundamental misconception about the nature of Judge Sentelle's role in selecting an Independent Counsel. In upholding the constitutionality of the Independent Counsel law in *Morrison v. Olson*,[13] the Supreme Court had made clear that federal judges are not exercising judicial power under Article III of the Constitution when choosing Independent Counsel, Judge Edwards declared. Rather, like executive-branch officials, they are acting under the Appointment Clause of Article II. It made little sense to think that Judge Sentelle could exercise this executive-type power, Judge Edwards reasoned, without consulting people, including the President's political opponents.

In a significant sense, Judge Edwards' opinion brought the "appearance of impropriety" principle full circle. The principle was first codified after the Black Sox scandal to assure the public about the integrity of judges when acting as judges. Judging, however, is a special activity. It cannot sustain public support unless seen as essentially nonpartisan and unbiased. Political decisions are different. To borrow Judge Edwards' words, they are not and cannot be the product of "a cloistered, apolitical judicial 'proceeding.'"[14] The "appearance" standard's extraordinary rise in prominence since Watergate has created mischief in substantial part because political decisions are not the same as judicial decisions, yet we have pretended that they can and should be.

In any event, while the ethics charges against Judge Sentelle were pending, both the White House and Ken Starr remained under appearance assault. And both responded by calling in reinforcements who had earned their ethical stripes during Watergate. At the White House, the President established a legal defense fund to avoid continued appearance charges about his legal bills. No matter how well Hillary Clinton may have done in the cattle futures market, there was no way the Clintons could afford to pay on a regular basis what for most individuals would be staggering legal expenses. To avoid an appearance of impropriety, the President and his advisors determined that the legal defense fund would place a ceiling on individual donations, publicly disclose the donor's identity, and be administered by a bipartisan group of trustees. For added protection, the list of trustees included two Watergate heroes: former Nixon Attorney General and Saturday Night Massacre victim Elliot Richardson, and the late Barbara Jordan, an outspoken Democratic member of the House Judiciary Committee that had voted to impeach Nixon.

Starr responded in analogous fashion to the appearance attacks against him. On September 28, the *Chicago Tribune* reported that Starr's name had been included in a list of advisory committee members on the letterhead of a Republican candidate who was attacking President Clinton for his "personal scandals."[15] A spokesman for Starr said it was a mistake; Starr's name was supposed to have been removed from any partisan-appearing material after his appointment on August 5. Clinton lawyer Bob Bennett leaped to the microphone: "This raises real concerns on my part because the justification for removing Fiske, and appointing Starr, was one of appearances." On October 5, after the five former ABA presidents had joined the attack against the improper appearances surrounding his selection, Starr wisely decided to hunker down for the remainder of his tenure with his own ethics counsel. He hired Georgetown University legal ethics professor and former chief counsel to the Senate Watergate Committee Samuel Dash. Professor Dash announced that he had been retained to help his client avoid the appearance of impropriety.[16]

And so he did. Later that month, for example, when Starr was criticized for continuing to represent a conservative foundation that allegedly was bankrolling President Clinton's Whitewater critics, Dash rose to Starr's defense.[17] When the propriety of Starr's privately representing tobacco companies while Independent Counsel was debated, Dash opined that Starr had avoided both actual conflict and the "appearance" and "perception" of conflict.[18] (The latter issue was raised by a number of Starr's critics, including Whitewater defendant Arkansas Governor Jim Guy Tucker, who said the tobacco companies had "axes to grind" with him because of Arkansas' tax policies.)[19] And when the *Nation* ran a cover story revealing that, in 1993, the RTC had sued Starr's law firm, Kirkland & Ellis, in an "eerily parallel" case to the RTC's case against Hillary Clinton's former firm, the Rose Law Firm, Starr parried the article's thrust with citation to Professor Dash's favorable review of his ethics in the matter.

On some of these issues, Dash found himself on the opposite side of the ethical battlefield from Stephen Gillers, a New York University law professor. Professor Gillers is one of the country's leading legal ethics specialists. News organizations repeatedly called upon him during the Whitewater investigation to comment on the propriety of someone else's conduct. Gillers criticized on appearance grounds the Sentelle-Faircloth-Helms lunch, the House Republicans' letter to Judge Sentelle opposing Fiske's reappointment, Starr's working relationship with Republican Senator Al D'Amato, and Starr's continued representation of numerous private clients while Independent Counsel. (According to the *Boston Globe,* Professor Gillers was a longtime friend of Bob Fiske,[20] yet Gillers himself apparently escaped appearance attack for criticizing Fiske's replacement while having "links" to Fiske.) On the other hand, Professor Gillers defended the appearances created by Bernie Nussbaum's protection of White House files,[21] as well as Hillary Clinton's representation of private clients before Arkansas regulators while her husband was governor.

The latter opinion provided considerable comfort to the Clintons in the appearance wars. So much so that President Clinton twice quoted Professor Gillers at a presidential news conference as authority for the proposition that the First Lady had behaved ethically when in private practice in Arkansas. Gillers' defense of the First Lady drew a spirited reply, however, from another leading legal ethics expert, Professor Monroe Freedman of Hofstra University Law School. Professor Freedman argued that Hillary Clinton had been bound by the appearance of impropriety standard while in practice in Arkansas, that her representation of clients before state regulators had violated this standard, and that excusing her behavior on the ground that spouses should be free to pursue conflicting careers was "paternalism cross-dressing as feminism."

The Gillers-Freedman debate boiled over into heated exchanges over the airwaves, in legal magazines, and even in cyberspace. At one point observers were treated to the spectacle of the two ethics professors' attacking each other for such things as furnishing a "misleadingly narrow" answer, offering a "snide conclusion," quoting selectively from statements for "rhetorical advantage," obscuring one's own errors, and providing "a misleading half-truth" to the public. Neither ethicist retreated from his initial position on whether Hillary Clinton had acted unethically in her legal practice—one of the few ethical issues in the years-long Whitewater debate that actually had to do with how the Clintons had behaved in Little Rock. The professors' dialogue for the most part hinged on technical arguments about applicable rules, although there were isolated moments—as when Professor Freedman asked why Hillary Clinton had chosen to represent clients before state regulators while her husband was governor—when the Clintons' motivation was discussed.

Of course, few Americans were inclined to try to puzzle through the rightness or wrongness of the Clintons' conduct in Whitewater. And who could blame them? It was difficult enough to attempt to work out the rightness or wrongness of the conduct of those investigating and judging the Clintons. And we haven't even mentioned the appearance volleys fired into and out of the offices of Senator Al D'Amato. While occupying key positions in Bob Dole's presidential campaign (and reportedly contemplating various cabinet positions in a Dole administration), D'Amato was busily attacking the Clintons during the Senate Whitewater Committee hearings he chaired. Senator D'Amato's detractors repeatedly pointed out this conflict and listed a variety of ethical problems that D'Amato himself had faced in the past. D'Amato's chairmanship of an ethics-type investigation became fodder for late-night comedy monologues on the fox-guarding-the-henhouse theme.

Nor have we mentioned the appearance problems that arose in selecting jurors for the McDougal-Tucker criminal trial—in many ways an epigrammatic skirmish in the Whitewater appearance wars. One of the high points occurred when prosecutors and defense counsel accepted Barbara Adams as an alternate juror. Adams had come to court each day dressed in a *Star Trek* commander's uniform, complete with communicator badge, tricorder, and phaser. Susan McDougal's attorney maintained that Adams' appearance was less important than her character. After a careful voir dire examination, he said he believed the thirty-one-year-old print-shop supervisor would be a good juror if called to serve. On CNN's "Burden of Proof," however, a prominent defense attorney said Adams was obviously "a clown" and "a screwball," and a law professor said Adams' choice of garb, although constitutionally protected, "holds our country up to ridicule in the world." The *Arkansas Democrat-Gazette* reported that the "media mob" soon became "obsessed" with Adams's clothing.[22]

Adams briefly defended herself to inquiring reporters one day by explaining that she was a devotee of the *Star Trek* series "because it is an alternative to 'mindless television' and promotes inclusion, tolerance, peace and faith in mankind." She said she wore the uniform to all "formal proceedings."[23] Unfortunately, these comments earned the wrath not of Khan but of the presiding U.S. District Judge, George Howard, Jr. (Judge Howard had replaced Judge Henry Woods, disqualified on appearance grounds by the Eighth U.S. Circuit Court of Appeals, upon motion by Ken Starr, because of Woods' "links" to the Clintons.) Judge Howard dismissed Adams from the jury for violating a court order barring discussions with the media.

Adams said she hadn't thought she was violating his order because her brief remarks had been unrelated to the trial. No matter. The transgression gave Judge Howard an excuse to dismiss someone whose appearance threatened the solemnity of the proceedings. Adams' dismissal prompted the Associated Press to poll an assortment of "media and legal ethicists." The ethicists, AP reported, criticized both Adams and the crew of the syndicated television show that had interviewed her.[24]

Yet Adams should have taken some comfort in the fact that she wasn't the only juror to have created an appearance controversy. To prevent "an appearance of impropriety," for instance, Judge Howard had earlier dismissed a potential juror who had said he "thought" he could put aside preconceptions about the case. A more interesting disqualification involved a forty-eight-year-old cashier who forthrightly admitted prejudging Governor Tucker based on his appearance. "I don't like his looks," she told the court. "He looks crooked."[25] This bit of honesty resulted in the putative juror's being herself cashiered. As well it should have—for fastening on appearances in a matter of national importance that demanded perspective, and a fair and common sense judgment on the underlying facts.

Notes

Chapter 1

1. *See generally* Richard Serrano, *Militias: Ranks Are Swelling*, Los Angeles Times, Apr. 18, 1996, at A1; Randy E. Barnett, *Guns, Militias, and Oklahoma City*, 62 Tennessee Law Review 443 (1995).
2. The statistic is in Serrano, *supra* note 1.
3. Richard Hofstadter, *The Paranoid Style in American Politics,* in Richard Hofstadter, The Paranoid Style in American Politics and Other Essays 3–41 (1996).
4. Todd Ackerman, *Baylor Accused of Putting Religion Above Academics*, Houston Chronicle, Sept. 16, 1996, at 11.
5. Sandra Barber, *Online School Board Approved*, Times-Picayune, June 7, 1996, at B3.
6. Carol Bowers, *Ethics Panel Finds No Wrongdoing in Donation,* Baltimore Sun, Sept. 29, 1995, at 4B.
7. Alan Abrahamson, *Boy Scout Issue Splits State's Judges*, Los Angeles Times, Feb. 8, 1995, at B1.
8. Christopher Ringwald, *Sexual Abuse Cases Prompt Insurers to Limit Coverage for Clergy*, Times Union, Aug. 11, 1994, at A1.
9. *Id.*
10. Olive Talley, *Preacher to Explain Sex Charge*, Dallas Morning News, June 12, 1994, at 35A.
11. Wendi Thomas, *Animaland Shelter Closed: Future Remains Uncertain*, Tennessean, June 21, 1996, at 4B.
12. See Chapter 6.
13. *CNN & Company* (CNN Broadcast, January 31, 1994) (transcript available on NEXIS).
14. Ann Toner, *Corn Growers Ask Commodity Agency to Tighten Rules*, Omaha World Herald, Oct. 3, 1996, at 24.
15. *Cheese Exchange Ready for New Whey*, UPI Newswire, Oct. 7, 1996, BC cycle (available on NEXIS).

Chapter 2

1. Henry Fielding, The History of Tom Jones, A Foundling 615 (Martin C. Battestin & Fredson Bowers eds., Wesleyan Univ. Press, 1975).
2. I.E. Sanborn, *Williams Wild, Passes Giving Reds Victory*, Chicago Tribune, Oct. 3, 1991, at 1.
3. Eliot Asinof, Eight Men Out: The Black Sox And The 1919 World Series 85 (H. Holt, 1963).
4. *Id.* at 13.
5. *Id.* at 13, 136.
6. *The Most Gigantic Sporting Swindle in the History of America!* N. Am., Sept. 27, 1920, *quoted in* Asinof, *supra* note 3, at 168.
7. Eddie Cicotte (p), Happy Felsch (cf), Chick Gandil (1b), Shoeless Joe Jackson (1f), Fred McMullin (if), Swede Risberg (ss), Buck Weaver (3b), Lefty Williams (p).
8. Major League Agreement art. I, § 4, *quoted in* Matthew B. Pachman, Note, *Limits on the Discretionary Powers of Professional Sports Commissioners: A Historical and Legal Analysis of Issues Raised by the Pete Rose Controversy*, 76 Virginia Law Review 1409, 1415 (1990).
9. American Bar Association, Report of the Forty-Fourth Annual Meeting 61–67 (1921); *Wants a Landis Inquiry: Welty Urges Congress to See If He Can Be Judge and Baseball Arbiter*, N.Y. Times, Feb. 3, 1921, at 5; *Further Action by Welty: Representative Wants to See Copy of Landis's Baseball Contract*, N.Y. Times, Feb. 4, 1921, at 13; *Would Bar Landis as Baseball Head: Representative Welty Proposes Bill Limiting Federal Judges to Government Salaries*, N.Y. Times, Feb. 12, 1921, at 3; *Volstead Opposes Landis Impeachment: Presents Minority Report Upholding Judge's Acceptance of Office Baseball Arbiter*, N.Y. Times, Mar. 4, 1921, at 4.
10. American Bar Association, Report of the Forty-Seventh Annual Meeting 68 (1924); John P. MacKenzie, The Appearance of Justice 180–82 (Scribner, 1974); Shirley S. Abrahamson, *Foreword* to Jeffrey M. Shaman, Steven Lubet & James J. Alfini, Judicial Conduct and Ethics vii (Michie Co., 1990). The ABA had designated committees to draft canons of judicial ethics as early as 1909. American Bar Association, Report of the Thirty-Second Annual Meeting 88 (1909).
11. Canon 4 provided: "A judge's official conduct should be free from impropriety and the appearance of impropriety; he should avoid infractions of law; and his personal behavior, not only upon the Bench and in the performance of judicial duties, but also in his every day life, should be beyond reproach." ABA Canons of Judicial Ethics Canon 4 (1924).
12. The federal statute that made it a crime for private parties to provide supplemental compensation to federal government employees, 18 U.S.C. § 209(a) (1988), is one example. *See Crandon v. United States*, 494 U.S. 152, 164–65 (1990):

Congress appropriately enacts prophylactic rules that are intended to prevent even the appearance of wrongdoing and that may apply to conduct that has caused no actual injury to the United States. Section 209(a) is such a rule. [Such legislation] . . . is supported by the legitimate interest in maintaining the public's confidence in the integrity of the federal service.

The prohibition in legal ethics codes against a lawyer's commingling the lawyer's funds with those of the client is another example. *See* ABA Model Rules of Professional Conduct Rule 1.15 (1990); ABA Model Code of Professional Responsibility DR 9-102(A) (1980); ABA Canons of Professional Ethics Canon 11 (1933).

13. ABA Model Code of Professional Responsibility EC 9-6 exhorts attorneys to strive to avoid not only professional impropriety but also "the appearance of impropriety." *See also id.* Canon 9 (entitled "A Lawyer Should Avoid Even the Appearance of Professional Impropriety").

14. ABA Comm. on Ethics and Professional Responsibility, Formal Op. 342 n.17 (1985).

15. ABA Model Rules of Professional Conduct 53 (Proposed Final Draft 1981) (citing Note, *Appearance of Impropriety as the Sole Ground for Disqualification*, 31 University of Miami Law Review 1516 (1977)); Victor H. Kramer, *The Appearance of Impropriety Under Canon 9: A Study of the Federal Judicial Process Applied to Lawyers*, 65 Minnesota Law Review 243 (1981); Neil D. O'Toole, *Canon 9 of the Code of Professional Responsibility: An Elusive Ethical Guideline*, 62 Marquette Law Review 313 (1979).

16. Robert N. Roberts, White House Ethics: The History of the Politics of Conflict of Interest Regulation 76–89, 117 (Greenwood Press, 1988).

17. Exec. Order No. 11,222, 3 C.F.R. 306 (1964–1965), *revoked,* Exec. Order No. 12,674, 3 C.F.R. 215 (1990).

18. *See, e.g.,* Roberts, *supra* note 16, at 131, 162. A 1990 Congressional Research Service study identifies four instances in which an "appearance of impropriety" standard was used as a basis to discipline federal executive branch employees. Morton Rosenberg & Jack H. Maskell, *Congressional Intervention in the Administrative Process: Legal and Ethical Considerations* 70 & n.241 (Congressional Research Service, Sept. 7, 1990). Special Counsel Bennett filed a memorandum in the Keating Five Hearings to support the proposition that "appearance of impropriety" has historically been an enforced ethical rule. *Preliminary Inquiry into Allegations Regarding Sens. Cranston, DeConcini, Glenn, McCain, and Riegle, and Lincoln Savings and Loan: Hearings Before the Select Comm. on Ethics,* United States Senate, 101st Cong., 2d Sess. (1990) (hereinafter *"Keating Five Hearings"*), *Exhibits of Special Counsel,* pt. 3, at 520 (Special Counsel's Analysis of Relevant Law and Applicable Standards). The memorandum cites only two cases involving impropriety in the executive branch.

19. The OGE issued 18 informal advisory letters and formal opinions on appearance problems in the first ten years of its existence. Office of Government Ethics, The Informal Advisory Letters and Memoranda and Formal Opinions of the Office of Government Ethics, 1979–1988, Nos. 83 x 18, 83 x 20, 84 x 5, 84 x 6, 84 x 11, 85 x 2, 85 x 10, 85 x 13, 85 x 14, 85 x 17, 85 x 19, 86 x 5, 86 x 10, 87 x 8, 87 x 11, 88 x 10, 88 x 13, 88 x 17 (1989).

20. *See supra* note 18.

21. ABA Model Code of Judicial Conduct Canon 2 (1990). This canon expands the injunction in the 1924 Canons that a judge should avoid the appearance of impropriety in the judge's *official* activities. *See also* Robert A. Ainsworth, Jr., *Impact of the Code of Judicial Conduct on Federal Judges*, 1972 Utah Law Review 369, 369 (praising the Code as a necessary and useful guide for judicial conduct).

22. Abrahamson, *supra* note 10, at v.

23. Kramer, *supra* note 15, at 243 & n.3. Only two of the twenty-six state and federal cases, and none of the law review articles, cited in Charles W. Wolfram, Modern Legal Ethics § 7.1.4 (1986), were published before 1975. The 1990 ABA Model Code of Judicial Conduct carries forward the rule that a judge must avoid the appearance of impropriety in all of the judge's activities. Model Code of Judicial Conduct Canon 2 (1990).

24. Paragraph 5 of the Code of Ethics for Government Service, which may or may not apply to senators, comes close. *See Keating Five Hearings, supra* note 18, *Exhibits of Special Counsel,* pt. 3, at 547 (Special Counsel's Analysis of Relevant Law and Applicable Standards). The Special Counsel argued that:

> The requirement that lawmakers avoid the appearance of impropriety is embodied in the Code of Ethics for Government Service, which is applicable to Members of Congress. Paragraph 5 of the Code states that a government employee should never accept "favors and benefits under circumstances which might be construed by reasonable persons as influencing the performance of his governmental duties."

> *Id.* (quoting House Committee on Standards of Official Conduct, 100th Cong., 1st Sess., Ethics Manual for Members, Officers, and Employees of the U.S. House of Representatives 195 (Comm. Print 1987).

25. *See id.* at 535–36 (discussing Robert Baker investigation); *id.* at 550 (statement of Select Committee on Standards and Conduct).

26. In 1977, the Senate established the Senate Code of Official Conduct as part of the Standing Rules of the Senate, and formed the Senate Select Committee on Ethics. S. Res. 110, 95th Cong., 1st Sess. (1977) (enacted); *see also* Senate Special Comm. on Official Conduct, Senate Code of Official Conduct to Accompany S. Res. 110, S. Rep. No. 49, 95th Cong., 1st Sess. 2 (1977).

27. Senate Select Comm. on Ethics, Korean Influence Inquiry, S. Rep. No. 1314, 95th Cong., 2d Sess. 5–6 (1978) (investigation into whether South Korea

was improperly purchasing the favor of congressmen through campaign contributions).

28. *See Keating Five Hearings, supra* note 18, *Exhibits of Special Counsel,* pt. 3, at 546–47 (investigation into whether Senator Durenberger's book deal violated Senate rules on outside income).

29. Statement of the Select Committee on Ethics Following Hearings Involving Senators Cranston, DeConcini, Glenn, McCain and Riegle 4–5 (1991). The committee found that the conduct of Senators DeConcini and Riegle "gave the appearance of being improper," but concluded that no further action was warranted. *Id.* (Decision of the Committee Concerning Senator DeConcini, Decision of the Committee Concerning Senator Riegle). The committee cleared Senators Glenn and McCain of everything except poor judgment, *id.* (Decision of the Committee Concerning Senator Glenn, Decision of the Committee Concerning Senator McCain); it recommended a formal investigation of Senator Cranston's conduct, *id.* (Resolution for Investigation). The committee "strongly and severely reprimand[ed]" Senator Cranston in its final report. 1 Senate Select Comm. on Ethics, Investigation of Senator Alan Cranston, S. Rep. No. 223, 102d Cong., 1st Sess. 36 (1991). In so doing, the committee rejected Senator Cranston's defense that he had engaged only in an appearance of impropriety. *See* 137 Cong. Rec. S18,826–28 (daily ed. Dec. 18, 1991) (statement of Sen. Rudman).

30. *Keating Five Hearings, supra* note 18, at 58.

31. *Id.*

32. *See generally* Dennis F. Thompson, Ethics in Congress: From Individual to Institutional Corruption (Brookings Institute, 1995).

33. An Act for the Better Regulation of Attornies and Solicitors, 1728, 2 Geo. 2 ch. 23, § 1 (Eng.), *reprinted in* A.H. Manchester, Sources of English Legal History: Law, History and Society in England and Wales, 1750–1950, 51, 60 (Butterworths, 1984); *see also* C.W. Brooks, Pettyfoggers and Vipers of the Commonwealth: The "Lower Branch" of the Legal Profession in Early Modern England 265–66 (Cambridge Univ. Press, 1986); Alan Harding, A Social History of English Law 287 (Penguin Books, 1966).

34. Martin C. Battestin, *Fielding's Definition of Wisdom: Some Functions of Ambiguity and Emblem in "Tom Jones,"* 35 English Literary History 188, 305 (1968).

35. William de Britaine, Humane Prudence: or, The Art by Which a Man May Raise Himself and His Fortune to Grandeur (n.p. 1680). The book reached a 12th edition by 1729. *See* Battestin, *supra* note 34, at 198.

36. William de Britaine, Humane Prudence: or, The Art by Which a Man May Raise Himself and His Fortune to Grandeur 61 (12th ed., printed for J. & J. Knapton et al., 1729), *quoted in* Battestin, *supra* note 34, at 198–99.

37. Fielding was *the* so-called "Active" or Court Magistrate of the period 1749–54. *See generally* Martin C. Battestin *with* Ruthe R. Battestin, Henry Fielding: A Life (Routledge, 1989). Fielding made the legal and socioeconomic problems of his time the subject of several excellent pamphlets. *E.g.,*

Henry Fielding, An Enquiry Into the Causes of the Late Increase of Robbers, &c. (2d ed., printed for A. Millar, 1751), *in* An Enquiry Into the Causes of the Late Increase of Robbers And Related Writings 61 (Malvin R. Zirker ed., Wesleyan Univ. Press, 1988). His *Amelia* was the first novel of social protest and reform in English, a genre that culminated in Dickens's fiction a century later. Henry Fielding, Amelia (1751) (Martin C. Battestin ed., Wesleyan Univ. Press, 1983).

38. *See* Henry Fielding, *An Essay on the Knowledge of the Characters of Men* (1743), in 1 Miscellanies by Henry Fielding, Esq. 12–30 (Henry Knight Miller ed., 1972); John H. Langhein, *Shaping the Eighteenth-Century Criminal Trial: A View from the Ryder Sources*, 50 University of Chicago Law Review 1, 60–67 (1983).

39. Henry Fielding, A Proposal for Making an Effectual Provision for the Poor (printed for A. Millar, 1753).

40. B.M. Jones, Henry Fielding: Novelist and Magistrate 113–17, 121 (G. Allen & Unwin, 1933); Pat Rogers, Henry Fielding: A Biography 180 (Scribner, 1979).

41. Jones, *supra* note 40, at 234–45.

42. *E.g.,* Battestin *with* Battestin, *supra* note 37, at 497–98, 523.

43. *Id.* at 459–60.

44. Fielding, *supra* note 38, at 153.

45. On the latter point, Fielding, *supra* note 37.

46. Fielding, *supra* note 38, at 154.

47. *Id.*

48. *See* Glenn W. Hatfield, Henry Fielding and the Language of Irony 193–94 (Univ. of Chicago Press, 1968). A sermon preached by Thomas Manningham in 1693 reflects apprehension in the church as well. Manningham declared that "tho' Prudence in the common acceptation of the World passes now for any Cunning Contrivance, for any dextrous Management of an Affair, whatever means are us'd; yet the ancient Moralists never allow'd a wicked Man to be call'd Prudent." Thomas Manningham, *Of Religious Prudence: A Sermon Preach'd Before the Queen, . . . on Sunday, Sept. 17, 1693* (1694), *quoted in* Hatfield, at 193.

49. The Nicomachean Ethics vi.13 (p. 158) (Oxford Univ. Press, 1988). Aristotle's treatise has been called "the most brilliant set of lecture notes ever written." Alisdair MacIntyre, After Virtue: A Study in Moral Theory 147 (Univ. of Notre Dame Press, 2d ed. 1984).

50. *See generally* Alisdair MacIntyre, A Short History of Ethics 74–76 (Collier Books, 1966).

51. The Nicomachean Ethics, *supra* note 49, at vi.5 (p. 143).

52. *Id.* at vi.12 (p. 156).

53. *See* Hatfield, *supra* note 48, at 192.

54. *See, e.g.,* Fielding, *supra* note 38, at 154. Fielding borrowed this term from one of the ethical handbooks, Thomas Powell, The Art of Thriving, or the Plaine Pathway to Preferment (n.p. 1635). Professor Battestin has called this

"false prudence"—the "shadow and opposite" of *prudentia*—"the characteristic of the whole 'tribe' of hypocrites and politicians, of whom . . . Machiavelli was 'the great patron and *coryphoeus.*'" Battestin, *supra* note 34, at 196 (quoting Robert South, *The Wisdom of this World, in* Sermons Preached Upon Several Occasions 140 (n.p. 1843)).

55. Letter from Captain Lewis Thomas (Apr. 3, 1794), *quoted in* J.P. Feil, *Fielding's Character of Mrs. Whitefield,* 39 Philological Quarterly 508, 509 (1960).

56. Fielding, *supra* note 1, at xxv.

57. *Id.* at 141.

58. *See, e.g.,* Kathleen Day, *Bank Board Chief, Critic Feuding,* Wash. Post, Sept. 20, 1986, at A1; Kathleen Day, *Bank Board Lived Well Off S&Ls,* Wash. Post, Dec. 8, 1986, at A1; Monica Langley, *Thrifts' Trade Group and Its Regulators Get Along Just Fine,* Wall St. J., July 17, 1986, at 1.

59. *See, e.g., Keating Five Hearings, supra* note 18, *Exhibits of Special Counsel,* pt. 2, at 378 (memorandum, dated Dec. 16, 1986, from Laurie A. Sedlmayr to Senator DeConcini).

60. *See* Kathleen Day, *When Hell Sleazes Over: Judgment Day for S&L Slimeballs,* New Republic, Mar. 20, 1989, at 26; *see also, e.g., Keating Five Hearings, supra* note 18, pt. 1, at 180, 189 (opening statement of Robert S. Bennett, Nov. 15, 1990); *id., Exhibits of Special Counsel,* pt. 2, at 378 (memorandum, dated Dec. 16, 1986, from Laurie A. Sedlmayr to Senator DeConcini); *cf. id., Exhibits of Special Counsel,* pt. 4, at 113 (memorandum, dated June 14, 1989, from Senator DeConcini to two aides, in which the Senator instructs them to "[d]iscredit Gray").

61. *Keating Five Hearings, supra* note 18, pt.1, at 25 (opening statement of Senator DeConcini, Nov. 19, 1990).

62. *Id.* Keating founded the antipornography organization, Citizens for Decent Literature, in Cincinnati during the 1950s. Gay Talese, Thy Neighbor's Wife 366 (Ivy Books, 1980). Cincinnati headline writers dubbed Keating "Mr. Clean," *id.,* even though several states barred CDL from seeking contributions within their borders because CDL spent an enormous percentage of the money it raised (67 percent, for example, in 1972) on administration and additional fund raising. David Corn, *Dirty Bookkeeping: Charles Keating's Porno Library,* New Republic, Apr. 2, 1990, at 14.

In 1969, President Nixon appointed Keating to the President's Commission on Obscenity and Pornography, from whose later findings—e.g., that there is "no evidence to date that exposure to explicit sexual materials plays a significant role in the causation of delinquent or criminal behavior among youth or adults," Commission on Obscenity and Pornography, Report of the Commission on Obscenity and Pornography 27 (1970)—Keating dissented in a scathing separate statement, *id.* at 511–49. Warning that "the moral fiber of our nation seems to be rapidly unravelling," *id.* at 548, Keating accused the commission of advocating "moral anarchy," *id.* at 515, and even called for a congressional investigation into the commission's activities, *id.* at 517–18.

63. *Keating Five Hearings, supra* note 18, pt. 1, at 25–26 (opening statement of Senator DeConcini, Nov. 19, 1990).

64. *E.g.,* James Ring Adams, The Big Fix: Inside the S&L Scandal 41–49, 195–209, 226–49 (John Wiley & Sons, 1990); Martin Mayer, The Greatest-Ever Bank Robbery: The Collapse of the Savings and Loan Industry 116–64, 194–202, 228–45 (Scribner, 1990); Stephen Pizzo, Mary Fricker & Paul Muolo, Inside Job: The Looting of America's Savings and Loans (McGraw-Hill, 1989).

65. Mayer, *supra* note 64, at 1.

66. J. Paul Hunter, Occasional Form: Henry Fielding and the Chains of Circumstance 122 (Johns Hopkins Univ. Press, 1975).

67. Stephen E. Ambrose, Eisenhower: Soldier and President 25–26 (Simon & Schuster, 1990) (footnote omitted).

68. Daniel J. Boorstin, The Image: A Guide to Pseudo-Events in America 200–01 (Vintage, 1992).

69. Tim Golden, *Kennedy Nephew Pleads Not Guilty to Charges of Assault and Rape,* N.Y. Times, June 1, 1991, at 6.

70. Jeffrey Travers & Stanley Milgram, *An Experimental Study of the Small World Problem,* 32 Sociometry 425 (1969).

71. The *Post* cited random examples: Joseph Barnes, a homeless man who sleeps on the streets; Brenda and Bill Sutton, an accountant and a UPS driver in suburban Maryland; Krista Conaway of suburban Virginia, who works for a company that sells mailing lists—are all just three people away from the President. D'Vera Cohn, *Three Degrees of Separation from Clinton,* Wash. Post, Mar. 19, 1995, at B1.

72. 4 Plutarch's Lives 98 (Arthur Hugh Clough ed., Dryden trans., 1905).

73. Matthias Gelzer, Caesar: Politician and Statesman 59–60 (Peter Needham trans., Blackwell, 1968); 4 Plutarch's Lives, *supra* note 72, at 96.

74. Guglielmo Ferrero, The Life of Caesar 191 (A.E. Zimmern trans., Norton, 1933).

75. 4 Plutarch's Lives, *supra* note 72, at 98.

76. J.P.V.D. Balsdon, Julius Caesar: A Political Biography 49–50 (Atheneum, 1967); Michael Grant, Julius Caesar 62–65 (McGraw-Hill, 1969); 4 Plutarch's Lives, *supra* note 72, at 98.

77. Fielding, *supra* note 1, at 960.

78. James Q. Wilson, Bureaucracy: What Government Agencies Do and Why They Do It 196–97 (Basic Books, 1989) (citations omitted).

79. Erving Goffman, The Presentation of Self in Everyday Life 33 (Archer, 1959).

80. Michael Lewis, *California, Here They Come,* New Republic, Aug. 19/26, 1996, at 26.

81. Suzanne Garment, Scandal: The Culture of Mistrust in American Politics 1 (Times Books, 1991).

82. Letter from Richard Olney, Attorney General under President Cleveland, to

Charles E. Perkins, President of the Chicago, Burlington & Quincy Railroad, *quoted in* Kenneth Culp Davis, Administrative Law Text 6 (3d ed. 1972).

83. Roberts, *supra* note 16, at 168.

84. President Carter's Remarks at a State Democratic Party Rally, 2 Pub. Papers 1866 (Oct. 26, 1978).

85. For example, the rules exempt gifts from the sponsor of a widely attended event. This exception, however, does not apply unless either (1) the member or employee is speaking or performing a ceremonial function at the event, or (2) attendance is appropriate to the performance of the official duties or representative function of the member or employee. The House Committee on Standards of Official Conduct issued a memorandum to House members explaining these nuances through the following—and other similar—examples: If Owen Owner, the owner of a sports team, invites Manny Member to view an upcoming game from his sky box, Manny Member must buy his own ticket. Calvin Congressman, on the other hand, may attend a dinner hosted by Big Corporation if the dinner is in honor of Calvin's long and distinguished career in public service. Likewise, Chloe Congresswoman without fear of censure may attend a symphony celebrating her public work.

86. Larry Wheeler, *Turnpike Commission Moved Quickly to Recruit Eppard,* Gannett News Services, Apr. 5, 1995.

87. William L. Roberts, *Ex-Aide's Ties to Shuster Raise Questions of Ethics,* Pittsburgh Post-Gazette, Aug. 6, 1995, at A12; Pat Griffith, *Eppard Defends her Dual Role as Lobbyist, Shuster's Adviser,* Pittsburgh Post-Gazette, Feb. 20, 1996, at A1.

88. Griffith, *supra* note 87.

89. Roberts, *supra* note 87.

90. Don Phillips, *Congressman, Lobbyist Blast Report's "Innuendo,"* Wash. Post, Feb. 10, 1996, at D10.

91. *Id.*

92. *Ineffective Reform: Campaign Finance Laws Miss the Target,* Rocky Mountain News, June 16, 1996, at 56A.

93. William Proxmire, *Take the Pledge: No More Special Interest Money,* Roll Call, Sept. 17, 1990, at 5. For a provocative discussion of other campaign finance reform proposals, *see Frameworks of Analysis and Proposals for Reform: A Symposium on Campaign Finance,* 18 Hofstra Law Review 213 (1989).

94. Proxmire, *supra* note 93, at 5.

95. *Id.*

96. Terry Atlas, *Scandal Builds Around Lincoln S&L,* Chicago Tribune, Nov. 19, 1989, at B7.

97. Proxmire, *supra* note 93, at 5.

98. *See* Senate Select Comm. on Ethics, 101st Cong., 1st Sess., Interpretive Rulings of the Select Comm. on Ethics 1, 121, 143–44 (Comm. Print 1989).

99. Stuart Taylor, Jr., *Bribery & Politics,* Legal Times of Washington, June 24, 1996, at 23.

100. Henry Fielding, *An Essay on Conversation, in* 1 Miscellanies by Henry Fielding, Esq., *supra* note 38, at 119, 135; *see* Hatfield, *supra* note 48, at 183.

101. Fielding, *supra* note 100, at 135.

102. Hatfield, *supra* note 48, at 183.

103. For example, Blifil at one point sets Sophia's pet bird free, feigning concern about the cruelty of the bird's confinement. While Thwackum, Square, and an attorney debate the ethics and legality of Blifil's conduct, Sophia alone understands that it was wrong *because* it was a malicious act (done out of jealousy of her preference for Tom), just as she sees Blifil's later courtship of her as wrong because it is driven by cupidity and a desire to inherit her father's wealth. Hatfield, *supra* note 48, at 183; *see also* Fielding, *supra* note 1, at 158–65.

104. Fielding, *supra* note 1, at 344.

105. James B. Stewart, Blood Sport: The President and His Adversaries 411 (Simon & Schuster, 1996).

106. Robert H. Frank, Passions Within Reason: The Strategic Role of the Emotions (Norton, 1988). Opportunists want their rewards now. It is therefore very difficult for them to pretend to be unopportunistic, Professor Frank contends, because this requires them to delay gratification. *Id.* at 134–35.

107. Fielding, *supra* note 38, at 155.

> [H]owever cunning the Disguise be which a Masquerader wears: however foreign to his Age, Degree, or Circumstance, yet if closely attended to, he very rarely escapes the discovery of an accurate Observer; for Nature, which unwillingly submits to the Imposture, is ever endeavouring to peep forth and shew herself; nor can the Cardinal, the Friar, or the Judge, long conceal the Sot, the Gamester, or the Rake.

108. Asinof, *supra* note 3, at 93–94.

109. Fielding, *supra* note 100, at 124 (citing Matthew 7:12 and Luke 6:31).

110. *Id.* at 152.

111. *Id.*

112. 1 Thessalonians 5:22.

113. John 7:24.

Chapter 3

1. Neal Stephenson, Zodiac 69–70 (Bantam, 1995).

2. Maureen Dowd, *Boom! Goes the White House,* N.Y. Times, June 13, 1996, at A29.

3. *Id.*

4. Wash. Post, Jan. 28, 1996, at A1.

5. Dan Balz & Richard Morin, *A Tide of Pessimism and Political Powerlessness Rises,* Wash. Post, Nov. 3, 1991, at A1 (emphasis added).

6. *Id.*

Chapter 4

1. Stephen E. Ambrose, Nixon: The Education of a Politician 1913–1962, 624 (Simon & Schuster, 1987) *("Nixon I")*.
2. Dino A. Brugioni, Eyeball to Eyeball: The Inside Story of the Cuban Missile Crisis 44 (Random House, 1991); Christopher Andrew, For the President's Eyes Only: Secret Intelligence and American Presidency from Washington to Bush 242–46 (Harper Collins, 1995).
3. David Wise & Thomas B. Ross, The U-2 Affair 78–94 (Random House, 1960).
4. Stephen E. Ambrose, Eisenhower: Soldier and President 509–10 (Simon & Schuster, 1990) *("Eisenhower")*.
5. *See* Peter W. Morgan, *The Undefined Crime of Lying to Congress: Ethics Reform and the Rule of Law,* 86 Northwestern University Law Review 177, 178–79 (1992).
6. David Wise, The Politics of Lying: Government Deception, Secrecy, and Power 35 (Random House, 1973).
7. Stanley L. Kutler, The Wars of Watergate: The Last Crisis of Richard Nixon 53 (Alfred A. Knopf, 1990).
8. Robert S. McNamara, In Retrospect: The Tragedy and Lessons of Vietnam 20–21 (Times Books, 1995).
9. *Id.* at 20. The U-2 photos had convinced Eisenhower, he later wrote, "that the horrors of the alleged 'bomber gap' and the later 'missile gap' were nothing more than imaginative creations of irresponsibility." Dwight D. Eisenhower, The White House Years, 1956–61: Waging Peace 572 n. (Heinemann, 1966).
10. Deborah Shapley, Promise and Power: The Life and Times of Robert McNamara 97–98 (Little, Brown, 1993).
11. *Id.* at 98.
12. *Id.*
13. Robert Hotz, *The Credibility Gap,* Aviation Week & Space Technology, June 15, 1964.
14. William Safire, Safire's New Political Dictionary 157–58 (Random House, 1993).
15. Murrey Marder, *Credibility Gap: Greater Skepticism Greets Administration Declarations,* Wash. Post, Dec. 5, 1965, at A21.
16. Stanley Karnow, Vietnam: A History 248 (Penguin, 1988).
17. William Prochnau, Once Upon a Distant War 21 (Random House, 1995).
18. Shapley, *supra* note 10, at 293–94; *see also* Ambrose, *Eisenhower, supra* note 4, at 34.
19. Ambrose, *Eisenhower, supra* note 4, at 116.
20. Lt. Gen. Harold G. Moore (Ret.) & Joseph L. Galloway, We Were Soldiers Once . . . and Young: Ia Drang: The Battle That Changed the War in Vietnam 53 (Harper Collins, 1993).

21. *E.g., id.;* Neil Sheehan, A Bright Shining Lie: John Paul Vann and America in Vietnam 287 (Random House, 1988).
22. Sheehan, *supra* note 21, at 280.
23. *Id.* at 282.
24. Karnow, *supra* note 16, at 254.
25. Sheehan, *supra* note 21, at 289–90.
26. Andrew F. Krepinevich, Jr., The Army and Vietnam 36–52 (Johns Hopkins Univ. Press, 1986).
27. *Id.* at 66–68.
28. *See* Sheehan, *supra* note 21, at 124, 326, 338, 540; Karnow, *supra* note 16, at 323–24.
29. Krepinevich, *supra* note 26, at 69.
30. Karnow, *supra* note 16, at 257. Indeed, one of the South Vietnamese officials in charge of the program was a secret Communist operative who deliberately pushed to accelerate the program so as to maximize the peasants' alienation from the South Vietnamese regime and their American sponsors. *Id.*
31. David Halberstam, The Best and the Brightest 207 (Random House, 1972).
32. Colin L. Powell, *with* Joseph E. Persico, My American Journey 100 (Ballantine, 1996); *see also id.* at 140–44.
33. Prochnau, *supra* note 17, at 358.
34. *Id.* at 130, 360, 403.
35. *Id.* at 301–02.
36. *Id.*
37. McNamara, *supra* note 8, at 280.
38. John McNaughton, *Publish or Perish . . . An Author of Pentagon Papers Notes That Their Publication Gave Them Life,* St. Louis Post-Dispatch, June 18, 1991.
39. A.M. Rosenthal, Address, "The New York Times and the Pentagon Papers" 12–13 (accepting John Peter Zenger Award for Freedom of the Press and the People's Right to Know) (1971).
40. Karnow, *supra* note 16, at 398.
41. No matter how many contingency military plans were being drafted in the late summer of 1964, for example, President Johnson "was in no hurry to plunge into a conflict." *Id.*
42. Sanford J. Ungar, The Papers and The Papers 17–18 (Columbia Univ. Press, 1989); Gerald S. Strober & Deborah Hart Strober, Nixon: An Oral History of His Presidency 205 (Harper Collins, 1994).
43. Ungar, *supra* note 42, at 110; Strober & Strober, *supra* note 42, at 210–11.
44. *E.g.,* Kutler, *supra* note 7, at 108–12.
45. *New York Times Co. v. United States,* 403 U.S. 713, 727–40 (1971) (Stewart, J., concurring; White, J., concurring).
46. *Id.* at 729.
47. Floyd Abrams, *The Pentagon Papers a Decade Later,* N.Y. Times, June 7, 1981, § 6, at 22 (quoting Professor Benno Schmidt).

48. Ben Bradlee, A Good Life: Newspapering and Other Adventures 317 (Simon & Schuster, 1995).

49. Fred Emery, Watergate: The Corruption of American Politics and the Fall of Richard Nixon 72–73 (Times Books, 1994).

50. *Id.* at 52–53.

51. Conversation No. 24-124, May 15, 1972 (White House telephone).

52. Dan Baum, Smoke and Mirrors: The War on Drugs and the Politics of Failure 24-25 (Little, Brown, 1996).

53. *E.g.,* Kutler, *supra* note 7, at 115.

54. Conversation No. 739-11, June 21, 1972.

55. Richard M. Nixon, Six Crises 340 (Doubleday, 1962).

56. Stephen E. Ambrose, Nixon: Ruin and Recovery 1973–1990, 585 (Simon & Schuster, 1991) *("Nixon III")*.

57. Conversation No. 342-16.

58. Conversation No. 739-4. Nixon indeed had dramatically reduced the level of U.S. troops in Vietnam—from approximately 540,000 when he took office to around 140,000 by the end of 1971—and within six months Nixon would present the signed Paris Peace Accords.

59. Conversation No. 739-4.

60. Conversation No. 741-002.

61. Conversation No. 745-2, June 30, 1972.

62. *E.g.,* August 29, 1972 press conference.

63. H.R. Haldeman, The Haldeman Diaries: Inside the Nixon White House 704 (Berkley Books, 1995).

64. *E.g.,* Conversation No. 037-175, 176, Mar. 20, 1973; Conversation No. 886-008, Mar. 21, 1973; Conversation No. 422-020, Mar. 22, 1973; *see also* Conversation No. 855-010, Feb. 14, 1973.

65. Conversation No. 856-004, Feb. 14, 1973.

66. Haldeman, *supra* note 63, at 716.

67. *Id.* at 719.

68. *Id.* at 735.

69. Conversation No. 897-011, Apr. 16, 1973.

70. *See* Haldeman, *supra* note 63, at 813.

71. *See* Kutler, *supra* note 7, at 263.

72. Emery, *supra* note 49, at 367–68.

73. *Id.* at 277.

74. *See* Thomas C. Reeves, A Question of Character: A Life of John F. Kennedy 240, 244, 320 (Free Press, 1991).

75. Ambrose, *Nixon III, supra* note 56, at 335.

76. *United States v. Nixon,* 418 U.S. 683, 705 (1974).

77. J. Anthony Lukas, Nightmare: The Underside of the Nixon Years 559 (Viking Press, 1976), *cited in* Ambrose, *Nixon III, supra* note 56, at 419.

78. *U.S. Intelligence Agencies and Activities: Risks and Control of Foreign Intelligence: Hearings Before the House Select Committee on Intelligence* (Part 5), 94th Cong., 1st Sess. 1662 (1975) (statement of Rep. Robert McClory [R-Ill.]).

79. *Public Officials Integrity Act of 1977, Blind Trusts and Other Conflict of Interest Matters: Hearings Before the Senate Committee on Governmental Affairs,* 95th Cong., 1st Sess. 3 (1977).

80. *Id.* at 9 (statement of John M. Harmon, Acting Assistant Attorney General, Office of Legal Counsel, Department of Justice).

81. *E.g.,* Senate Committee on Governmental Affairs, S. Rep. No. 95-170 (1977), to accompany S. 555, at 6, 32, *reprinted in* 1978 U.S.C.C.A.N. 4216, 4222, 4248.

82. Karnow, *supra* note 16, at 415.

Chapter 5

1. Mark Twain, Following the Equator, flyleaf of first edition (American Publishing Co., 1897).

2. The Independent Counsel legislation is codified at 28 U.S.C.A. §§ 591–599 (West Supp. 1996). Its constitutionality was upheld in *Morrison v. Olson,* 487 U.S. 654 (1988). For some other views on the subject, see Symposium, *Addressing the Constitutionality of the Independent Counsel Statute,* 38 American University Law Review 255 (1989) (various authors); Beth Nolan, *Removing Conflicts of Interest from the Administration of Justice: Conflicts of Interest and Independent Counsels Under the Ethics in Government Act,* 79 Georgetown Law Journal 1 (1990); Stephen L. Carter, *The Independent Counsel Mess,* 102 Harvard Law Review 105 (1988).

3. *See* Harold J. Krent, *Executive Control over Criminal Law Enforcement: Some Lessons from History,* 38 American University Law Review 275 (1989). Krent correctly points out that, contrary to statements by Justice Scalia in his *Morrison v. Olson* dissent, criminal prosecution has never been a sole prerogative of the Executive. Nonetheless, the institutional differences between ordinary prosecutors and Independent Counsels remain significant—perhaps not from a separation-of-powers perspective, but certainly from a policy perspective.

4. The history of the Jordan affair is nicely summarized in Suzanne Garment's Scandal: The Culture of Mistrust in American Politics 50–56 (Times Books, 1991).

5. *United States v. Nofziger,* 878 F.2d 442 (D.C. Cir.), *cert. denied,* 493 U.S. 1003 (1989).

6. *The Deaver Case,* Wash. Post, Dec. 19, 1989, at A22.

7. Philip Sherman, *Deaver Prosecutor Seeks Paid Appearances to Discuss Ethics,* N.Y. Times, Sept. 19, 1988, at A20.

8. Though it is beyond the scope of this book, it is worth noting that the past several decades' dramatic improvement in surveillance technologies, coupled with the growth and increased complexity of federal criminal law over the same period, has exacerbated this problem in every context, not just the ethics-law area. It is now child's play to reconstruct an individual's movements, telephone contacts, purchases, and so forth using computer databases

often available to law enforcement officials without even the requirement of a search warrant. In addition, aerial (and sometimes even satellite) surveillance expands the reach further, again often without a warrant.

9. Reid Beddow, *Michael Deaver and the Perils of Power,* Wash. Post, Jan. 17, 1988, at X1.

10. Pub. L. No. 95-521, 92 Stat. 1824 (codified as amended in scattered sections of the United States Code).

11. 5 U.S.C.A. App. §§ 401–408 (West Supp. 1996).

12. 5 U.S.C.A. App. § 1–7 (West Supp. 1996).

13. Dwight Davis—Complimentary Airline Ticket—Official Travel, B-257704, Nov. 14, 1994. Federal employees could read about this edifying decision in Government Ethics Newsgram, Summer 1995, at 7. The same publication also told them about such details as the application of criminal conflict-of-interest statutes to high school students who work for the government in the summer (at 6), and the availability of a special video that "follows three SGEs [Special Government Employees] through many of the ethical hurdles they face in the course of their government service" (at 7).

14. Peter G. Crane, *Let My People Write,* Wash. Post, Feb. 8, 1994, at A19.

15. *United States v. National Treasury Employees Union,* 115 S. Ct. 1003 (1995).

16. Crane, *supra* note 14.

17. Brief of Amicus Curiae Common Cause in Support of Petitioners (No. 93-1170) (June 10, 1994).

18. Brief Amicus Curiae of Public Citizen, Inc. in Support of Respondent (July 29, 1994); Brief of Amici Curiae Freedom to Read Foundation, Association of American Publishers, Inc., People for the American Way, Pen American Center and the National Writers Union in Support of Respondents (July 28, 1994).

19. These observations on direct mail are based largely on the experience of one of us (Reynolds) as a board member and former chief executive officer of a nonprofit that raised nearly all of its funds by direct mail. For some writings on the subject, see Tracy Weber, *Making Politics Pay: Cashing in on Causes,* Los Angeles Times, Mar. 3, 1996, at A1; Tracy Weber, *Making Politics Pay: Trafficking in Donors' Names,* Los Angeles Times, Mar. 4, 1996, at A1; Matthew Ebnet, *Funding Crunch Is MADD's Driving Force,* Kansas City Star, Feb. 12, 1996, at A1. As usual, some of the most revealing accounts can be derived from insider trade publications. *See, e.g.,* Kevin Van Groesbeck, *4 Keys to Using Emotion,* Target Marketing, Feb. 1996, at 26; Jeffrey O'Brien, *Nonprofit Conscience Check,* Direct, June 1995, at 1.

20. Katherine Dunn, *Fibbers: The Lies Journalists Tell,* New Republic, June 21, 1993, at 18.

21. *Id.*

22. According to Larry Sabato, "the Watergate scandal . . . had the most profound impact of any modern event on the manner and substance of the press's conduct," and drew all sorts of new entrants to the journalistic field— in no small part because they saw Woodward and Bernstein played by Robert

Redford and Dustin Hoffman in the movie version of *All the President's Men*. Larry Sabato, Feeding Frenzy 61 (Free Press, 1991).

23. Ruth Marcus & Walter Pimus, *Enid Waldhotz: Savvy Politician or Duped Wife?* Wash. Post, Nov. 26, 1995, at A1.

24. Doug Bandow, *Ethics and Excellence: Cooperation and Integrity in Business,* 85 Business & Society Review 60 (1993).

25. *See* Gordon Adams, The Iron Triangle (Council of Economic Priorities, 1981). The term has spread to cover the relationship among special interests, bureaucrats, and congressional overseers in a variety of fields. *See, e.g.,* William Kristol, *Term Limitations: Breaking Up the Iron Triangle,* 16 Harvard Journal of Law and Public Policy 95 (1993); Harold McDougall, *Lawyering and the Public Interest in the 1990s,* 60 Fordham Law Review 1 (1991).

26. John Milton, Paradise Lost, Bk. II, lines 907–09 (London, 1667).

27. Eliza Newlin Carney, *Uneasy Umpires,* National Journal, May 18, 1996, at 20.

28. American Bar Association Committee on Government Standards, Cynthia Farina, Reporter, *Keeping Faith: Government Ethics and Government Ethics Regulation,* 45 Administrative Law Review 287, 290 (1993).

Chapter 6

1. *Quoted in* Geoffrey James, Business Wisdom of the Electronic Elite: 34 Winning Management Strategies From CEOs at Microsoft, COMPAQ, Sun, Hewlett-Packard, and Other Top Companies 189 (Times Business, 1996).

2. *Quoted in* Joseph L. Badaracco, Jr. & Allen Webb, *Business Ethics: A View From the Trenches,* 37 California Management Review 8 (1995).

3. Sallie Gaines, *Teaching Ethics: Uproar Makes B-Schools Bristle,* Chicago Tribune, May 17, 1987, at C1.

4. *See, e.g.,* Tad Tuleja, Beyond the Bottom Line: How Business Leaders Are Turning Principles into Profits ix (Facts on File, 1985) (over 2,000 business ethics articles were published from 1976 to 1980); Caroline Price, *Right or Wrong: Used to Be, Temptations Were of the Immoral, Illegal or Fattening Kind, Now They're Probably Unethical Too,* 6 Michigan Business 22 (Aug. 1989) (the Center for Business Ethics found a 500 percent increase in business ethics instruction between 1975 and 1980).

5. The President's Blue Ribbon Commission on Defense Management (the "Packard Commission") studied problems in the defense contracting area in depth in its Final Report to the President, "A Quest for Excellence," in June 1986. The government contracting scandals prompted the defense industry to reemphasize business ethics. (*See* Final Report pages 39 *et seq.,* and Appendix M, "Defense Industry Initiatives on Business Ethics and Conduct.")

6. *See, e.g.,* Thomas R. Piper, Mary C. Gentile & Sharon Daloz Parks, Can Ethics Be Taught? Perspectives, Challenges, and Approaches at Harvard Business School 118 & n.2 (Harvard Business School, 1993).

7. U.S. Sentencing Commission, Guidelines Manual, Chapter 8 (Nov. 1991).

8. *Ethics for Hire,* Business Week, July 15, 1996; Lynnette Khalfani, *Companies Making Big Expenditures on Ethics Training Programs,* Houston Chronicle, Aug. 11, 1996, at 10.

9. *Id.*

10. Only two factors can reduce the "culpability multiplier" that is used to calculate a convicted corporation's fine: cooperation with the prosecution and an effective program to prevent and detect violations of law. These factors can reduce a corporation's fine by as much as 90 percent. *See, e.g.,* Jeffrey W. Nunes, Comment, *Organizational Sentencing Guidelines: The Conundrum of Compliance Programs and Selfreporting,* 27 Arizona State Law Journal 1039, 1046 (1995). In certain cases, "compliance" can discourage the government altogether from prosecuting.

11. Manuel G. Valasquez, *Corporate Ethics: Losing It, Having It, Getting It,* in Peter Madsen & Jay M. Shafritz eds., Essentials of Business Ethics 228, 229 (Meridian, 1990). Some of the well-known companies that were convicted of multiple crimes include American Airlines, Ashland Oil, Bethlehem Steel, Braniff International, Diamond International, Firestone, Goodyear, Gulf Oil, International Paper, National Distillers, Northrop, Occidental Petroleum, Pepsico, Phillips Petroleum, R.J. Reynolds, Schlitz, Seagram, Tenneco, and United Brands.

12. Dan K. Webb & Stephen F. Molo, *Some Practical Considerations in Developing Effective Compliance Programs: A Framework for Meeting the Requirements of the Sentencing Guidelines,* 71 Washington University Law Quarterly 375, 375 (1993) (citing Columbia University Law School Professor John C. Coffee).

13. August 14, 1996 interview with Frank Navron, Ethics Resource Center, Washington, D.C.

14. *See generally* Carrie Mason-Draffen, *Rising Awareness Fuels Harassment Charges,* Newsday, Sept. 15, 1996, at F10; Kirstin Downey Grimsley, *Learning Where to Draw the Line; Lawsuits Spur Companies to Offer Special Training,* Wash. Post, Aug. 25, 1996, at H1; Saundra Torry, *Economy, Business, Government Fuel Hot Specialties,* Wash. Post, Jan. 1, 1996, at F7; Saundra Torry, *Harassment Case Award Strikes a Chord with Firms,* Wash. Post, Sept. 5, 1994.

15. Dan Cordtz, *ETHICSPLOSION!,* Financial World, Aug. 16, 1994, at 58.

16. Piper, Gentile & Parks, *supra* note 6, at 2.

17. *Id.*

18. Victor Futter, *An Answer to the Public Perception of Corporations: A Corporate Ombudsperson?* 46 Business Lawyer 29, 31 (1990).

19. *Id.*

20. Piper, Gentile & Parks, *supra* note 6, at 2.

21. *The Washington Post/*Kaiser Family Foundation/Harvard University Survey Project, "Why Don't Americans Trust the Government?" at 3 (1996).

22. Harrison Rainie, Margaret Lioftus & Mark Madden, *The State of Greed,* U.S. News & World Report, June 17, 1996, at 62 (citing a February 1996 Journal of Business Ethics study).

23. *See* Dwight R. Lee & Richard B. McKenzie, *How the Marketplace Fosters Business Honesty,* 92 Business & Society Review 5 (1995).

24. Patrick E. Murphy, *Corporate Ethics Statements: Current Status and Future Prospects,* 14 Journal of Business Ethics 727 (Sept. 1995).

25. *Id.*

26. *Id.; see also* Gary R. Weaver, *Corporate Codes of Ethics: Purpose, Process and Content Issues,* 32 Business and Society 44 (1993).

27. *Introductory Commentary* to Guidelines Manual, Chapter 8 (italics deleted).

28. *Id., Application Note* 3.(k) to § 8A1.2.

29. Weaver, *supra* note 26, at 44.

30. *See infra* note 53.

31. James Q. Wilson, *Capitalism and Morality,* Public Interest, Fall 1995, at 42.

32. Thomas C. Kohler, *Civil Virtue at Work: Unions as Seedbeds of the Civic Virtues, in* Mary Ann Glenden & David Blankenhorn, Seedbeds of Virtue: Sources of Competence, Character, and Citizenship in American Society 131 (Madison Books, 1995) (citing Juliet B. Schor, The Overworked American: The Unexpected Decline of Leisure 17–43 (Basic Books, 1991)).

33. *Ethics for Hire,* Business Week, July 15, 1996, at 26.

34. Stanley J. Modic, *Corporate Ethics; From Commandments to Commitment,* Industry Week, Dec. 14, 1987, at 33.

35. *Quoted in* Kurt Eichenwald, *The Two Faces of Texaco,* N.Y. Times, Nov. 10, 1996, § 3, at 1.

36. *See, e.g., id.*

37. Robert Jackall, Moral Mazes: The World of Corporate Managers (Oxford Univ. Press, 1988).

38. *Id.* at 6.

39. *Id.* at 59.

40. *See id.* at 22, 56, 59.

41. *See id.* at 59, 87–89, 111, 133, 141, 147.

42. *Id.* at 111.

43. Badaracco & Webb, *supra* note 2, at 8.

44. *Id.* The interviewees had all taken an elective course on business ethics while at Harvard, and thus could arguably be seen to represent a disproportionately "sensitive" sample. But the results of the interviews are consistent with other data from larger sample studies. *See id.* at n.3.

45. Michael Lewis, Liar's Poker: Rising Through the Wreckage on Wall Street 70 (Penguin Books, 1990).

46. H.J. Aibel, *Corporate Counsel and Business Ethics: A Personal Review,* 59 Missouri Law Review 427, 435 (1994).

47. Peter F. Drucker, *Ethical Chic,* Forbes, Sept. 14, 1981, at 160.

48. James Fallows, Breaking the News: How the Media Undermine American Democracy 10–16 (Pantheon, 1996).

49. Thomas J. Peters & Robert H. Waterman, Jr., In Search of Excellence: Lessons from America's Best-Run Companies 8 (Warner Books, 1982).

50. Hedrick Smith, Rethinking America xxi (Random House, 1995).

51. *E.g.,* Geoffrey James, Business Wisdom of the Electronic Elite (Times Business, 1996).

52. Smith, *supra* note 50, at 34–35.

53. The Johnson & Johnson story also teaches how ethics codes *can* work well when they *reinforce* the actual message that management *both* intends to communicate *and* in fact does communicate, by words and deeds throughout all levels of the organization—just as, Adam Smith observed, "custom and fashion" can heighten our moral sentiments when they happily coincide with "natural principles of right and wrong." Since the 1940s, Johnson & Johnson has had a relatively simple corporate Credo. The Credo's opening sentence announces the company's "first responsibility." It is "to the doctors, nurses and patients, to mothers and fathers and all others who use our products and services." (For the complete text of the Credo, see Francis J. Aguilar, Managing Corporate Ethics: Learning from America's Ethical Companies How to Supercharge Business Performance 66 (Oxford Univ. Press, 1994).) This duty was tested as the Tylenol crisis unfolded in 1982. As it turns out, Johnson & Johnson at the time had "dozens of people making hundreds of decisions and all on the fly." *Id.* at 67. These decisions were mutually reinforcing and were all directed toward protecting the consumers of Johnson & Johnson's products. This happened because the decision makers independently believed that the company truly wanted them to think of consumers first. *Id.* at 67–68; *see also* Tuleja, *supra* note 4, at 78–79; Valasquez, *supra* note 11, at 235–36. So, the businessmen erred on the side of safety and good citizenship. Yet Johnson & Johnson had been pounding away at its employees for half a century that the company means what it says in its Credo, especially in the "first principle."

54. Tuleja, *supra* note 4, at 11 (quoting an unnamed business writer).

55. Harvey L. Pitt & Karl A. Goskaufmanis, *When Bad Things Happen to Good Companies: A Crisis Management Primer,* 15 Cardozo Law Review 951, 951 (1994).

56. Jackall, *supra* note 37, at 141.

57. For a long-term study of a group of sixty-four "ethical resisters" whom the authors describe as acting from appropriate moral motives, see Myron Peretz Glazer & Penina Migdal Glazer, The Whistleblowers: Exposing Corruption in Government and Industry (Basic Books, 1989).

58. *See* Deborah Frazier, *Whistleblower Angers Farmers,* Rocky Mountain News, May 4, 1995, at 14A.

59. *Frederick v. Department of Justice,* 73 F.3d 349 (Fed. Cir. 1996).

60. *Serrao v. Merit Systems Protection Board,* No. 95-3562, 1996 U.S. App. LEXIS 24402 (Fed. Cir. Sept. 17, 1996).

61. *Ward v. Merit Systems Protection Board,* 981 F.2d 521 (Fed. Cir. 1992).

62. *Szepesi v. Department of Agriculture,* No. 94-3439, 1995 U.S. App. LEXIS 5079 (Fed. Cir. Mar. 14, 1995).

63. Ellen Newborne, *Whistle-Blowers Pipe Up More Frequently,* USA Today, July 22, 1996, at 28.

64. *See, e.g.,* Aguilar, *supra* note 53, at 7–15, 150; Peters & Waterman, *supra* note 49, at 122, 218.

65. Andrew W. Singer, *1-800-SNITCH; Corporate Hot Lines,* 32 Across the Board 16 (Sept. 1995).

66. *Id.*

67. *Id.*

68. *See generally* Tuleja, *supra* note 4, at 174–75.

69. Ralph Nader, *The Anatomy of Whistle-Blowing, in* Madsen & Shafritz, *supra* note 11, at 152, 157.

70. 31 U.S.C. §§ 3729–3731 (1994).

71. The Financial Institutions Reform, Recovery and Enforcement Act of 1989 (FIRREA) provides rewards to whistle-blowers in connection with savings and loan frauds, and the Insider Trading Sanctions Act authorizes the SEC to offer rewards for information leading to civil insider-trading penalties.

72. *See, e.g.,* Dee De Pass, *He Never Gave Up,* Star Tribune, Dec. 14, 1995, at 1D.

73. Calvin Sims, *Trying to Mute the Whistle-Blowers,* N.Y. Times, Apr. 11, 1994, at D1 (describing Metwest former sales manager Christopher (Jack) Dowden); *see also* Mark Pazniokos, *Document Shows How UTC Tried to Limit Report of Fraud,* Hartford Courant, June 26, 1994, at A1 ($22.5 million award to Douglas D. Keeth, formerly of United Technology Corporation's Sikorsky Aircraft Division).

74. Http://www.whistleblowers.com.

75. Richard C. Paddock, *Whistle-Blower Still Shaking up Stanford,* L.A. Times, Feb. 14, 1992, at A3.

76. Marcia Barinaga, *John Dingell Takes on Stanford,* Science, Feb. 15, 1991, at 734.

77. *Crown Jewels at Risk,* N.Y. Times, Feb. 9, 1992, at 4–16.

78. October 17, 1994 Statement, *quoted in* David Folkenflik, *What Happened to Stanford's Expense Scandal?* Sun (Baltimore), Nov. 20, 1994, at 4F. Ultimately, a federal district court in California agreed with Stanford that federal employees such as Biddle should not be entitled to rewards under the False Claims Act. Other federal courts have reached the opposite conclusion, however. As of this writing the issue remains in doubt.

79. Paddock, *supra* note 75.

80. *Id.*

81. *Film View: My Hero May Be Your Stoolie,* N.Y. Times, Aug. 27, 1989, at 2–1.

82. Modic, *supra* note 34, at 53.

83. Piper, Gentile & Parks, *supra* note 6, at 92.

Chapter 7

1. Isaac Asimov, Foundation 112 (Doubleday, 1966).

2. See, for example, the Supreme Court's opinion in *Edwards v. Aguillard,* 482 U.S. 578 (1987), which struck down a statute requiring the teaching of "creation science" on the ground that it was religious interference with science

forbidden by the First Amendment. *See also* Steven Goldberg, *The Reluctant Embrace: Law and Science in America,* 75 Georgetown Law Journal 1241 (1987).

3. For a discussion of such protections, see Richard Delgado & David Millen, *God, Galileo & Government: Toward Constitutional Protection for Scientific Inquiry,* 53 Washington & Lee Law Review 349 (1978); John A. Robertson, *The Scientists' Right to Research: A Constitutional Analysis,* 51 Southern California Law Review 1203 (1978); James R. Ferguson, *Scientific Inquiry and the First Amendment,* 64 Cornell Law Review 639 (1979).

4. Steven Goldberg, Culture Clash: Law and Science in America 62 (NYU Press, 1994). Goldberg's book contains clear and up-to-date discussions of all of the issues discussed in this paragraph.

5. Yale law professor Stephen L. Carter has argued that sometimes the answer to this question should be no. Stephen L. Carter, *The Bellman, the Snark, and the Biohazard Debate,* 3 Yale Law & Policy Review 358 (1985). Carter has, however, come under significant criticism for this attitude. *See, e.g.,* Lewis Thomas, *Introduction: Regulating Biotechnology,* 3 Yale Law & Policy Review 309, 310 (1985); Goldberg, *supra* note 4, at 182–84.

6. *See generally* Robert J. Levine, Ethics and Regulation of Clinical Research (Urban & Schwarzenberg, 1981); *see also* Charles W. Lidz et al., Informed Consent: A Study of Decisionmaking in Psychiatry (Guilford Press, 1984).

7. James Gleick's biography of Richard Feynman, Genius (Vintage, 1993), gives a good sense of the prewar era. Before the war,

> The membership of the American Physical Society still fell shy of two thousand, though it had doubled in a decade. Teaching at a college or working for the government in, most likely, the Bureau of Standards or the Weather Bureau, a physicist might expect to earn a good wage of from three thousand to six thousand dollars a year.

Id. at 53. Research budgets were still measured in the thousands of dollars. After the war, on the other hand,

> Science as an institution—organized science—ranked second only to the military as a guarantor of what was being called national security. President Harry S Truman told the Congress that fall that America's role in the world would depend directly on research coordinated by universities, industrial companies and the government: "The events of the past few years are both proof and prophecy of what science can do."

Id. at 209.

8. *Id.*

9. Robert Wilson, *Book Review,* Scientific American, Dec. 1958, at 145.

10. There is an extensive literature on the subject of science fraud and misconduct, going far beyond the short historical summary here. For more on the

subject, see William J. Broad & Nicholas Wade, Betrayers of the Truth (Simon & Schuster, 1982); Research Fraud in the Behavioral and Biomedical Sciences (David J. Miller & Michel Hersen eds., John Wiley & Sons, 1992).

11. For more on the Summerlin affair, see Broad & Wade, *supra* note 10, at 153–57; Joseph Hixson, The Patchwork Mouse (Doubleday, 1976).

12. Broad & Wade, *supra* note 10, at 158–60.

13. *Id.* at 63–73.

14. *Fraud in Biomedical Research: Hearings Before the Subcommittee on Investigations and Oversight of the Committee on Science and Technology,* U.S. House of Representatives, 97th Congress, March 31, April 1, 1981 (U.S. Govt. Printing Office No. 77–661, 1981).

15. *Quoted in* Broad & Wade, *supra* note 10, at 11.

16. *Id.*

17. *Id.* at 86–87.

18. Daniel E. Koshland, Jr., *Fraud in Science,* 235 Science 141 (1987).

19. James H. Jones, Bad Blood: The Tuskegee Syphilis Experiment (Free Press, 1993).

20. Barbara Culliton, *Inside the Gallo Probe,* 248 Science 1494 (1990); Kathy A. Fakcelmann, *Trouble in the Laboratory: Probing the Science of a Controversial Paper,* 137 Science News 200 (1990).

21. Broad & Wade, *supra* note 10, at 12.

22. 42 U.S.C. § 289b (1988), Pub. L. No. 99–158, 99 Stat. 874. In 1993, this section was amended to provide specifically for the creation of the Office of Research Integrity. 42 U.S.C. § 289b (1988 & Supp. 1995), Pub. L. No. 103–43, 107 Stat. 140, 142 (1993).

23. 42 C.F.R. § 50.102 (1993). The guidelines, however, explicitly exclude "honest error or honest differences in interpretations or judgments of data" from this definition. *Id.* For more on the development of this standard, see Elizabeth Howard, *Scientific Misconduct and Due Process: A Case of Process Due,* 45 Hastings Law Journal 309 (1994).

24. For example, the Office of Management and Budget, which reviews most proposed regulations, commented on the draft that "your proposal goes beyond the mandate of Section 493 of the Public Health Services Act, which deals with scientific fraud, by attempting to regulate the broader area of scientific misconduct." *Id.* at 318 n.52; *see also* Robert M. Andersen, *The Federal Government's Role in Regulating Misconduct in Scientific and Technological Research,* 3 Journal of Law & Technology 121 (1988).

25. Malcolm Gladwell, *The Fraud Fraud: Up Close, the Alleged Sins of Scientists Look Minor,* Wash. Post, Nov. 14, 1993, at C1.

26. *See generally id.*; Steve Twedt, *Minor Error Brought On Costly, Grueling Ordeal,* Pittsburgh Post-Gazette, Dec. 28, 1994; John Schwartz, *U.S. Loses Science Fraud Case on Appeal,* Wash. Post, Aug. 11, 1993, at A13; Michell Ruess, *Panel Clears Clinic, Researcher of Misconduct,* Cleveland Plain Dealer, Aug. 12, 1993, at 11A.

27. Twedt, *supra* note 26; also telephone interview with Steve Twedt, journalist, Aug. 24, 1995.

28. According to Healy, Dingell "never would have been interested in the Sharma case if I hadn't been NIH director." *Id.*

29. John D. Dingell, *Misconduct in Medical Research,* 328 New England Journal of Medicine 1610–15 (1993).

30. Twedt, *supra* note 27.

31. Schwartz, *supra* note 26.

32. Gladwell, *supra* note 25.

33. Mika Popovic et al., *Detection, Isolation and Continuous Production of Cytopathic Retroviruses (HTLV-III) from Patients with AIDS and Pre-AIDS,* 224 Science 497 (1984) (first of four key papers).

34. Gladwell, *supra* note 25.

35. *Id.*

36. *Id.*

37. *Id.*

38. As Bernadine Healy recounts, "My staff saw the contents of a computer used exclusively by one of these employees. It contained drafts of demanding letters from Mr. Dingell to me—and to the Secretary and Assistant Secretary of Health and Human Services—about the inquiry, as well as a near-complete draft of what was to be the subcommittee's report on Dr. Gallo. As if all this were taken from 'The Wizard of Oz,' an N.I.H. bureaucrat appeared to be ghost-writing the intimidating word of the mighty Congressional chairman." Bernadine Healy, *The Dangers of Trial by Dingell,* N.Y. Times, July 3, 1996, at A23.

39. Daniel J. Kevles, *The Assault on David Baltimore,* New Yorker, May 27, 1996, at 94, 102. The Kevles article is the best single source from among the enormous literature on the Baltimore/Imanishi-Kari affair. For some other useful accounts, see Gina Kolata, *A Venomous Rift in U.S. Science,* International Herald Tribune, June 27, 1996; Maxine Singer, *Assault on Science,* Wash. Post, June 26, 1996, at A21; David Warsh, *Left Alone, Science Heals Itself,* Chicago Tribune, July 1, 1996, at 4.

40. Singer, *supra* note 39.

41. *Scientists' Legal Aid,* Legal Times, July 1, 1996, at 3.

42. *Quoted in* Rick Weiss, *Proposed Shifts in Misconduct Reviews Unsettle Many Scientists,* Wash. Post, June 30, 1996, at A6.

43. *Quoted in* Kolata, *supra* note 39.

44. Gladwell, *supra* note 25.

45. Gleick, *supra* note 7, *passim.*

46. Goldberg, *supra* note 4, at 13.

47. This is discussed in Glenn Reynolds, *Between Pilate and Galileo,* 35 Jurimetrics: Journal of Law, Science & Technology 349 (1995).

48. *See, e.g.,* Michael H. Graham, Federal Practice and Procedure: Federal Rules of Evidence § 6822 (interim edition Supp. 1995).

Chapter 8

1. N.Y. Times, June 6, 1980, at A28.
2. Ellen M. Kozak, *The ABCs of Avoiding Plagiarism,* Writer's Digest, July 1993, at 40.
3. Alexander Lindey, Plagiarism and Originality 64–65 (Harper & Bros., 1952). Lindey's book is probably the most influential single work on plagiarism. For other useful treatments, see Francoise Meltzer, Hot Property: The Stakes and Claims of Literary Originality (Univ. of Chicago Press, 1994); Thomas Mallon, Stolen Words: Forays into the Origins and Ravages of Plagiarism (Ticknor & Fields, 1989); K.R. St. Onge, The Melancholy Anatomy of Plagiarism 79–89 (University Press of America, 1988); Harold Ogden White, Plagiarism and Imitation During the English Renaissance (Harvard Univ. Press, 1935).
4. Lindey, *supra* note 3, at 64–65.
5. *Id.* (citing Alexander Pope).
6. *Quoted in id.*
7. White, *supra* note 3, at 16.
8. A good summary of the classical theory of imitation is contained in White, *supra* note 3, at 3–19; *see also* Lindey, *supra* note 3, at 62–77.
9. Harold Ogden White notes that Thomas Churchyard spent the latter part of the sixteenth century arguing that those who practiced the classical theory of imitation were thieves. White also notes that "he alone of all English writers before 1600 takes this position." White points out that Churchyard accused all and sundry of stealing his rather uninspired (if original) work, although White also comments that Churchyard is rather vague on "[w]ho stole from him, and what, and, hardest of all to explain, *why.*" White, *supra* note 3, at 117. Churchyard also thundered against poets who tried to exalt themselves by tearing down their competitors, though White notes that "as far as extant works show, the only Elizabethan whom this description fits is Churchyard himself." *Id.* at 116.
10. According to Harold Ogden White, Shakespeare's

> practise of imitative composition is too well known to require comment. It is a commonplace to say that the originality of his genius never appears more clearly than when one of his works is compared with the sources which he found useful in writing it. Whatever he wanted, he took; the results compose the best possible body of proof for the classical theory that literary excellence depends, not on the writer's ability to fabricate plots, but on his power to do something original *with* a plot, wherever he gets it.

> *Id.* at 106.

11. Mallon, *supra* note 3, at 24.
12. *Id.* at 3–4.
13. Lindey, *supra* note 3, at 2.

14. *Id.* at 63.
15. *Id.* at 60.
16. Joseph Gibaldi & Walter Achtert, MLA Handbook 4 (Modern Lang. Ass'n., 1980).
17. St. Onge, *supra* note 3, at 53 (italics added).
18. These quotations are from James Risen & Richard E. Meyer, *No Time to Cite Source, He Says: Biden Stirs Row by Using Lines from Briton's Talk,* Los Angeles Times, Sept. 13, 1987, at 1. *See also* Eleanor Randolph, *Plagiarism Suggestion Angers Biden's Aides,* Wash. Post, Sept. 13, 1987, at A6. For an insightful retrospective of Biden's problem, see St. Onge, *supra* note 3.
19. *Id.* at 81.
20. William Safire, *No Heavy Lifting,* N.Y. Times, Sept. 27, 1987, Magazine, at 12.
21. Jon Margolis, *For Joe Biden, as with Hart, It's the Stupidity that Hurts,* Chicago Tribune, Sept. 22, 1987, at 15.
22. Michael White, Washington correspondent for the *Manchester Guardian, quoted in* Randolph, *supra* note 18 (Kennedy); John Corry, *Senator Biden's Drama,* N.Y. Times, Sept. 21, 1987, at C18 ("Mr. Kinnock may have borrowed that time span from George Lucas: 'For a thousand generations the Jedi were the guardians of peace and justice.' That's media politics, too.").
23. St. Onge, *supra* note 3, at 81.
24. *Id.*
25. *Id.* at 88, 89.
26. *Quoted in* Mallon, *supra* note 3, at 119.
27. "And why beholdest thou the mote that is in thy brother's eye, but perceivest not the beam that is in thine own eye?" Luke 6:41.
28. *Quoted in* Richard Stone, *Feder and Stewart, Historian Trade Charges,* 260 Science 151 (1993). For other discussions of the plagiarism search, see Christopher Anderson, *Robocops: Stewart and Feder's Mechanized Misconduct Search,* 350 Nature 454–55, Apr. 11, 1991 (in particular, describing the plagiarism machine); Edward Dolnick, *Science Police,* Discover, Feb. 1994, at 56.
29. Dolnick, *supra* note 28, at 60.
30. David Streitfeld, *Plagiarism Ruling Has It Both Ways,* Wash. Post, Dec. 17, 1993, at C1, C6. The original of the Lindey quote appears in Lindey, *supra* note 3, at 60. In light of the popularity of the parallelism approach—and the way in which it is implemented in the Stewart and Feder detection scheme—it is worth setting out Lindey's warnings here:

> Whether the virtues of parallels outweigh the vices is open to debate. The fact remains that the vices are considerable.
>
> 1. Any method of comparison which lists and underscores similarities and suppresses or minimizes differences is necessarily misleading.
> 2. Parallels are too readily susceptible of manipulation. Superficial resemblances may be made to appear as of the essence.
> 3. Parallel-hunters do not, as a rule, set out to be truthful and impartial. They are hell-bent on proving a point.

4. Parallel-hunting is predicated on the use of lowest common denomina-
   tors. Virtually all literature, even the most original, can be reduced to
   such terms, and thereby shown to be unoriginal. So viewed, Mark
   Twain's *The Prince and the Pauper* plagiarizes Dickens' *David Copperfield*.
   Both deal with England, both describe the slums of London, both see
   their hero exalted beyond his original station. To regard any two books in
   this light, however, is to ignore every factor that differentiates one man's
   thoughts, reactions and literary expression from another's.
5. Parallel columns operate piecemeal. They wrench phrases and passages
   out of context. A product of the imagination is indivisible. It depends on
   totality of effect. To remove details from their setting is to falsify them.
6. Parallels fail to indicate the proportion which the purportedly borrowed
   material bears to the sum total of the source, or to the whole of the new
   work. Without such information a just appraisal is impossible.
7. The practitioners of the technique resort too often to sleight of hand.
   They employ language, not to record facts or to describe things accurately, but as props in a rhetorical hocus-pocus which, by describing different things in identical words, appears to make them magically alike.
8. A double-column analysis is a dissection. An autopsy will reveal a great
   deal about a cadaver, but very little about the spirit of the man who once
   inhabited it.
9. Most parallels rest on the assumption that if two successive things are
   similar, the second one was copied from the first. This assumption disregards all the other possible causes of similarity.

Id. at 60–61. Unfortunately, Lindey concludes, "Whatever his vices or
virtues, the parallel-hunter is a hardy species. He is destined, as someone has
said, to persist until Judgment Day, when he will doubtless find resemblances
in the very warrant that consigns him to the nether regions." *Id.* at 61.

31. *Id.*
32. *See* Jeffery Mervis, *NIH Takes Stewart and Feder off the Misconduct Beat,* 362
    Nature 686 (1993); Richard Stone, *Stewart and Feder Report for Desk Duty,*
    262 Science 19 (1993); *Two Scientific Watchdogs Are Leashed,* USA Today,
    Mar. 30, 1994, at 5D.
33. Lindey, *supra* note 3, at 53–54.
34. *Id.*
35. *Id.* at 61.
36. Andrew Rosenthal, *Two Top Aides to Dukakis Resign as One Admits Role in
    Biden Tape,* N.Y. Times, Oct. 1, 1987, at A1.
37. Edwin M. Yoder, Jr., *Hand-Me-Down Speeches,* Wash. Post, Sept. 22, 1987, at
    A21.
38. Charles Krauthammer, *In Defense of Joe Klein,* Weekly Standard, Aug. 5,
    1996, at 12.
39. Daniel J. Boorstin, The Image: A Guide to Pseudo-Events in America 19
    (Vintage, 1992).

40. *Id.*
41. Jerry Walker, *Majority of News Directors Air VNRs,* Jack O'Dwyer's Newsletter, Mar. 6, 1996, at 3.
42. Jack O'Dwyer, *Editorial,* Jack O'Dwyer's Newsletter, Mar. 30, 1994, at 8:

> This is the blindness of the print media, which uses tons of material from press releases every day without mentioning it in any way. The Columbia Journalism Review several years ago found that major dailies carry lengthy press releases with only a light rewriting. Some of the papers even attach bylines and datelines to the releases, making it look like the entire story was the work of an industrious, onsite reporter.

43. Nicholas Schoon, *Covering Itself in Glory: Greenpeace Has Hit the Headlines Again—But this Time the Media Claim They Have Been Duped,* Independent, Sept. 5, 1995, at 15.
44. Kevin Brass, *Press Release Use Causes Stir in Tribune Newsroom,* Los Angeles Times, July 17, 1989, § 6, at 2. The quote is from *Tribune* deputy editor Bob Witty.
45. Jay Levinson & Seth Godin, Guerrilla Marketing for the Home-Based Business 48 (Houghton Mifflin, 1995).
46. Interview with Professor Candace McKearney White, University of Tennessee Journalism Department, and material provided by Professor White.

Chapter 9

1. James B. Stewart, *The Illegal Loan,* New Yorker, July 15, 1996, at 36, 37 (the exchange occurred at a local restaurant in Little Rock, Arkansas between Jim McDougal and a high-school student).
2. *E.g.,* John C. Coffee, Jr., *From Tort to Crime: Some Reflections on the Criminalization of Fiduciary Breaches and the Problematic Line Between Law and Ethics,* 19 American Criminal Law Review 117, 119–26 (1981); Kathleen F. Brickey, *Corporate Criminal Liability: A Primer for Corporate Counsel,* 40 Business Lawyer 129 (1994).
3. Geraldine Szott Moohr, *Mail Fraud and the Intangible Rights Doctrine: Someone to Watch Over Us,* 31 Harvard Journal on Legislation 153, 164 n.40 (1993).
4. *See The Key Points,* Newsweek, Oct. 4, 1976, at 38.
5. Moohr, *supra* note 3, at 154.
6. *See, e.g.,* John C. Coffee, Jr., *Does "Unlawful" Mean "Criminal"? Reflections on the Disappearing Tort/Crime Distinction in American Law,* 71 Boston University Law Review 193, 194 & n.3 (1991) (citing, for example, T. Tyler, Why People Obey The Law (1990)).
7. 18 U.S.C. § 1951. The Hobbs Act makes it a crime for anyone to obstruct, delay, or affect commerce or movement of any article or commodity in commerce by robbery or extortion. The law defines extortion as the "obtaining of

property from another, with his consent, induced by wrongful use of actual or threatened force, violence, or fear, or under color of official right."

8. 18 U.S.C. §§ 1341, 1343, 1346.

9. 18 U.S.C. § 1961 *et seq.*

10. *See generally* Robert N. Roberts, *The Federalization of "Grass Roots" Corruption; Fighting Corruption with Federal Laws,* 66 Spectrum: The Journal of State Government 6 (1993).

11. 18 U.S.C. § 1346.

12. *United States v. Mandel,* 591 F.2d 1347, 1361 (4th Cir.), *aff'd on reh'g en banc,* 602 F.2d 653 (4th Cir. 1979), *cert. denied,* 445 U.S. 961 (1980).

13. 591 F.2d at 1366, 1380–81.

14. *Id.* at 1366.

15. *United States v. Bronston,* 658 F.2d 920, 926 (2d Cir. 1981).

16. Record at 1242–43, *quoted in* Coffee, *supra* note 2, at 132.

17. *Meinhard v. Salmon,* 249 N.Y. 458, 465, 164 N.E. 545, 546 (1928).

18. For a discussion of fiduciary theory and government ethics, see Kathleen Clark, *Do We Have Enough Ethics in Government Yet?: An Answer from Fiduciary Theory,* 1996 University of Illinois Law Review 57 (1996).

19. Coffee, *supra* note 2, at 143.

20. *United States v. Margiotta,* 688 F.2d 108 (2d Cir. 1982), *cert. denied,* 461 U.S. 913 (1983).

21. 483 U.S. 350 (1987).

22. *Id.* at 360.

23. For an excellent discussion of the importance of the rule of law in criminal cases, see John C. Jeffries, Jr., *Legality, Vagueness, and the Construction of Penal Statutes,* 71 Virginia Law Review 189 (1985).

24. *United States v. Mandel,* 591 F.2d at 1361.

25. *See* Craig M. Bradley, *Supreme Court Review: Forward: Mail Fraud After McNally and Carpenter,* 79 Journal of Criminal Law & Criminology 573, 573–74 (1988).

26. The provision is codified at 18 U.S.C. § 1346.

27. *See, e.g., United States v. Sawyer,* 85 F.3d 713, 728 (1st Cir. 1996) (vacating the mail-fraud conviction of an insurance lobbyist who had violated "a prophylactic civil prohibition [a state gift law] that addresses appearances of— but not actual—corruption").

28. *See* National Collegiate Athletic Association, 1991–92 NCAA Manual §§ 13.6.2.2–13.6.2.9 (1991).

29. Landis Cox, Note, *Targeting Sports Agents with the Mail Fraud Statute: United States v. Norby Walters & Lloyd Bloom,* 41 Duke Law Journal 1157, 1178 & n.115 (1992) (citing NCAA Const. art. 3, § 3(a)).

30. Steve Fiffer, *College Sports; Agents' Trial: Why Bother?* N.Y. Times, Apr. 16, 1989, § 8, at 5, col. 1.

31. Cox, *supra* note 29, at 1178.

32. *Id.* at 1179 & nn. 119, 122 (footnote omitted).

33. *See* Douglas S. Looney, *Cash, Check or Charge?* Sporting News, July 1, 1996,

at 38, 41 (citing a recent speech by Father Theodore Hesburgh, former Notre Dame president).

34. Fiffer, *supra* note 30.
35. Comments of Stanley S. Arkin at October 1990 conference at George Mason University, *cited in* Thomas Leary, *The Commission's New Option that Favors Judicial Discretion in Sentencing,* 3 Federal Sentencing Reports 142, 144 n.10 (1990).
36. 18 U.S.C. § 371.
37. James V. DeLong, *New Crimes, High Fines: The Criminalization of Nearly Everything,* 365 Current 21 (Sept. 1994).
38. Stephen J. Adler & Wade Lambert, *Common Criminals: Just About Everyone Violates Some Laws, Even Model Citizens,* Wall St. J., Mar. 12, 1993, at 1.
39. Linda Greenhouse, *Law Ill-Equipped for Politics,* N.Y. Times, Dec. 28, 1992, at A1.
40. James Fallows, Breaking the News 134 (Pantheon, 1996).
41. *Independent Counsel Has a Lonely Role,* Los Angeles Times, Jan. 31, 1987, at 5, col. 1.
42. *MacNeil/Lehrer Newsshow: Newsmaker Interview* (PBS television broadcast, April 12, 1990); *see also Has Case Peaked with Poindexter?* N.Y. Times, Apr. 15, 1990, at E7, col. 3; Lawrence Walsh, *Secretary and the Rule of Law,* 43 Oklahoma Law Review 583, 588–90 (1990).
43. The false-statement statute provides:

> Whoever, in any matter within the jurisdiction of any department or agency of the United States knowingly and willfully falsifies, conceals or covers up by any trick, scheme, or device a material fact, or makes any false, fictitious or fraudulent statements or representations, or makes or uses any false writing or document knowing the same to contain any false, fictitious or fraudulent statement or entry, shall be fined not more than $10,000 or imprisoned not more than five years, or both.

44. The provision was revised somewhat and codified in 1948, when Congress enacted the Criminal Code. The revisions and codification further support the points made in the following pages concerning the statute's inapplicability to statements made to federal courts or Congress. For a fuller discussion of the statute's legislative history and other points made herein, see Peter W. Morgan, *The Undefined Crime of Lying to Congress: Ethics Reform and the Rule of Law,* 86 Northwestern University Law Review 177 (1992).
45. *United States v. Yermian,* 468 U.S. 63, 82 (1984) (Rehnquist, Brennan, Stevens & O'Connor, JJ., dissenting).
46. For example, FDR would have been subject to prosecution for misrepresenting Nazi torpedo attacks on the U.S. destroyer *Greer* as unprovoked; Eisenhower for his denials of any U.S. role in helping insurgents in Indonesia as well as for his famous disavowal in the U-2 incident; Kennedy and Johnson, *inter alia,* for statements on Vietnam; Nixon, take your pick; Reagan, Iran-

contra; and Bush if you believe Rep. Henry Gonzalez's "Iraqgate" accusation that Bush misled Congress in 1990 by falsely fingering only European companies (and not U.S. suppliers) for arming Iraq.

47. *Hubbard v. United States,* 115 S. Ct. 1754 (1995).
48. The False Statements Accountability Act of 1996, Pub. L. No. 104–292.
49. *E.g.,* Comprehensive Crime Control Act of 1984, Anti-Drug Abuse Act of 1986, Anti-Drug Abuse Act of 1988, Crime Control Act of 1990, and (after a gun-control filibuster in 1992) Violent Crimes Control and Law Enforcement Act of 1994.
50. Glenn Harlan Reynolds, *Kids, Guns, and the Commerce Clause: Is the Court Ready for Constitutional Government?* CATO Policy Analysis No. 216, Oct. 10, 1994.
51. *E.g.,* 4 Va. Code Ann. § 18.2–344 (1966 repl. vol.). Courts typically refuse to entertain civil lawsuits challenging the laws (at least when brought by heterosexuals) on the ground that there is no real legal controversy because no one actually expects state officials to enforce them. *See, e.g., Doe v. Duling,* 782 F.2d 1202 (4th Cir. 1986) (refusing to hear challenge to Virginia's fornication statute).
52. Pub. L. No. 101–131, 103 Stat. 777 (amending 18 U.S.C. § 700).
53. 491 U.S. 397 (1989).
54. Robert Justin Goldstein, *The Great 1989–1990 Flag Flap: An Historical, Political, and Legal Analysis,* 45 University of Miami Law Review 13, 30 (1990).
55. *Remember Flag Burning? Congress Does,* U.S. News & World Report, Apr. 3, 1995, at 12.
56. Goldstein, *supra* note 54, at 102 (quoting University of Michigan historian Terrence McDonald).
57. *Id.*
58. *Id.* at 78.
59. *Id.* at 100 (citing Kennedy & Dewar, *Ruling Rekindles Amendment Debate,* Wash. Post, June 12, 1990, at A7, col. 1).
60. *My Flag, Your Shorts,* Time, July 3, 1995, at 62.
61. Goldstein, *supra* note 54, at 105.
62. James Q. Wilson, *Drugs and Crime, in* 13 Drugs and Crime 521, 543 (Michael Tonry & James Q. Wilson eds., Univ. of Chicago Press, 1990).
63. *Id.*
64. James Bowman, *The Spectator,* Jan. 27, 1990, *reprinted in* On Drugs: Opposing Viewpoints (Greenhaven Press, 1990).
65. Dan Brown, Smoke and Mirrors: The War on Drugs and the Politics of Failure 45 (Little, Brown, 1996); *see also* Mark H. Moore, *Supply Reduction and Drug Law Enforcement, in* 13 Drugs and Crime, *supra* note 62, at 109, 152–53.
66. James Bovard, Lost Rights: The Destruction of American Liberty 202 (St. Martin's Press, 1994).
67. Stuart Taylor, Jr., *Ten Years for Two Ounces,* American Lawyer, Mar. 1990, at 65.

68. Mark A.R. Kleiman & Kerry D. Smith, *State and Local Drug Enforcement: In Search of a Strategy, in* 13 Drugs and Crime, *supra* note 62, at 69, 98.

69. *Id.*

70. *See* Taylor, *supra* note 67, at 65.

71. Bovard, *supra* note 66, at 5.

72. *Id.* at 213.

73. *Id.*

74. *California's Prisons: Too Close for Comfort,* Economist, May 4, 1996, at 24.

75. *Violent and Irrational—and That's Just the Policy,* Economist, June 8, 1996, at 23, 25.

76. Stuart Taylor, Jr., *How A Racist Drug Swells Violent Crime,* American Lawyer, Apr. 1993, at 31.

77. *See generally* Thomas Muhammad, *National Concerns About Terrorism Are Misdirected,* Dallas Morning News, Aug. 21, 1996, at 23A (citing FBI data); Chitra Ragavan, *Experts Give Conflicting Reports on Rise of Terrorism,* All Things Considered (National Public Radio) (Aug. 7, 1996) (citing State Department report, *Patterns of Global Terrorism,* and former State Department Counterterrorism expert Larry Johnson).

78. James K. Glassman, *Hiding Behind the Smoke,* Wash. Post, June 18, 1996, at A13; *see also* Dick Feagler, *More Heat than Light on Black Church Fires,* Plain Dealer, June 21, 1996, at 2A.

Chapter 10

1. Scott Adams, The Dilbert Principle 269 (HarperBusiness, 1996).

2. James F. Dunnigan, How to Make War: A Comprehensive Guide to Modern Warfare 15 (Quill, 1983).

3. *Embrace Crunchiness,* Economist, Aug. 27, 1988, at 13.

4. Dunnigan, *supra* note 2, at 217.

5. *Id.* at 216.

6. For more on this, see *id.* at 240–48.

7. The Federalist No. 45, *in* Clinton Rossiter ed., The Federalist Papers 292 (Mentor, 1961).

8. Peter Pitts, *Wrong Answers in "Dirty Little Secrets,"* Indianapolis Star, May 11, 1996, at A11.

9. For a discussion of these issues, see Glenn H. Reynolds, *Is Democracy like Sex?* 48 Vanderbilt Law Review 1635 (1995); Gary Lawson, *The Rise and Rise of the Administrative State,* 107 Harvard Law Review 1231 (1994); David Schoenbrod, Power Without Responsibility: How Congress Abuses the People Through Delegation (Yale Univ. Press, 1993).

10. Fred Barnes, *The Parasite Culture of Washington: Take the Money and Stay,* New Republic, July 28, 1986, at 16.

11. Telephone conversation with D.C. Bar membership office, August 19, 1996.

12. Jonathan Rauch, Demosclerosis: The Silent Killer of American Government (Times Books, 1994).

13. *Id.* at 54, 56.

14. *Id.* at 57.

15. George Will, *"Influence Peddlers" to "Implementers,"* St. Louis Post-Dispatch, Jan. 2, 1993, at 3B. It is worth noting that such interest groups need not be looking for government money. The "benefits" they seek may be the non-monetary ones of enacting a particular social or ideological agenda. The de-sire to order other people's lives is one that rivals greed in its appeal, and politicians may actually be *more* willing to give in to such groups since doing so—say, by enacting the sort of symbolic criminal legislation we discussed in "Crime Follies"—doesn't cost money.

16. For a clear and insightful discussion of the delegation issue, see Schoenbrod, *supra* note 9.

17. Rauch, *supra* note 12, at 54.

18. *Id.* at 72–73.

19. George Will, *Some CEOs Are Looting the Corporations They Head,* Atlanta Journal & Constitution, Sept. 3, 1991, at A9.

20. *Move Over Ben Chavis,* New Republic, Jan. 9, 1995, at 9.

21. David Samuels, *Philanthropical Correctness: The Failure of American Founda-tions,* New Republic, Sept. 18, 1995, at 28.

Chapter 11

1. *See generally* Claus Jensen, No Downlink (Farrar, Strauss, Giroux, 1996); Diane Vaughan, The Challenger Launch Decision (Univ. of Chicago Press, 1996). As Jensen notes (at 364–65), "The course of events in the years lead-ing up to the *Challenger* disaster demonstrates, quite conclusively, how diffi-cult it is for unpalatable information to penetrate large organization[s]. . . . The faintest consonant whisper will always get through, while any conflicting views or dissonant information will have to be shouted from the rooftops, or writ very large, if it is ever to be received."

2. As Jensen notes about NASA, what is truly frightening about the *Challenger* disaster is not that it disclosed an inept, bumbling organization, but that it disclosed that even organizations that are better run than average can still be bumbling and inept at times. "There is no reason for believing that the peo-ple at NASA or at Morton Thiokol were any meaner or more irresponsible than the average employee in any large, modern organization. On the con-trary, there is every reason to suppose that, in many instances, they have been far more conscientious, and that their testing and safety procedures have been better than average. . . . But the agency still did not manage to pick up all the warning signals in time; nor could it discern the overall pattern formed by countless tortuous relationships both inside and outside the organization—not until it was too late." Jensen, *supra* note 1, at 364.

3. *See* Jeff Elliott, *Drug Prevention Placebo: How DARE Wastes Time, Money, and Politics,* Reason, Mar. 1995, at 7 (arguing that, according to a National Insti-tute of Justice study, the D.A.R.E. drug education program provides the ap-

pearance of doing something about the drug problem, but that "DARE doesn't have a measurable effect on drug abuse").

4. As Madison wrote, "The powers delegated by the proposed Constitution to the federal government are few and defined." The Federalist, No. 45 (Madison).

5. Christina Hoff Sommers, *Teaching the Virtues: A Blueprint for Moral Education,* Chicago Tribune Sunday Magazine, Sept. 12, 1993, at 18.

6. Robert Frank, Passions Within Reason: The Strategic Role of the Emotions 19, 249–50 (W.W. Norton, 1988).

7. Henry Fielding, The History of Tom Jones: A Foundling 167 (Martin C. Battestin & Fredson Bowers eds., Wesleyan Univ. Press, 1975).

8. (Free Press, 1996).

9. *Id.* at 162.

10. *Id.* at 136.

11. *Id.* at 65.

12. *Id.* at 156.

13. Stephen E. Ambrose, Eisenhower: Soldier and President 11 (Simon & Schuster, 1990).

14. *Id.*

15. Richard M. Nixon, *quoted in* Stephen E. Ambrose, Nixon: Ruin and Recovery, 1973–1990, 590 (Simon & Schuster, 1991).

16. 2 Henry Fielding, *Articles in the Champion, in Miscellaneous Writings, in* 15 The Complete Works of Henry Fielding, Esq. 167 (1903) (1793).

17. Fielding, *supra* note 7, at 344.

Appendix

1. Larry Ault, *Hale Co-Defendant Asks that Casey Prosecute His Case,* Arkansas Democrat-Gazette, Mar. 22, 1994, at 9A.

2. James B. Stewart, Blood Sport: The President and His Adversaries 411 (Simon & Schuster, 1996).

3. Daniel Klaidman, *Bennett Brings Clinton Firepower, Some Baggage,* Legal Times, May 9, 1994, at 1.

4. Independent Counsel Reauthorization Act of 1994, 28 U.S.C. §§ 519–599.

5. Bob Hohler, *Queries About His Whitewater Links Foreshadowed Fiske's Removal,* Boston Globe, Aug. 6, 1994, at 6.

6. *See, e.g.,* Clarence Page, *The Not-So-Impartial Whitewater Counsel,* Advocate, Aug. 16, 1994, at 7B.

7. Toni Locy & Marilyn W. Thompson, *Lunch Among "Old Friends" Causes Latest Whitewater Ripple,* Wash. Post, Aug. 24, 1994, at A3.

8. *In re Charge of Judicial Misconduct or Disability,* 39 F.3d 374 (Judicial Council Complaint Nos. 94-8, 94-9, 94-10; D.C. Cir. Nov. 1, 1994).

9. *Id.* at 375.

10. *Id.* at 381 (quoting Chesterfield Smith et al., Joint Statement Regarding Independent Counsel Selection Process 1 (Sept. 20, 1994)).

11. *Id.* at 381 n.6.
12. In accordance with the D.C. Circuit's rules governing such complaints, the opinion did not actually name Judge Sentelle, although everyone knew he was "the subject judge."
13. 487 U.S. 654 (1988).
14. 39 F.3d at 382.
15. *Whitewater Prober Hit on Partisanship,* Chicago Tribune, Sept. 28, 1994, at 16.
16. Jane Fullerton, *The Man Who Steers Starr from Troubled Waters,* Arkansas Democrat-Gazette, Oct. 8, 1995, at 1A.
17. Sam Skolnik, *Kenneth Starr's Conservative Conflict?* Legal Times, Oct. 23, 1995, at 1.
18. Leslie Phillips, *Whitewater Investigator Also Faces Questions,* USA Today, Apr. 2, 1996, at 6A; *Waxman Hits Starr Role in Tobacco Co. Matters,* National Journal's Congress Daily, May 11, 1995.
19. Joan I. Duffy, *Starr Won't Quit Whitewater Probe,* Memphis Commercial Appeal, Mar. 1, 1996, at 2B.
20. Michael Kranish, *GOP Expresses Misgivings on Fiske,* Boston Globe, Mar. 15, 1994, at 13.
21. *Who's Right, Bernie or Phil?* Legal Times, Aug. 14, 1995, at 6.
22. Grant Tennille, *Loose Lips Sink "Starship Officer" Juror,* Arkansas Democrat-Gazette, Mar. 15, 1996, at 12A.
23. Gary Borg, *Trekkie Beamed off Whitewater Jury,* Chicago Tribune, Mar. 15, 1996, at 9.
24. James Jefferson, *Appeals Court Reinstates Charge Against Arkansas Governor,* A.P. Wire, Mar. 15, 1996.
25. Joan I. Duffy, *Clinton Resists Testimony in Arkansas,* Memphis Commercial Appeal, Mar. 6, 1996, at 1A.

Index